P9-CCU-414

OFF THE BEATEN PATH® SERIES

NINTH EDITION

NEW HAMPSHIRE

OFF THE BEATEN PATH®

DISCOVER YOUR FUN

**BARBARA RADCLIFFE ROGERS
AND STILLMAN ROGERS**

REVISED BY AMANDA SILVA

Globe
Pequot
Guilford, Connecticut

All the information in this guidebook is subject to change. We recommend that you call ahead to obtain current information before traveling.

Globe Pequot

An imprint of The Rowman & Littlefield Publishing Group, Inc.
4501 Forbes Blvd., Ste. 200
Lanham, MD 20706
www.rowman.com

Distributed by NATIONAL BOOK NETWORK

British Library Cataloguing in Publication Information available

Library of Congress Cataloging-in-Publication Data available

ISBN 978-1-4930-3755-1 (paperback)
ISBN 978-1-4930-3756-8 (e-book)

∞™ The paper used in this publication meets the minimum requirements of American National Standard for Information Sciences—Permanence of Paper for Printed Library Materials, ANSI/NISO Z39.48-1992

Printed in the United States of America

In loving memory of George Radcliffe and Norman Rogers, the fathers who chose New Hampshire as our childhood home, and of James C. Cleveland, who as a US congressman worked so long and hard to preserve its character and protect its land.

Amanda Silva would like to thank her parents, who, no matter how far away their family's latest relocation took them, always made it possible to come home.

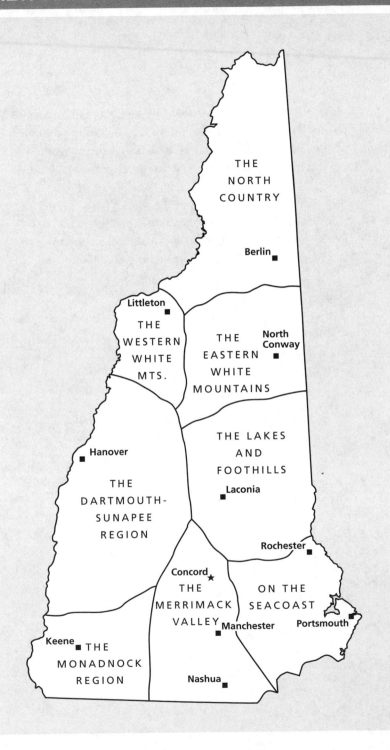

THE
NORTH
COUNTRY

Berlin ■

Littleton
■

THE
WESTERN
WHITE
MTS.

THE
EASTERN
WHITE
MOUNTAINS

North
Conway
■

THE LAKES
AND
FOOTHILLS

Hanover
■

Laconia
■

THE
DARTMOUTH-
SUNAPEE
REGION

Rochester
■

Concord ★

THE
MERRIMACK
VALLEY

ON THE
SEACOAST

Keene
■ THE
MONADNOCK
REGION

Manchester
■

Portsmouth
■

Nashua ■

Contents

Introduction

The tremendous diversity of New Hampshire's landscapes makes it visually exciting and also provides a wide variety of activities, particularly for those who enjoy the outdoors. The challenges of its terrain, soil, and climate have given its people a unique character—or perhaps such a place has always attracted those of independent and self-sufficient spirit.

New Hampshire people do tend to be an independent lot; most of them say exactly what they think. Another bewildering trait to those who don't know us well is that you can't always tell about us by our looks. The size of a person's fortune often bears no relation to the size of one's home or the make of one's car. It is often said of Boston ladies that they don't buy their hats; they have them. New Hampshire people are like that, too. The beautiful farmhouse may be all that's left several generations later and may be kept up by a lot of hard work alone; the tiny cottage with the gate askew may be the home of a millionaire. We tend to live in what we have.

The same trait is true of restaurants, which is very confusing to the traveler used to decorated interiors and flashy exteriors. You can't always judge a restaurant by its cover, and very often the plainest place or the most staid of inns may have a chef who retired to the country from a four-star bastion of haute cuisine. Surprises are what New Hampshire is full of, and they make each day a happy adventure.

"Off the beaten path" is a relative thing. By most standards, the whole state is off the beaten path. There are only three areas that are congested by traffic, even in the height of tourist season. When lodging is heavily booked during the most popular weeks, it is not because there are too many people here, but because resorts do not line our roads. Reservations are always a good idea during July and August and around the first week of October. Places such as

You Can't Get There from Here

As a rule of thumb, you can get north and south, but not east and west, on public buses. The main routes run from Boston to Montreal or Portland, Maine, passing through Portsmouth, Concord, Keene, Manchester, Nashua, and a few other cities farther north. But you can't get from Portsmouth to Keene without going back to Boston. The major bus lines are Concord Coach Lines (800-639-3317; concord coachlines.com) and Greyhound (800-231-2222; greyhound.com). You can fly into Manchester-Boston Regional Airport, served by four major airlines: American Airlines, Delta, Southwest, and United.

Garfield Falls, which even many local people have not seen, require travel on unpaved roads. But none of these require four-wheel-drive vehicles, except in winter or early spring, when some roads are muddy or not plowed.

Which brings us to the question of when to visit. New Hampshire is a seasonal state, and each month has its attractions. The best time for you to explore the Granite State depends upon your tastes and interests. Winter is glorious, filled with crystal-cold days for skiing or snowshoeing across white meadows with clear views of mountains through leafless trees. Night brings the stars so close you can spot constellations you never saw before and is a good time for a sleigh ride and a blazing fire in the hearth. Snow covers all the hardscrabble farms and rock-filled fields, and the air is clear and smells of wood smoke. But if you like little museums or want to hike to waterfalls, winter is not the best season.

Spring is good for country walks and hikes. Sugar houses come briefly to life, shrouded in steam and smelling of sweet maple syrup. With the end of the sap run, spring wildflowers carpet the woodlands, and the view of the mountains is softened, but not obscured, by leaves the size of mouse ears. Spring peepers fill the evening air with chirping. A lot of the little places aren't open yet, but people in those that are have time to chat and suggest other local gems

If You Don't Like It, Wait a Minute

Mark Twain (and just about everyone else) had some choice words about the "infinite variety" of New England weather. Most of the exaggerated stories you've heard are probably true. Average temperatures don't tell you much. One day it may be sunny and 80 degrees, the next day may be 50 degrees and raining, but the average temperature for the period will be calculated at 65, although neither day was 65. And the twenty-four-hour averages don't tell you what the daytime temperature was. That in mind, you may find the following "official" average temperatures remotely helpful: Jan, 21 degrees Fahrenheit; Feb, 23 degrees Fahrenheit; Mar, 32 degrees Fahrenheit; Apr, 44 degrees Fahrenheit; May, 56 degrees Fahrenheit; June, 65 degrees Fahrenheit; July, 70 degrees Fahrenheit; Aug, 67 degrees Fahrenheit; Sept, 60 degrees Fahrenheit; Oct, 49 degrees Fahrenheit; Nov, 38 degrees Fahrenheit; and Dec, 25 degrees Fahrenheit. In reality, expect most summer days to be in the 70s, spring and fall in the 50s and 60s, winter in the 20s and 30s. Humidity tends to be high year-round, which makes the cold seem colder and the hot seem hotter. The nice thing, as Mark Twain suggests, is that it never stays any way for very long. In general, the best weather tends to be in August, September, and October, with less rain than in the spring and fewer hot, humid days than earlier in the summer. The worst cold spells usually come in December and January. November is gray and March muddy, but both have some glorious days.

What's Going on Here?

The major cities have daily newspapers, and every area has its free weekly paper list-ing local events, festivals, church suppers, and just about everything else. The daily papers have special sections, usually late in the week, with entertainment and events calendars for the coming week. Many papers also print special summer sections, which are available free at information centers early in the summer. The major news-papers are the *Union Leader* (Manchester), *Keene Sentinel, Foster's Daily Democrat* (Dover), *Portsmouth Herald, Concord Monitor, Valley News* (Lebanon), *Telegraph* (Nashua), *News and Sentinel* (Colebrook), and *Coos County Democrat* (the North Country).

you won't want to miss. Bed-and-breakfast hosts have time to share a glass of sherry with you after dinner. Spring comes so fast that you can almost watch the apple blossoms unfold.

Summer is full of festivals celebrating almost everything from blueberries to zucchinis, and every little town has its historical society open. Days are long and not too hot to enjoy hikes and climbs. Lakeshores and mountain brooks offer swimming.

After Labor Day the weather is still summery, but there is a lull in the number of tourists until the end of the month. Farmers' markets are filled with produce and jars of glistening jellies. Hiking is at its very best, and the road-sides are brightened by patches of turning swamp maples.

Foliage paints the state, from north to south, in brilliant shades of red and gold. It begins in mid-September in the North Country and lasts until mid- to late October in the Monadnock region. The peak can vary by a week or so, depending on the weather, but any area will have at least two weeks of good color, usually more.

So plan your travel dates according to your own interests, or better yet, come often and enjoy the best of each season. You will, of course, need a good road map in order to plan your travels and to keep from getting lost on our wonderful winding country roads—although getting lost has its rewards, too, and may actually be the best way to see the state. But it's nice to know where you are when you finally emerge onto a main road. If you prefer to hold a map instead of your smartphone, consider investing in a copy of the *New Hampshire Atlas and Gazetteer* (Garmin).

Prices are a tricky thing to provide in a guidebook, but we have done it anyway. They change with economic conditions, even seasons and weather conditions, since restaurants depend on the markets for fresh produce and seafood. Lodging rates usually rise during the busiest times and drop during

Save on Dining Out

A number of New Hampshire restaurants are included in an annual book of dining discounts called *Entertainment*. Participants change with each edition but always cover all price ranges and styles, from fine dining to fast foods. New Hampshire is included in two different books, one covering southern New Hampshire and south coastal Maine, the other covering Vermont and bordering areas, which includes the entire Connecticut River Valley. The books cost about $30, and discounts are usually the price of one entree, which can be as much as a $24 savings on one dinner. In the back of the book are discount coupons for sports, such as kayak or ski rentals, and admission to museums and attractions in the area. For information call (800) 374-4464 or visit entertainment.com.

the slower ones. We have given dollar amounts when they seemed fairly likely to remain constant and elsewhere have used general ranges. For bed-and-breakfast places we consider $100 to $150 a night for two people to be moderate; for inns and hotels without breakfast, $90 to $125 is moderate. In restaurants, $15 to $25 is moderate for the main course, and we've further broken that into a high and low if the prices fall into a close range. How you add to that with other courses and wine will affect your bill, of course, but the entree price sets the base. Sometimes we've been even more specific, especially if the prices are exceptional.

To Find Out More

Write the **New Hampshire Office of Travel and Tourism,** P.O. Box 856, Concord, NH 03302, or call (800) 386-4664 to order a copy of *The Official New Hampshire Guidebook,* a handy compilation of advertising and listings. To speak to a representative, call (603) 271-2343 or (800) 258-3608.

The state's website at visitnh.gov gives general information on events, weather, and attractions. For an update on fall foliage conditions, call (800) 258-3608 or visit yankeefoliage.com. For alpine ski conditions call (800) 258-3608 or check out skinh.com. For a listing of private campgrounds, call (800) 822-6764 or (603) 846-5511; ucampnh.com.

White Mountains Attractions, North Woodstock, NH 03262, (800) 346-3687 or (603) 745-8720, can send you information on the northern part of the state, as will the **Mount Washington Valley Chamber of Commerce,** North Conway, NH 03860. Call (800) 367-3364 or visit mtwashingtonvalley.org.

Now to all the usual disclaimers, add the caveat emptor endemic to travel guides: Things change, especially in the restaurant business. Over the years, our authors have tried to choose places with consistent ownership, but when we discover a great new spot, we can't wait five years to share it with you. If you find our recommendations not up to our descriptions, there are several possible reasons. The restaurant in question may have changed owners or chefs, or it may have just plain gone downhill. Your taste in food may not be the same as ours. One person's pâté is another's "ptoooi," as Confucius wisely observed. There is no substitute for your own good judgment. If you get inside and don't think it's the right place for you, leave. In those memorable cases where a place we've recommended doesn't look like what it tastes like, we've mentioned that fact so that you will expect it. If in doubt, don't be embarrassed to ask to see a menu before you're seated. New Hampshire people don't buy pigs in a poke, and they don't expect you to either.

Enjoy New Hampshire as we do. We think that you'll agree, after you've met the state in person, that it's a place where familiarity breeds both respect and love.

On the Seacoast

New Hampshire has the shortest seacoast of any coastal state—only 18 miles long—but it's also one of the most historic. The first European inhabitants established a settlement at **Odiorne Point** in 1623, and later the same year a fishing village was established at Dover Point on the northern banks of the Piscataqua River on Little Bay. The Odiorne Point settlement was abandoned, but the Dover settlers built a meetinghouse and homes, which became the first permanent settlement in the colony.

The histories of this area, the American colonies, and the young nation are inextricably intertwined. The first American flag to be saluted by a foreign power flew from the mast of the *Ranger,* which sailed from Portsmouth in 1777. Portsmouth ladies sewed the flag, using fabric cut from their dresses. Portsmouth today, for all of its funky shops and bright eateries, still has the air of a prosperous eighteenth-century seaport.

Exeter, too, was a shipbuilding town and a lively port. Although it has lost its navigable link with the sea, its fine buildings still speak of the profitable West Indian trade. Inland from the shores of the Great Bay stretched almost unbroken

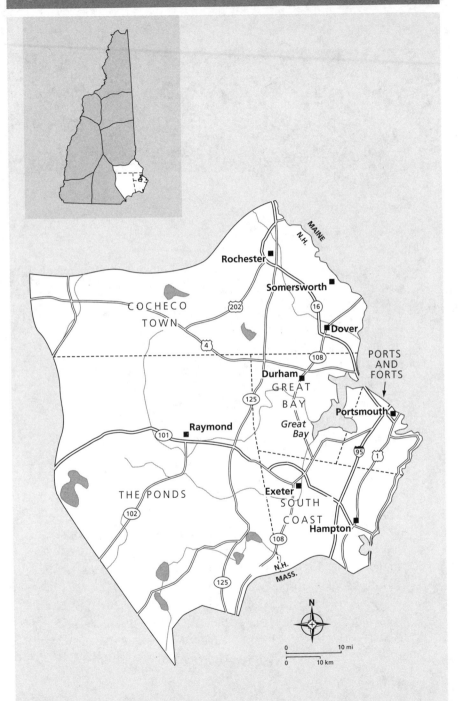

Rochester

Somersworth

202

16

4

Dover

108

PORTS AND FORTS

COCHECO TOWN

Durham

GREAT BAY

125

Portsmouth

Raymond

101

Great Bay

95

1

THE PONDS

102

Exeter

SOUTH COAST

Hampton

108

N.H.
MASS.

125

MAINE
N.H.

N

0   10 mi
0   10 km

farmland, and, although more heavily settled than other parts of the state, the area is still rich in farms and orchards.

Although most visitors' views of the New Hampshire coast are the traffic and commercialism of Route 1, there are lovely and quiet back roads to enjoy even in this playground area. Portsmouth, too, has its surprises, tucked away amid its tangle of old lanes and paths that grew into streets. New Hampshire, as a colony, began in this seacoast area, and it's an appropriate place for us to begin exploring the state.

Portsmouth and the seacoast are accessible by air and bus, but if you are taking a bus, make sure it stops at Market Square, downtown. Some of the buses use the Pease International Tradeport, out of town, and there is no bus service to the city, so if you arrive by air or your bus lets you off there, you'll have to call a cab. This is an odd gap in otherwise excellent public transportation. C&J Bus (ridecj.com, 603-430-1100, 800-258-7111) makes stops at the downtown Starbucks at 1 Market Square. Greyhound buses also serve the area from 54 Hanover Street (800-231-2222; greyhound.com).

You can travel throughout the seacoast area from Hampton through Portsmouth to Rochester and as far west as Exeter on the Coast transportation system. Its seven routes provide bus service from the Massachusetts border, all along the ocean and up the Maine border to Farmington and all the towns along Great Bay. The basic fare is $1.50; kids 5 and under ride free; half-fare ($0.75) is reserved for seniors (65 and over), and those with disabilities. Exact change is required, so bring a supply of ones and quarters. A complete fare and route guide is available at The Chamber Collaborative of Greater Portsmouth, town and city halls, local businesses, and on the buses. For specific route or

For Off-the-Beaten-Path Travelers

New Hampshire's state highway map, available free at most information offices, is an essential reference, of course, but those who like to know exactly where that interesting-looking road goes (or where it doesn't go) need the definitive set of road maps. DeLorme publishes a book of these large-format maps for nearly every state, and *The New Hampshire Atlas and Gazetteer* is required reading for explorers. Along with the roads, DeLorme maps show cemeteries, schools, streams, rail lines, and other landmarks to help you identify your whereabouts. Places of interest, such as parks, boat launches, campgrounds, covered bridges, waterfalls, and natural features, are shown by symbols and name. It's the natural companion for *New Hampshire Off the Beaten Path*. You'll find the maps in bookstores, or you can order copies online from the Garmin website.

fare questions, you can also call (603) 743-5777 from 6:30 a.m. to 10:30 p.m. Mon through Fri or 8 a.m. to 9:30 p.m. on Sat, or visit coastbus.org.

Seacoast Trolley Company offers reserved and customizable tours for groups of 15 or more passengers, which must be reserved at least 24 hours in advance, according to seasonal tour schedules. Weather permitting, the 1.5-hour seasonal tours start in April and run through October. The price of tickets is $15 for adults (16–65); $8 for juniors (3–15), toddlers (3 and under) are free, while senior (65+) passengers pay $13.

Ports and Forts

The link with the sea did not end with the sailing of the last clipper. Ships were built in Portsmouth for both world wars, and the forts that guarded the harbor during the American Revolution still dot the coast.

New Castle, once called Great Island, was the first seat of government and even now looks like the tiny prosperous fishing and seafaring village of its colonial origins. Streets too narrow for sidewalks are lined with houses whose doorways open directly onto the roadway. The numbers on them are not addresses, but dates, most of them from the 1600s and 1700s.

Fort Constitution had its beginning in 1632 with the earthworks and four "great guns"; a blockhouse was built in 1666; and at the end of the century a breastwork was added to protect the military stores. It was named Fort William and Mary.

EVENTS ON THE SEACOAST

Market Square Day
Second Sat in June, Portsmouth
(603) 433-4398
proportsmouth.org

Prescott Park Arts Festival
June–Sept., Portsmouth
(603) 436-2848
prescottpark.org

Seafood Festival and Sidewalk Sale
early Sept, Hampton Beach
(603) 926-8717
hamptonbeach.org

Strawbery Banke Candlelight Stroll
early Dec, Portsmouth
(603) 433-1100
strawberybanke.org

The Chamber Collaborative of Greater Portsmouth Events Calendar
portcity.org.

Paul Revere, the Boston silversmith and patriot, is best known for his ride on the night of April 18, 1775. But in New Hampshire, he's remembered for a ride almost four months earlier. On December 13, 1774, he brought a message that British troops were coming from Rhode Island to protect the garrison and secure it against the fractious Sons of Liberty. The next day, 400 of the latter converged on the fort and liberated one hundred barrels of gunpowder and some small arms, which they loaded on a gundalow (a type of boat built at Portsmouth and used to navigate tidal rivers) and sailed up the Oyster River to Durham. They hid the gunpowder in homes and under the pulpit of the meetinghouse until they could haul it by oxcart to Cambridge for use at Bunker Hill. On December 15, before the British could get reinforcements, another group helped itself to sixteen small cannons and whatever other military supplies could be carried off. It was the first active engagement of the Revolution.

Renamed Fort Constitution, it was used in 1812 and every other war until it was returned to the state of New Hampshire in 1961. Its walls and ramparts are a fine place for viewing the lighthouse, harbor, and Fort McClary, which guards the other side of this harbor entrance from Kittery Point, Maine. Visitors must observe the parking restrictions posted at the Coast Guard Station entrance now more than ever. For general information, visit nhstateparks.org/visit/historic-sites or call (603) 271-3556.

For access to the rocks and sandy beach of the neighboring shore, go through **_Great Island Common,_** a 32-acre park overlooking the harbor. From here you can see two lighthouses, islands, and Fort Constitution, as well as passing sailboats. Rocky tidal areas surround the park with pools to explore and a gentler tide than the one that crashes against the rocks along the ocean. While the beach isn't very long, it's set in a very attractive cove. The park provides picnic tables, a pavilion, and grills, as well as playgrounds, ball fields, and restrooms. There are no camping facilities. Open to the public 365 days per year, from 9 a.m. until 9 p.m., unless otherwise noted. Admission is $4 per person (ages 6–65); $2 for seniors (65+); $1 for handicapped visitors; and children (5 and under) are free. Admission is only charged for nonresidents from May through September, and no pets are allowed during this time.

Nearby, look for the entrance to Wild Rose Lane, which ends at 211, **_Fort Stark._** It is another of the seven forts built to protect Portsmouth Harbor and the naval shipyard. Although it was the site of earthworks during the Revolution and the War of 1812 and of a later stone fort, the present batteries were built at the turn of the twentieth century and were used in both world wars. The huge steel doors of the magazines stand ajar, grass grows from the cement, and one round gun emplacement has begun to slide down the crumbling cliff.

Interior access is closed due to vandalism. Open by appointment only; call (603) 271-3556.

Portsmouth brewing magnate Frank Jones bought a small hotel in New Castle at the end of the nineteenth century and rapidly expanded it into *Wentworth by the Sea,* a premier resort of the New England coast. In 1904 representatives of Japan and Russia negotiated an end to the Russo-Japanese War here, earning President Theodore Roosevelt the Nobel Peace Prize. By the 1970s, such grand hotels had lost their luster, and this one closed. After standing forlorn and empty for years, in 2003 this pride of the New Hampshire seacoast reopened its doors, its elegance regained in a multimillion-dollar restoration. Rooms have marble showers, leather-topped desks, and down pillows, and an in-house spa pampers guests. Reviving the dining traditions of the original Wentworth by the Sea, while improving on them significantly with a menu based on fresh local ingredients, the *Salt Kitchen & Bar* offers such main dishes as pan-seared chicken with forest mushrooms, herb-mustard crusted pork loin or pan-seared sea bass with black olive risotto and garlic-roasted Japanese eggplant. The pastry chef's signature is lemon curd tartlet with strawberry, almond, and honey tuile. The smaller waterside dining room, *Latitudes Waterfront and Latitudes Sky Bar* overlooks a marina of white boats bobbing in the waves, backed by the bay and a fringe of marsh grasses and trees on the opposite shore. The chef keeps diners' attention on the food with contemporary free-form china to frame a tempting selection of small dishes, possibly including crispy calamari with spicy peppers and toasted peanuts or a trio of bite-sized burgers, each different. Hearty salads and traditional entrees round out an appealing menu. Hotel rates are in the expensive range. The address is 588 Wentworth Rd., PO Box 860, New Castle 03854; (603) 422-7322 or (866) 384-0709; wentworth.com.

Facing New Castle Island and Fort Stark is *Odiorne Point,* where the first Europeans in the state settled. Site of Fort Dearborn during World War II, the grass-covered hills are actually camouflaged casemates for gun emplacements and their support systems. The entire point is now a nature center, with diverse coastal habitats to explore. Along with the rocky shore and salt marsh, there are a freshwater marsh and coastal woods. A drowned forest of pine, birch, and hemlock stumps is firmly rooted about 2 feet below tide level at the south end. Throughout the natural habitat you can see signs of human habitation as well. Stone walls of old farmlands and a colony of summer cottages cross the area, and you may see the hardy remnants of some of the formal gardens of the long-gone cottages. Day use for adults is $4; children (ages 6–11) cost $2. Boat launch fee $5 to $8. No pets. Route 1A, Rye; (603) 436-7406; nhstateparks .com/odiorne.html.

Read All About It

New Hampshire's history is a microcosm of American history, beginning with the earliest settlements on the coast dating from the early 1600s. The book *It Happened in New Hampshire* (Globe Pequot Press) records thirty-one events and incidents that illustrate life and times from those early settlers to the twenty-first century. The stories are anecdotal, some serious, and some humorous (such as how George Washington got a black eye during his presidential visit to Portsmouth). Others detail little-known events, such as the secession of the Indian Stream Republic and the role of the Concord coach in winning the West. A few shed new light on places: President Wilson's Summer White House in Cornish, a World War II prisoner-of-war camp in Stark, and the last of the great log drives in the North Country.

Visitors to Odiorne Point might also want to check out the **Seacoast Science Center** (seacoastsciencecenter.org), dedicated to educating park visitors about the area's wildlife. Center hours run daily 10 a.m.–5 p.m. beginning in mid-February through October 31; Saturday through Monday, starting November 1 through mid-February, and by appointment Tuesday through Friday, with hours open during school vacation days. Admission is $4 for adults, $2 for children (6–11 years); children 5 years and younger, as well as residents 65 and older, are free.

Portsmouth is a lively city with warrens of back streets to explore. The path to its abundant historic homes is part of the **Portsmouth Harbour Trail.** A full-color map and thirty-two-page guide are available ($2) and provide a handy and excellent reference to historic buildings and sites and varied architectural styles along the way. Write or call the Chamber Collaborative of Greater Portsmouth, 500 Market St., #16A, Portsmouth 03801; (603) 610-5510; order online at portsmouthnh.com/listing/portsmouth-harbour-trail, or go to the visitor kiosk at Market Square during the summer.

Most people are surprised to learn that slavery was a part of early colonial life in New Hampshire. In 1775, the eve of the American Revolution, there were 656 slaves in the state. The stories of their lives are told on the **Portsmouth Black Heritage Trail.** The twenty-four sites on the trail include Long Wharf, where slaves were unloaded and sold; the William Pitt Tavern at Strawbery Banke; the Governor John Langdon House; and the Portsmouth Children's Museum, which served as the state's first black church in the late nineteenth and early twentieth centuries. *Portsmouth Black Heritage Trail* brochures, which describe the sites and contain a map, can be purchased for $2 from the Portsmouth Black Heritage Trail, 10 Middle St., Portsmouth 03801;

(603) 380-1231. For a list of sites and some excerpts from the booklet, visit seacoastNH.com/Black-History or pbhtrail.org.

Much of Portsmouth is best seen on foot, and the city has wisely provided a good parking garage right in the center of town on Hanover Street. It's very inexpensive and saves you the hassle of trying to find a legal space on the narrow streets of this ancient port town. It's just 1 block north of Market Square, off Market Street.

The original name for the settlement here was ***Strawbery Banke,*** after the riverbanks reddened with the fruit in the late spring. A museum preserving nearly four centuries of this old waterfront neighborhood, saved from demolition in the 1950s, now uses the name Strawbery Banke. Thirty of the thirty-five historic homes here stand on their original foundations. The unusual feature of the restoration is that instead of returning the neighborhood to any single period and showing what things looked like then, the buildings and their furnishings show the evolution of homes, gardens, shops, and daily life throughout the entire period of its existence.

blackheritage

Portsmouth has an intriguing black heritage. For more see *Black Portsmouth: Three Centuries of African-American Heritage,* Sammons & Cunningham, University of New Hampshire Press.

The most dramatic example of this whole-history approach is at the ***Drisco House,*** built in 1795. The house changed with the times, and when it was acquired, one side of the duplex was a "frozen-in-time" 1950s apartment. It has been saved as it stood, but the other half of the house has been restored to its origins as the store and home of an eighteenth-century mid-level tradesman. This, too, is unusual, for the homes that are usually saved and restored are those of wealthy and prominent citizens—homes far more elegant and ornate than the Drisco House. This one building, with its 1795 and 1955 halves, spans the history of the Puddle Dock neighborhood in Portsmouth.

The process of discovery and restoration is a continuing one, and visitors are invited to share in it through a number of exhibits showing cutaway walls and structural details. The ***Jackson*** and ***Sherburne Houses*** are dedicated entirely to old-house archaeology, showing not only how the homes were built but also how historians can detect the changes made over the centuries. To anyone restoring an older home, looking inside the mechanics of original and renovated construction is an invaluable lesson. To the more casual visitor, it's just plain interesting.

Portsmouth was a major shipyard during World War II, and life on the home front in a coastal city is illustrated at the ***Abbott Grocery Store,*** restored

Thanks, Gov!

Royal Governor John Wentworth unwittingly helped train and equip three regiments of New Hampshire soldiers for the Continental Army, which were ready from the first shots of the Revolution. Wentworth had vigorously supported these as a local militia to defend Portsmouth in case of an attack from French or other enemies of the Crown; all they had to do was change their names and march off to Bunker Hill. These three regiments fought in nearly every major encounter and were credited with an important role in winning the war.

to its 1943 appearance and contents. The storekeeper's apartment next door and exhibits in the rear of the building all show how life on the home front changed during the war.

For more than fifty years the family of a New Hampshire governor of the Civil War era lived in the **Goodwin Mansion**, and his wife's detailed and spirited diaries provide information that has made it possible to restore not only the house but her remarkable gardens as well. At various times in summer and fall, Victorian teas are served in these gardens.

In keeping with the museum's philosophy, its newest restoration tells the story of a Russian Jewish family that settled in Puddle Dock at the turn of the twentieth century. **Shapiro House** celebrates the lives of the family of Abraham and Shiva Shapiro and is restored to the 1910 period. From the kosher kitchen to the bedrooms on the second floor, and even to family treasures and a boarder's room on the third floor, this is an immersion in the immigrant experience of adaptation to life in a new country. Holidays appropriate to the family are celebrated here.

Without major endowment, Strawbery Banke continues to grow, as funds are available, usually from local donations or entry fees. It is exciting to watch the restorations take place, and each visit gives visitors an appreciation of being part of its progress. Even the gifts purchased at the museum shop help fund the restoration. It's like giving twice when you do your Christmas shopping there.

Speaking of Christmas, on the first two weekends of December, the village opens for a **Candlelight Stroll**. Candles light the windows as you wander through the streets with costumed carolers and musicians. The houses are decorated for the holidays and offer free refreshments to visitors. Craftspeople are at work, and you can shop for gifts in their workshops or in the museum store. Each year brings new features, and it's an occasion for local people to enjoy the winter quiet of Strawbery Banke. The stroll takes place on six evenings only; 5 to 9 p.m. on Saturday, and 4 to 8 p.m. on Sunday. Tickets cost

$25 for adults, $12.50 for children (ages 5–17); children 4 years and younger are free. Packages are offered for families and groups.

The restored buildings are open daily May through October, 10 a.m. to 5 p.m., and November through April, Saturdays 10 a.m. to 2 p.m., and Sundays noon to 2 p.m. Guided ninety-minute walking tours leave on each hour. Admission is $19.50 for adults, $9.00 for children (ages 5–17), and free for children under 5. Write Strawbery Banke, 14 Hancock St., Portsmouth 03801; call (603) 433-1100; or visit strawberybanke.org.

Gardeners should stop at *Prescott Park* across the street to see the All-America Show Garden, where each year's All-America selections are grown. Show gardens such as this are located in different parts of the country to demonstrate which flowers perform best in various climates. Northerners who spot boxwood at Strawbery Banke may wonder how it grows in New Hampshire. The answer is that Portsmouth and a tiny coastal strip are in a different gardening zone from the rest of the state, due to the moderating effect of the sea. In addition to the garden, the park has an active marina and hosts almost daily activities throughout the summer. The *Prescott Park Arts Festival,* which begins in June and runs through September, offers twilight and Sunday brunch concerts, theater, art shows, and craft shows. On the Saturday of Memorial Day weekend (or the first Saturday in June) area restaurants compete in a *Chowderfest* at the park, and on the Saturday of Columbus Day weekend they meet again for a *Chili Cook-Off* at midday. Check prescottpark.org for details.

holdyourtongue

As "witches" were being hanged in neighboring Massachusetts, based on no more than the testimony of children, Goody Walford of Portsmouth, described as an old crone and accused of witchcraft, brought a defamation suit against her accusers and was awarded damages by the court.

Rich, creamy chowders made from scratch are a fine art that's been perfected at *Geno's Chowder and Sandwich Shop* (603-427-2070) near Prescott Park. Geno's daughter, Francesca Marconi, keeps up a tradition that Geno began in the 1960s, adding a changing selection of other savory soups and legendary meaty lobster rolls. Boat owners can even tie up here to eat on Geno's deck.

Another lively Portsmouth event is the annual *Market Square Day,* the second Saturday of June (603-431-4398). Music, food booths, activities, art exhibits, and crafts shows all end with fireworks. The city is ablaze with color, balloons, and throngs of people having fun. Check out proportsmouth.org for more information. Visitors can find specifics on these or other activities, such as *First Night,* by calling the Chamber Collaborative of Greater Portsmouth at (603) 436-1118.

St. John's Church on Chapel Street, just off Bow Street, is a masterpiece of colonial architecture with later trompe l'oeil painting decorating its galleried interior. The bell in the steeple, still used to summon worshippers each Sunday, was captured at the French fortress at Louisbourg, Nova Scotia, in 1745, brought to Portsmouth, and presented to this church. The bell fell during a fire in 1806 and was recast by Paul Revere. Queen Anne gave the church its silver; and the Brattle organ, built in England in 1662, is a pure baroque organ of the sort J. S. Bach played, and is the oldest operating pipe organ in America. E. Power Biggs made a recording on it for the 1976 bicentennial celebrations. The church also has a copy of the rare "Vinegar Bible." Royal Governor Benning Wentworth is buried in the adjacent churchyard. You can see all of these things with the help of a little brochure that you will find in the front of the church. We hope you'll leave a contribution for the building's upkeep and repair when you leave.

Built at the Portsmouth Naval Shipyard in 1953, the *USS* **Albacore,** now at the *Port of Portsmouth Maritime Museum,* never went to war. Its mission was an experimental one. The intent was to redesign and adapt it as the prototype for the submarine of the future. The teardrop hull design made the *Albacore* the fastest submarine ever put in the water. That and dive brakes, sonar systems, and other new theories tested onboard have become part of modern submarine design. The fascinating story of this experimental submarine and how its fifty-five-member crew lived in its 205-foot-by-27-foot confines during its nineteen years of commission is told during a ten-minute video and a half-hour tour of the vessel. Now sunk in a dry basin so you can see the entire hull, the USS *Albacore* looks a bit like a beached whale up close. It's the only one of its kind; so even if the sea and its ships don't interest you at all, don't pass up the chance to see it. Open daily Memorial Day to Columbus Day 9:30 a.m. to 5:30 p.m. Winter hours Thurs through Mon 9:30 a.m. to 4 p.m. Adults $8, children (ages 7–17) $3, children under 7 years free, family $16. You'll find the *Albacore* on the Market Street Extension, or Route 1 bypass, 600 Market St., Portsmouth; (603) 436-3680 or ussalbacore.org.

For entertainment in Portsmouth you can't do better than *The Music Hall.* This nicely restored theater is run by a local nonprofit organization and offers current movies, classic and foreign films, live theater, ballet, and music. Touring groups, such as the Acting Company, perform here on a regular basis. Located at 28 Chestnut St., Portsmouth; call (603) 436-2400, or call the twenty-four-hour film line at (603) 436-9900 for information. Visit themusichall.org for pricing information or to purchase tickets online. *Seacoast Repertory Theatre,* a professional company, presents a full entertainment calendar (603-433-4472, seacoastrep.org). One night a month, Portsmouth's art galleries host Art Round Town gallery walks, with refreshments and artists on hand to discuss their work (603-436-7007). You might also want to check the "Spotlight" section of the *Portsmouth Herald,* a weekly supplement to the paper, which covers music, theater, and the visual arts throughout the seacoast area, with addresses and phone numbers of clubs.

Portsmouth has developed a reputation for some of the best dining in the state, with a range of styles to choose from. Voted 2018's Most Romantic Restaurant in NH by *Food & Wine* magazine, restaurateur Massimo Morgia's **Ristorante Massimo** offers an impeccable Italian dining experience in an elegant, yet cozy environment. Established in 1994, Ristorante Massimo features Italian cuisine from every region of Italy, fusing them with flavors unique to New England. The menu includes intriguing appetizers of duck, peekytoe crab, and rabbit; and entrees of rib eye steak finished with hedgehog mushroom-bordelaise, sweet potato–sage encrusted veal rib eye finished with a cognac and peppercorn demi-glace, and grilled Australian rack of lamb with a lavender-chestnut demi-glace. Pasta courses (all pasta is made on premises) run about $11 to $12 and Secondi entrees $22 to $34. Reservations are strongly encouraged. Dinner service begins at 5 p.m. Mon through Sat. Massimo is at 59 Penhallow St.; call (603) 436-4000 or visit ristorantemassimo.com.

"Setting seafood standards since 2002," **Surf** Portsmouth is the sister restaurant of the original and ever-popular Surf in Nashua (see page 33), owned by Chef Michael Buckley. Diners visiting the New Hampshire seacoast are smart to get their seafood fix at Surf in Portsmouth, which features New England favorites like haddock and lobster rolls, along with some spicier, more exotic fare in the form of shrimp vindaloo and shrimp and pork belly ramen. Complete with a full sushi menu, along with a raw bar, offering oysters and clams on the half shell, as well as oyster shooters, true seafood fanatics are sure to leave Surf satisfied. Hours of operation are Thur through Sun from 11 a.m. to 4 p.m. for lunch; dinner is served Mon through Sun from 4 p.m. to 9 p.m., with hours extended to 10 p.m. on Fri and Sat. Surf is located at 99 Bow St.; (603) 334-9855; surfseafood.com/menu/Portsmouth.

Because not every visitor to the seacoast is necessarily a fan of seafood, **The Library Restaurant,** nestled on the corner of State Street, is one of Portsmouth's culinary and architectural gems. Offering brunch, lunch, and dinner, The Library Restaurant redefines steakhouse. Boasting an award-winning menu, this is place to go for an elevated steak dinner experience. Enjoy dining any time of day, ensconced in historic surroundings and New England charm. Open daily from 11:30 a.m., The Library Restaurant is an especially cozy environment during the fall and winter months. Located at 401 State St.; (603) 431-5202; libraryrestaurant.com.

The former chef at Lindbergh's Crossing, Evan Mallett, has opened his own restaurant at the same location. *Black Trumpet Bistro* has the same cozy atmosphere, retaining the low-beamed, brick dining room, and upstairs wine bar. An expert mycologist, Chef Mallet literally steps out his back door for ingredients, finding a garden of exotic mushrooms in the woods behind his home. He makes and cures the sausages he serves in the restaurant and works closely with local farmers to find wholesome, unusual, pesticide-free ingredients from which he creates a constantly changing seasonal menu. Mallet delights in interesting game dishes and in artistic presentations that are as enticing to the eye as to the palate. For example, elk rib eye is served with cherry-pepper coulis on a square plate, beside a tangerine shell filled with pistachio rice pudding. Quickly seared sashimi-quality yellowfin tuna might be fanned over a mound of shoestring blue-potato fries. Black Trumpet Bistro is at 29 Ceres St.; (603) 431-0887; www.blacktrumpetbistro.com.

Ceres Bakery, at 51 Penhallow St., bakes incomparable breads, cookies, tortes, and coffee cakes. Nowhere else will you find such generous slices of the last two served up at reasonable prices. Hearty thick soups are served with a slice of their daily bread, or you can choose quiches or salads. The bakery opens Mon through Fri 7 a.m. to 5 p.m., Sat 7 a.m. to 4 p.m., Sun 8 a.m. to 1 p.m. (603-436-6518 or ceresbakery.com).

Martin Hill Inn is the kind of place you create in your mind when you're traveling and tired, but you know you'll never find. Right downtown, within a few blocks of restaurants and shops, this engaging inn is country-quiet, with a large, shady garden where you can stroll amid periwinkles and tulips in May or peonies and lilies in the summer—or just relax with a book. Inside it's all antiques and elegance, but the kind you want to sink into instead of tiptoe through. Each room has its own character, colors, and style, and we like them all, especially the master bedroom, in shades of China blue, complemented by an Abigail Adams bedspread. Although the historic building is restored and decorated in antiques, modern conveniences abound: ample reading lights and brand-new plumbing and fixtures. Full breakfast is served in a lovely period room. The inn is at 404 Islington St., Portsmouth; (603) 436-2287; martinhillinn.com.

Within walking distance from Strawbery Banke and most of the other attractions of Portsmouth, the *Ale House Inn* occupies the top floor of a harborside building that once housed a brewery. Tastefully decorated rooms with queen-size brass beds frame views of the harbor. Restaurants and Market Square are close by. The inn is at 121 Bow St., Portsmouth; (603) 431-7760; alehouseinn.com.

Out of town, where the Little Harbor Road ends at the water's edge, is the **_Wentworth-Coolidge Mansion._** It is one of the very few residences of a royal governor virtually unchanged since the Revolution. The governor lived well. The home that he built in 1750 was originally even larger and was the most elegant of its day. It was not only his residence, but the center of government as well. You can tour the original rooms and the Governor's Council Chamber, where he signed the charters for land grants and towns throughout New Hampshire and Vermont. The grounds, where you are welcome to picnic, are planted with the first lilacs brought to the New World. They are the state flower, and if you visit New Hampshire in May you will see them blooming in dooryards and gardens and at the sites of long-deserted farms throughout the countryside. Although technically an "exotic" here, lilacs have a long history in the state and have been accepted as native.

Although the Wentworth-Coolidge Mansion grounds are free to enjoy, including free parking, a tour of the mansion itself is well worth the cost of admission. Tours run Wed through Sun, 10 a.m. to 4 p.m. from Memorial Day through Labor Day; Fri through Sun from Labor Day to the end of Oct. All tours depart on the hour, and the last tour of each day leaves at 3 p.m. Admission is $5 for adult non-NH residents (18 years and over); $4 for adults NH residents (aged 18–64); $3 for nonresident youth passes (ages 6–17); NH residents over 65, NH youths (ages 6–17), and children under 5 admitted free. Since hours tend to vary with each season, it's always a good ideas to call ahead or consult the website. The Wentworth-Coolidge Mansion is located at 375 Little Harbor Rd., off Route 1A in Portsmouth; (603) 436-6607; wentworthcoolidge.org/visit/hours.

South of Portsmouth, not far from Route 1, is the 150-acre property of the **_Urban Forestry Center._** A beautiful place to visit for its gardens, woodland, and salt marsh landscapes, it is also an attractive demonstration area, the purpose of which is not only to protect this piece of land, but to show others how they can protect and enhance their own property as well. Individuals, municipalities, developers, and conservation commissions all look to the center for inspiration and advice. Throughout the property are mailboxes where you will find extensive information on each project. Plant-by-plant descriptions are available at the perennial border, and a thorough booklet on herb culture and uses, prepared by Tanya Jackson (one of New England's leading herb experts), is free at the herb garden. The center sponsors lectures, field trips, and programs on natural history, wildlife, gardening, and New Hampshire forests. Visit nhstateparks.org for more information.

A "Garden for the Senses" trail, created especially for the visually and physically impaired, emphasizes plants selected for flavor, fragrance, color, and texture, with wide paths and raised beds for easy access. An arboretum contains examples of trees for street plantings, cold-hardy trees, and those with unusual and interesting flowers, bark, or leaves. Several plantations and trails as well as ample space for watching birds that live in the marsh and shore areas add to the center's attractions. Free and open year-round, the trails are favorites of cross-country skiers and snowshoe hikers (no motorized recreational vehicles). Trail hours are 7 a.m. to 8 p.m. daily, while the office is open Mon through Fri from 8 a.m. to 4 p.m. The center is at 45 Elwyn Rd. (off Lafayette Road) in Portsmouth; call (603) 431-6774 for more information.

Off the coast, shared with Maine but with access from New Hampshire, and visible only in clear weather, are the ***Isles of Shoals.*** Described by the writer and poet Celia Thaxter, who grew up there, they were painted by the impressionist artist Childe Hassam, who came to the summer arts colony that developed there. His work includes more than 400 paintings of the islands, many of which were done to illustrate Thaxter's *An Island Garden,* a classic of garden writing as fresh in its facsimile reprint as it was in its original printing at the turn of the twentieth century. These islands are as wrapped in tales of shipwrecks, pirates, ghosts, and buried treasure as they

Whodunit?

John and Maren Hontvet shared their cottage on Smuttynose, one of the Isles of Shoals, with John's brother, Maren's brother, and his beautiful wife, Anethe, all freshly arrived from Norway. Maren's sister, Karen, was visiting. A friend, Louis Wagner, lived in Portsmouth and was jobless. Thus the scene is set for the night of March 5, 1873.

The three men from Smuttynose decided to spend the night in Portsmouth, and they mentioned this to Louis, whom they met there. From here, the story has two distinctly different versions. The accepted one, based more on contemporary public opinion and sentiment than on the actual trial and testimony, is that Louis rowed a stolen dory 10 miles out to the island and, in an attempt to rob the house, hacked Anethe and Karen to death with an axe while Maren managed to escape and hide all night in the rocks along the shore. She identified him as the murderer, and he was caught, almost lynched by incited mobs, tried, and hanged.

While popular opinion of the era would not accept the idea of a family woman committing murder, the trial evidence points to Maren as the villain and shows no evidence that Wagner was even on the island that night. But anyone who knew the truth was dead, and Maren and John moved to Portsmouth, without either brother or the pretty sister-in-law. Smuttynose is uninhabited today.

are in fog. Craggy and barren as they were when Captain John Smith called them "barren piles of rock," the islands still fascinate visitors. *The Isles of Shoals Steamship Company* at 315 Market St. offers a selection of river, harbor, and island tours. They also provide guided walking tours of Star Island with time to explore the terrain on your own. All tours are narrated and regale the history of Portsmouth Harbor, the Isles of Shoals, and the New Hampshire seacoast in entertaining detail. The popular Extended Star Island Walking Tour departs on select summer afternoons at 12:25 p.m., and affords guests a guided walking tour of the island, complete with information about Captain John Smith, Pocahontas, pirates Blackbeard and Captain Kid, along with the lady ghost of White Island. Guests are also free to explore independently during the ninety minutes of time spent on the island. Check out the website for the full range of tour options—each voyage lists duration, along with time spent at the destination before sailing back to port. To confirm hours and cruise operation, call (603) 431-5500, (800) 441-4620, or visit islesofshoals.com.

Whale-watching, fishing, harbor, and Great Bay cruises from Portsmouth are also offered by Portsmouth Harbor Cruises at Ceres Street Dock, 64 Ceres St., Portsmouth; (603) 436-8084; portsmouthharbor.com. Between May and October they offer harbor, bay, and river cruises. You can also take cruises there from Rye Harbor (see next section).

The South Coast

The shoreline in Rye is less developed than elsewhere, with long stretches of open salt marsh (some of it a wildlife preserve) and rocky coast broken by beaches. *Atlantic Fishing Fleet* offers deep-sea fishing trips and whale-watches on board *Atlantic Queen II* from April through mid-October. You might catch flounder, mackerel, or, cod. The trip is fun, whatever the catch, and offers an education about the fishing industry. Atlantic Fishing Fleet can be found at 1870 Ocean Blvd., Rye. For a schedule call (603) 964-5220.

Island Cruises operates tours to the Isles of Shoals and lobster tours from Rye Harbor. The two-hour island tour is narrated with historical facts and tales of mysterious doings. On the one-hour lobster tour you learn all about the elusive crustaceans and how they are harvested, coming face to face with one when a trap is brought aboard. During July and August, the island tour operates several times each day and the lobster tour goes out Sat through Wed at 10 a.m. In June and September, tours operate on weekends only. Contact them at Rye Harbor State Marina, 1870 Ocean Blvd., (603) 964-5545, or uncleoscar.com.

For a shore bound excursion that gives you nature on one side and human nature on the other, walk or bicycle around **Little Boar's Head.** A 2-mile path runs the ridge of a rocky promontory, with waves crashing on the rocks below. Inland stands a row of beach "cottages" built in the pre–income tax days, when wealthy city dwellers moved their families and household staffs to the shore for the summer. In the early summer, wild roses bloom along the path.

Roses at **Fuller Gardens** are clearly not wild: 1,500 carefully tended rose-bushes thrive in the sea air in an All-America Rose Display Garden, once part of a fine old Boar's Head estate. Both roses and perennial beds are at their peak in June, but the gardens are filled with blooms all summer and late into the fall. Don't miss the gate in the hedge leading to the cool, cedar-shaded Japanese garden with its pool, bridge, and stone lantern. Marble walkways surround a terraced formal garden. Open 10 a.m. to 5:30 p.m. daily, mid-May through mid-Oct, the gardens are at 10 Willow Ave., which leaves Route 1A just north of its intersection with Route 101D in North Hampton. The telephone is (603) 964-5414. Admission is $9 for adults, $4 for children under 12, and $8 for seniors. You may also visit fullergardens.org.

The town of Hampton lies inland, out of hearing distance of raucous Hampton Beach. Follow Park Avenue east from Route 1 to find the original settlement at Meetinghouse Green. The old common is now a memorial park to the first settlers, with a stone for each of the pioneer families placed by their descendants. Across the street is the **Tuck Museum,** operated by the Hampton Historical Society, a group of buildings that includes an old one-room schoolhouse, a museum of early farm implements, the Seacoast Fire Museum, and a variety of exhibits on the area's history. It isn't the Smithsonian, but it is a very approachable collection; most items are not in glass cases but right where you can see them. A playground on the shady lawn outside will amuse the children if your attention span exceeds theirs. Open 1 to 4 p.m. Wed, Fri, and Sun from mid-June to mid-Sept. Admission is free. The museum is at 40 Park Ave., Hampton; call (603) 929-0781 or visit hamptonhistoricalsociety.org for news of special events.

When you've satisfied your appetite for Hampton's history, grab a bite to eat at one of the town's popular eateries. Known for its charm and blend of traditional American with Mediterranean fare, **The Galley Hatch** offers creative dishes influenced by the seasons. Open Mon through Sun, The Galley Hatch serves mouthwatering lunches and dinners, with a variety of weekly lunch specials available during the summer months. Located at 325 Lafayette Rd.; (603) 926-6152; galleyhatch.com.

For affordable comfort food on the fly, **Lupe's 55 Authentic & Fresh** offers wholesome, fresh Mexican comfort food, with plenty of vegetarian-friendly options. Open daily from noon to 10 p.m., Lupe's is a popular place for consistently delicious meals before or after a day at the beach. Visit 107 Ocean Blvd.; (603) 601-7772.

With more than forty summer seasons under its belt, the *Sea Ketch* is a Hampton Beach staple for breakfast, lunch, dinner, and coastal cocktails. Enjoy live entertainment on the deck while taking in some sunshine and salty seaside air afforded by the 360-degree view. Family-friendly and casual, the Sea Ketch is a quality spot for summer dining. Swing by anytime Mon through Sun, between 7 a.m. and 11:45 p.m. The Sea Ketch Restaurant is at 127 Ocean Blvd. (Top of G St.); (603) 926-0324; seaketch.com.

Bordering Route 1 near the state line in Seabrook is the *Hampton Harbor Marsh,* New England's largest salt marsh, with more than 5,000 acres of sea grass, mudflats, and sandbars. It's an important migratory stop for more than twenty-one species of shorebirds. Exeter, like Portsmouth, is a nice place for walking. Fine homes line its streets, and three of the finest Federal mansions face the bandstand in the center of town. The *Gilman Garrison House* was built of massive hewn logs in the late 1600s as a fortified garrison. In the mid-1700s the house was enlarged and remodeled, adding a wing and more formal rooms in which its owner felt more comfortable entertaining John Wentworth, the royal governor, during his visits to Exeter. These visits ended abruptly when the governor had to take refuge in Fort William and Mary and finally flee altogether at the outbreak of the Revolution. (Since Portsmouth was considered a hotbed of Toryism, the seat of the state's government moved to Exeter—making it the state's first capital.) Later, Daniel Webster boarded in this house while he was a student at Phillips Exeter Academy. Tours by appointment only. The Gilman Garrison House is located at 12 Water St. in Exeter; call (603) 436-3205 for an appointment.

Also in the center of town is the *American Independence Museum,* a newly established combination of the Ladd-Gilman House (home of New Hampshire's governor during the Revolution) and the Folsom Tavern, featuring the archives of the Society of the Cincinnati. The collections in the two eighteenth-century buildings feature furnishings from the 1600s, two annotated drafts of the US Constitution, and historic artifacts. Open Tues through Sat from 10 a.m. to 4 p.m. Call to make a reservation or book a group tour. Tickets are $6 for adults, $5 for seniors, $3 for students and children over the age of 6; free admission for children under 6 years of age. The American Independence Museum is located at 1 Governor's Lane (off Center Street), Exeter; (603) 772-2622; independencemuseum.org.

Known best to students, parents, and alumni of Phillips Exeter Academy, the *Exeter Inn* offers a wide variety of rooms that retain the charm of a historic

Where's the Beach?

New Hampshire's shoreline just can't seem to sit still. As glaciers melted away and raised the ocean level about 12,000 years ago, the tide line reached as far west as Route 125 in Barrington and Lee, with Stratham Hill as an offshore island. However, as glaciers continued to melt away, their weight stopped pressing down on the land behind. So it rose, pushing the shoreline farther east, until it reached the Isles of Shoals. Once the land stopped this process of readjustment, known as isostatic recovery, the shoreline settled into its present place.

But don't get complacent. Ocean levels are on the rise again, at the alarming rate of $\frac{1}{25}$ inch each year. That means a rise of about 3½ feet by the year 3000, so you'd better build that sand castle farther back.

hotel while providing modern and stylish lodgings. The spacious lobby sets the tone of approachable elegance. The inn's Epoch Restaurant gets high scores for fine dining and for favoring—and crediting on the menu—local producers, such as Sandwich Creamery's cheddar in the dauphine potatoes and North Country Smokehouse bacon in the corn fritters. Seafood gets the attention it deserves in dishes such as olive oil poached ahi tuna, served with asparagus risotto. A vegetarian dish is always offered, getting every bit as much attention to detail as the other entrees; perhaps orange-ginger tofu brochettes with roasted tomatillo quinoa, grilled pineapple, and toasted pepper coulis. The restaurant is busy during special events at the academy, so call ahead to be sure of a table. The inn is found at 90 Front St., Exeter; call (603) 772-5901, or visit theexeterinn.com.

Great Bay

Past Portsmouth Harbor, the Piscataqua River opens into Little Bay, which is fed by the Oyster River and *Great Bay.* At 5 miles long, Great Bay is the largest inland body of salt water in New England, but it's very hard to see since only one road, Route 4, passes within sight. Even that restricts views to the northern end. The towns that lie along the rivers feeding it are all far from its tidal shores.

The best way to see this area is from the water, on a *Piscataqua River Cruise,* a three-hour trip from Portsmouth to Durham, with a stop at the site of the Bickford Garrison to learn how, in 1694, one farmer cleverly defended it by changing coats and voices to make the post seem well-manned. The tour includes a buffalo farm (see below) and a chance to sample a buffalo burger as well. Offered on weekends in the fall, when the foliage along the wooded shores is at its best, cruises are run by Isles of Shoals Steamship Company, 315 Market St., PO Box 311, Portsmouth 03802; call (603) 431-5500 or visit islesofshoals.com.

Another way to see this area from the water is to paddle your own canoe or kayak, putting in at **Hilton Park,** on Dover Point, on the north side of the big highway bridges. Paddlers should be aware that the current under the bridges is among the strongest on the East Coast, a place to avoid. But you're going the other way, north along the shore of Dover Neck and the Piscataqua River. You have two possible destinations from here: The Piscataqua is formed by the **Cocheco** and **Salmon Falls Rivers.** The first leads to Dover (about 6 miles) and the second to South Berwick, Maine, about 7 miles away. The shores of both are fairly undeveloped, so either makes a scenic trip.

The Little Bay Buffalo Company is a family-run farm on rolling meadows and woodlands extending to the waters of Little Bay. It is a habitat for a number of wildlife species and a migratory stop for waterfowl. The bison here are not for petting, but they are usually visible in the pasture, often at close range. Also at the farm are displays on the interrelationship between the bison and the Native Americans' way of life, as well as information on local Native Americans who camped here in the summer to fish and hunt. The Company Store sells buffalo meat, hides, and related products such as buffalo tooth necklaces. The clear message here, well stated by the Langley family, is that using resources requires responsibility. To reach the farm, take Durham Point Road from Route 108 and watch for the small sign on Langley Road to the left. Open daily mid-April through late Nov, 9 a.m. to 5 p.m.; observation area open until sunset. Contact the company at 50 Langley Rd., Durham 03824; (603) 868-3300 or (800) 380-3311.

Durham is best known for the **University of New Hampshire,** which dominates the town and brings it to life. Beside Thompson Hall on the campus is a lovely ravine filled in May with lilacs of every shade from white to dark purple. **The Art Gallery at the University of New Hampshire** is a little-known treasure trove of fine arts located in the Paul Creative Arts Center. The permanent collection includes 1,500 paintings, prints, drawings, and sculpture works, most from the nineteenth and twentieth centuries. Among these are works by Durer, Hogarth, Abbott Thayer, Corot, Frank Benson, Hiroshige, Daumier, Homer, Lotte Jacobi, Whistler, Miro, Roualt, Klimpt, Frank Shapleigh, and a host of other luminaries, as well as a major collection of Japanese woodcuts and historic works, including pre-Columbian and African art. Major exhibitions bring other works on a regular basis. The Art Gallery is at 30 Academic Way; (603) 862-7222.

Off Durham Point Road, on the way to Newmarket, is the ***Great Bay Estuarine Research Reserve,*** more than 4,000 acres of tidal waters, mud flats, salt marsh, tidal-creek woodlands, fields, and meadows on Adams Point. There is no nature center or organized visitor program here, but the habitat is filled with the flora and fauna peculiar to tidal estuaries. A boat put-in and parking area are reached by a stone-wall-bordered road that ends at the Jackson Laboratory, an estuarine research center. Park there to reach the viewing platform (wheelchair accessible) overlooking rolling meadows with the bay in the background. The air is filled with the trill of birds. The bay is a kayaker's heaven, with protected waters formed by an almost endless supply of rivers. Their tidal estuaries meander through grassy marshlands rich in bird life and past forested shores that turn gold and crimson in the fall. For information on the Great Bay Reserve, call New Hampshire Fish and Game at (603) 868-1095, or contact the preserve at (603) 778-0015; greatbay.org.

From Adams Point, you can canoe or kayak along the shore and up the ***Squamscott River*** to Exeter. Look for the chained gate to Adams Point (open 4 a.m. to 10 p.m.) to find the put-in. Paddle along the shore to your right, watching for birds and other wildlife on this undeveloped shore where bald eagles winter. High tide is best; tides are fairly high here, and at low tide you'll see vast expanses of mud. The first big channel you come to is the Lamprey River, which you can follow to Newmarket for a shorter trip. Past that is the Squamscott River; if you go all the way to Exeter, it is about a 10-mile paddle one-way.

Emery Farm was established in 1655, which, eleven generations later, makes it high on the list of the nation's oldest family farms. Here you can pick your own strawberries, blueberries, or raspberries. Juicy, tree-ripened peaches and garden produce, as well as local maple syrup, honey, and fresh home-baked breads, are sold; New Hampshire crafts and pottery add to the unique farm stand. In the spring, they sell herb plants and garden flats from their greenhouse. The farm is open every day, Easter through Christmas Eve (they also sell Christmas trees) from 9 a.m. to 6 p.m. Emery Farm is on Route 4, 2 miles east of Durham (603-742-8495 or emeryfarm.com).

The elegant ***Three Chimneys Inn,*** overlooking the mill pond in Durham, serves memorable meals in its dining room, or more casual and less expensive—but good—dinners in its ***ffrost Sawyer Tavern.*** In the silver-set dining room, expect the likes of pork tenderloin wrapped in bacon with raisin-apple-onion compote and sweet potato–leek hash, finished with bacon sherry vinaigrette, or tenderloin of beef stuffed with smoked Gouda, roasted red pepper, and basil, wrapped in applewood smoked bacon and accompanied by cognac Dijon sauce. It's open for lunch Tues through Sat; dinner is served daily from 5 p.m. to 9 p.m.. Deep-hued guest rooms have the air of an English estate, with ornate, hand-carved beds and rich tapestries, set in Durham's oldest house, which dates from 1649. Rooms are upwards of $220 with breakfast and dinner for two, but out of the ordinary in terms of decor, with the original fireplaces restored and working, whirlpool tubs, and several thoughtful details. The Three Chimneys is at 17 Newmarket Rd., Durham; call (603) 868-7800, or visit three-chimneysinn.com.

Just west of Durham, the village of Lee was once covered in farmland. Many of the fields have been reclaimed by forest, but one of the old family farms has taken on a new life as ***Flag Hill Winery.*** Unlike many northern wineries that buy in the juice, Frank Rheinholt has planted French hybrid grapes, producing several fine wines literally from the ground up. Flag Hill also makes wine from plums, apples, and raspberries. After the success of their wines, they became New Hampshire's first distillery, producing General John Stark Vodka in 2004. Flag Hill Chef Ted McCormack holds tasting dinners deeply rooted in the philosophy of locally grown foods. "Locavore" menus feature ingredients from nearby farms, and Friday evening cooking classes offer hands-on food experiences. You can visit the vineyards, learn about the process, and taste the wines, which are also served at esteemed local restaurants. Flag Hill is on Route 155, near the Route 125 intersection, at 297 North River Rd., and is open for tours and tastings Wed through Sun 11 a.m. to 5 p.m.; call (603) 659-2949 for information or visit flaghill.com.

On leaving the winery, go right, following Route 155 north through Lee. In the town cemetery, opposite the schoolhouse, look for a large boulder near the center, with a plaque marking it as the grave of Sherwood (Woody) Sherburn. He was so incensed at vandals knocking over cemetery stones that he vowed he'd find one they couldn't budge. He seems to have succeeded.

Wine and Cheese

Vineyards and cheese dairies are both relative newcomers to the state's agricultural landscape. Although dairy farms have long been part of the New Hampshire scenery, only recently have they turned their attention to cheesemaking. In 2008, the wineries and dairies joined with a cider maker to create the *New Hampshire's Wine & Cheese Trails,* in conjunction with New Hampshire Made. Their brochure is available at state tourist information centers and on the website visitnh.gov. When planning travels to smaller farms and vineyards, it is always a good idea to call first to be sure they will be open.

The historic towns of Greenland and Stratham lie along the southern shore of Great Bay, whose ecosystem and history are explored at *Sandy Point Discovery Center.* Interactive displays inside show the importance of tidal estuaries as habitats and how they cleanse polluted waters. A look at the bay's history shows fishing and salt hay harvesting. Trails lead to various ecosystems along the shore and estuary, and nature pamphlets help you identify the birds and other wildlife you'll meet there. The center is open May through Oct, Wed through Sun 10 a.m. to 4 p.m.; admission is free. To find the center, which is signposted from Route 33, take Depot Road and turn left at the T; (603) 862-6700.

Cocheco Town

Dover was the scene of repeated Native American attacks during the early years of the settlement; so nearly all of its garrison houses were destroyed. The only one still surviving is the 1765 *Damm Garrison,* which is protected by a roofed lattice portico between two brick buildings of the *Woodman Museum.* In original condition, this heavy log structure houses a collection of early furnishings and implements. To learn the story of the Dover Massacre, which this garrison house survived, read *It Happened in New Hampshire,* an anecdotal history of the state with thirty-one incidents that tell its story from the first settlements to the fall of the Old Man of the Mountain in 2003.

The two exhibition buildings of the Woodman Museum are a tribute to the inquiring minds of the Victorians who assembled their contents. At the Woodman House you'll find collections of mounted animals, including specimens of most of the mammals native to the state and many, such as an 8-foot-tall polar bear, which are not. In addition to an extensive collection of rocks, minerals, and butterflies, the museum displays fine examples of Sioux beadwork. President Lincoln's saddle, used in his last review of troops and inherited by his aide, Colonel Daniel Hall, after Lincoln's assassination, highlights the Civil War collection on the third floor. The Hale House contains fine antique furniture and a variety of collections from the nineteenth century. Open April through mid-Dec, the Woodman Museum's hours are 10 a.m. to 5 p.m., Wed through Sun. The Woodman Museum is located at 182 Central Ave., Dover; call (603) 742-1038 or visit woodmanmuseum.org.

Kids and their parents love the *Children's Museum of New Hampshire,* just off the Lower Square on the banks of the Cocheco River. The 2009 facility explores the river in a multifaceted "Cochecosystem" exhibit that looks at both natural and industrial history. Visitors can see the river from a beaver's perspective as it builds its dam, or learn how Native Americans fished for alewives. Kids can also board a Piscataqua River gundalow to help load and unload cargo or "navigate" the boat down the river. A human-sized kaleidoscope fascinates everyone, as they see themselves reflected in every direction, but the museum's pièce de résistance is "Build It, Fly It." This aerodynamics exhibit teaches by doing, as budding engineers design their own flying machine from interlocking foam pieces in different shapes, then crank it up to the ceiling for a test flight. If it flops, the exhibit helps them redesign it until it flies. The museum is open Tues through Sat 10 a.m. to 5 p.m. and Sun from noon until 5 p.m., and on Mon from 10 a.m. to 5 p.m. during the summer, school vacations, and some holidays. Children's Museum of New Hampshire is located at 6 Washington St., Dover. Call (603) 742-2002 or visit childrens-museum.org for admission prices and additional information.

Along the Cocheco River in the center of Dover's downtown is an impressive complex of brick mill buildings, and facing these across Central Avenue are rows of classic mercantile buildings. Views and reminiscences of old Dover are posted along the sidewalk at various points, noting stores that were once there, and other historical anecdotes. A walking path follows the river through a park. On Central Avenue, near the Lower Square is a local institution that has provided generations with wedding and birthday cakes for more than half a century, run by the same family. **Harvey's Bakery** now has a coffee shop, so you can enjoy their famous maple bars with a cup of coffee at a booth, or have a more filling breakfast or lunch. Coffee shop hours are Mon through Sat 5:30 a.m. to 3 p.m. The bakery is open Mon through Fri 6 a.m. to 5 p.m. and Sat 6 a.m. to 4 p.m. Harvey's Bakery is at 376 Central Ave., Dover; call (603) 742-6029 for the bakery and (603) 749-3564 for the coffee shop, or visit harveysbakery.com.

Salmon Falls Stoneware is a potters' studio where they make salt-glazed stoneware and decorate it by hand with traditional designs. It is open daily from 9 a.m. to 5 p.m. You can find Salmon Falls Stoneware in the old Boston and Maine Engine House at 75 Oak St. in Dover; (603) 749-1467, (800) 621-2030 or salmonfalls.com.

Dover is a good place to use as a base while visiting the seacoast area. Quieter than Portsmouth or the beach towns, it is easier to find lodging here, especially in the summer. To sleep in the midst of history, head on over to Dover's **Silver Fountain Inn.** Built in 1871, the former private mansion has been converted to an inn which offers nine rooms representative of post-Civil War era elegance—Austrian crystal doorknobs, imported stone fireplaces, and hand-painted wall coverings. The inn also offers guests modern conveniences and amenities, including Wi-Fi and cable TV. However, you'll be so close to a variety of area attractions that you'll likely not need either during your stay. The Silver Fountain Inn is at 103 Silver St., Dover; (603) 750-4200; silverfountain.com.

New to the Dover area, ***The Garrison Hotel*** fuses historic charm with updated amenities to create the ideal home base for any New Hampshire trip. Situated just about halfway between Boston and Portland, Maine, this boutique hotel is a quick ten-minute jaunt from Portsmouth and a short hour from the White Mountains and Lake Winnipesaukee. In other words, if you're looking for the perfect point to leverage the most adventures from a single spot, The Garrison Hotel is it. Located at 200 Sterling Way in Dover. For rate and availability information, call (603) 842-6783 or visit thegarrisonhotel.com.

North of Dover is Rochester, where the ***Rochester Opera House*** has a tipping floor that rises on one end to provide better views of the stage and lowers to make a flat dance floor. By 1996, when the second effort to restore the magnificent 1908 theater began, no one remembered how the unique floor mechanism worked, and it seemed unlikely that it could be restored to working order. But the UNH engineering school began investigating and discovered its secret—a large screw, well hidden inside a column at the back of the auditorium. The mechanism has been restored, and the floor once again rises and falls. The Opera House is at 31 Wakefield St. in Rochester; (603) 335-1992; rochesteroperahouse.com. Route 6 of the COAST bus stops at the city hall; check coastbus.org.

Off Routes 4/202, west of Northwood, is ***Northwood Meadows State Park.*** This undeveloped parkland along the Lamprey River has several walking trails and fishing platforms, which are accessible to wheelchairs; call (603) 436-1552 for information.

The Ponds

Pawtuckaway State Park has both boat and canoe launches on the lake, two campgrounds with tent sites, a beach, and several hiking trails. One of these leads to the ***Pawtuckaway Boulders,*** a forest filled with huge glacial erratics that were broken off the cliffs on the three small mountains nearby, and carried by the glacier to their present location a few thousand feet away in a valley to the east. The boulders vary in size, with some as long as 60 feet and over 30 feet high. Paths also lead to the summits of the three small mountains, two of which offer open views to the south. The campgrounds are open from mid-June to Labor Day, with camping through Oct. Write Pawtuckaway State Park, RFD #1, 128 Mountain Rd., Nottingham 03290; call (603) 895-3031 or (603) 271-3628 for reservations.

Until recently, the town of ***Fremont*** was home to a relic of early Americana, which, sadly, closed a few years ago. Spaulding & Frost Cooperage had made white pine barrels since 1874. It was the oldest and largest cooperage

Missing: A 48-Foot White Rock

New Hampshire is covered in glacial erratics, those giant boulders the glaciers picked up in their travels and left off someplace else. A WPA guidebook written in the 1930s refers to one in Raymond as follows: "South of the railroad station is an erratic boulder of white quartz that was transported several hundred feet. It is 48 feet long, 39 feet wide, and from 24 to 30 feet high. Two pine trees have found lodgement in crevices."

However, this massive geological marker seems to have disappeared. That's a pretty hefty rock to carry off, unless you're a glacier, so it must either be there (perhaps now covered in moss and pine needles) or have been a figment of someone's imagination. Many of these erratics were quarried, but quartz is an unlikely building stone. So where did the rock go?

Bob Hart, a Raymond native, took on the challenge of finding it. He began by searching the location described in the WPA guide, but he extended his search in other directions. He combed the area north of the railway station, as described in that 1930s book, but the stone was actually south of the station. Unfortunately for rockhounds, it's in someone's backyard, surrounded by trees and covered in lichen, so it no longer stands out as a white beacon. Though readers can no longer visit the rock, at least the mystery has been solved.

in the world, and you can still see their building, marked by yet another state historic marker. This is not far from the old gunsmith shop, where John and Andrew Brown, prominent New Hampshire gunsmiths, had their shop from 1845 to 1907. Their shop served as the recruiting office where local men could enlist to serve in the Civil War. Route 107 crosses Route 101 near Raymond, east of Manchester, and Fremont is just to the south.

The small town of Fremont, where you will see an abundance of state historic markers, was a hotbed of historical happenings, one of which was the Mast Tree Riot in the mid-1700s, when locals, in the oft-used guise of Indians, attacked an agent of the king who came to investigate reports of locals cutting mast trees reserved for the Royal Navy. The 1800 *Fremont Meeting House* is one of only two in the United States with twin-ended porches and stairwells. Note also its high pulpit and box pews, typical of such early meetinghouses. The Fremont Meeting House is open by appointment and for the town's lively Old Home Days, the third Sunday in August (603-895-4032 or 603-887-6100).

The *Sandown Depot* is housed in a restored 1873 railroad station. It is thought to have been the busiest single-line railroad line in the country, with eighteen freight and sixteen passenger trains passing through Sandown each

Mast Tree Riot

In 1734, more than four decades before Lexington and Concord, rebellious colonists in Fremont instigated an event known as the Mast Tree Riot. At that time, white pine trees over a certain girth (perfect for masts for the Royal Navy's ships) were the property of the king of England, and colonists were forbidden from cutting any of these. When the king's surveyor came to inspect some illegally cut trees in Fremont, locals threatened his life. He wisely retreated, but when he returned with reinforcements, they were attacked by a band of "Indians," a handy, if politically incorrect disguise. It was one of the earliest armed encounters between colonists and representatives of the Crown.

day. Most of the original railroad equipment is still in place, including the telegraph office. Open on Saturdays from May through Oct, hours run from 10 a.m. to 2 p.m. Admission is free. The museum is on Route 121A at 6 Depot Rd. in Sandown. Call (603) 887-6100 or visit sandownnhdepot.org.

Inquire at the museum to see if the ***Sandown Meeting House*** on Fremont Road is open to visitors. Built in 1773 and 1774, it is the finest and best-preserved church structure in the state. It still has its original hand-wrought hinges and latches on the paneled doors, as well as the square pews and slave gallery. (It surprises many to learn that owning slaves was a fairly common practice among wealthier New England families—although never to the extent it was in the South.) The pulpit is goblet-shaped, with a canopy that acts as a sounding board. If you are interested in early construction techniques, ask to see the loft, reached by a ladder from the gallery. Crossbeams are staggered, and mortised joints are held by wooden keys. According to a local tale, the church took longer to construct than was anticipated, and the rum supply ran out. The workmen refused to continue until the supply was replenished. Just down Route 121A from the depot is ***Zorvino Vineyards,*** open daily from 11 a.m. to 5 p.m. At tasting dinners, the chef pairs their wines with various food styles, including Asian and Caribbean. Zorvino Vineyards is at 226 Main St., Sandown; call (603) 887-8463 or visit zorvino.com.

The ***Chester Village Cemetery*** dates from 1751 and contains monuments by a number of colonial master stone carvers. Look especially at the faces of the angels, a common motif on tombstones of the period. The story is that stoneworker Abel Webster, who lived in Chester in the 1700s, had a running theological quarrel with the townspeople. To get even with them, he put frowns on the faces of all the angels on the tombstones. The cemetery is located at the crossroads of Routes 121 and 102 in Chester.

ALSO WORTH SEEING ON THE SEACOAST

John Paul Jones House
43 Middle St., Portsmouth
(603) 436-8420
The 1758 house where Captain "Don't
Give up the Ship" lived when he was in
Portsmouth.

New Hampshire's coast has several
beaches, the best of which is Jenness
State Beach in Rye. Larger and more
crowded, with a perpetual carnival
atmosphere, is Hampton Beach; (603)
548-6002.

Northwood
on Routes 4/202, west of Dover, is an
antiques center, with more than a dozen
shops and group antiques markets lining
the road.

Route 121 leads from Chester to Auburn, past Lake Massabesic, where the Audubon Society has created a center for education and wildlife viewing. The **Massabesic Audubon Center** has miles of trails through fields and forests on a 135-acre point of land surrounded by water. Nature exhibits at the center include birds of prey, reptiles, and a garden to attract birds and butterflies. Frequent programs feature a variety of nature experiences and include day camps for children in the summer. From Route 101, follow Bypass 28 to Spofford Road, following signs to the center, which is at 26 Audubon Way, Auburn; (603) 668-2045; nhaudubon.org.

Bed-and-breakfast accommodations are surprisingly rare in this part of the state, so visitors are happy to discover **Stillmeadow B&B,** one of several well-restored mid-nineteenth-century homes on Route 121, 545 Main St. in Hampstead. Rooms are moderately priced, warm, and welcoming, with private baths, nicely chosen color schemes, and pleasant views. Breakfast is served with elegance in the dining room and features home-baked breads and muffins. Write to PO Box 565, Hampstead 03841, or call (603) 329-8381 or visit still-meadow.com. Reservations are required.

More Places to Stay on the Seacoast

DURHAM

Hickory Pond Inn
1 Stagecoach Rd.
(603) 659-2227 or
(800) 658-0065
Adjoining its own golf course, the inn has a homey feel, despite its motel-like rooms. There is cross-country skiing and a skating rink in the winter. Rooms include continental breakfast. Moderate rates.

HAMPTON

Lamie's Inn
490 Lafayette Rd.
(603) 926-0330
oldsaltnh.com
An inn in a 1740 home with a well-thought-of restaurant, and thirty-two rooms. Rates high-moderate.

HAMPTON BEACH

The Seascape Inn at Plaice Cove
955 Ocean Blvd.
(603) 926-1750
Motel style, nineteen rooms. Doubles moderate, lower off-season.

PORTSMOUTH

The Hotel Portsmouth
40 Court St.
(603) 605-8120
thehotelportsmouth.com
Located right downtown; blends the best of larger hotel amenities with the quaint comfort of a bed-and-breakfast.

The Port Inn
505 US Highway 1 Byp.
(603) 436-4378
Vintage charm and convenient location.

ROCHESTER

Governor's Inn
78 Wakefield St.
(603) 332-0107
governorsinn.com
Suites in an elegant mansion in downtown Rochester. Prices moderate.

(For additional dining and lodging, remember that Portsmouth is only 12 miles away.)

More Places to Eat on the Seacoast

CENTER BARNSTEAD

The Crystal Quail
202 Pitman Rd.
(603) 269-4151
crystalquail.com
Game meats are a favorite of chef/owner Harold Huckaby, who describes the three choices on the prix fixe menu to guests. Expect to hear about dishes such as rabbit in a mushroom cream sauce inside delicate crepes, pheasant breast sauced with red wine, or pheasant ravioli with wild boar bacon. Dinner by reservation only. Expensive.

TO LEARN MORE ABOUT THE SEACOAST

The Chamber Collaborative of Greater Portsmouth,
500 Market St., Portsmouth;
(603) 610-5510
portsmouthchamber.org

DOVER

La Festa
300 Central Ave.
(603) 743-1400
lafestabrickandbrew.com
Variety of brick oven pizzas, calzones, baked pastas, and hot grinders. For lighter fare, check out the cold grinders, salads, and appetizers. Free parking behind restaurant.

Newick's Lobster House
431 Dover Point Rd.
(603) 742-3205
newicks.com
A seafood staple of the New Hampshire coast since 1948. Try the legendary lobster roll or new local favorites like seafood shepherd's pie.

EXETER

11 Water Street
11 Water St.
(603) 773-5930
11waterst.com
The lunch and dinner menus offer a good variety, from mainstream to chicken saltimbocca and rosemary-smoked pork tenderloin. Moderate.

HAMPTON

The Old Salt at Lamie's Inn
490 Lafayette Rd., #9
(603) 926-8322
oldsaltnh.com
Chicken pot pie to prime rib, in a colonial setting. The chef insists on native clams and shrimp, and scrod from local waters, as well as using as much locally grown produce as possible. Inexpensive to moderate.

PORTSMOUTH

Jumpin' Jay's Fish Cafe
150 Congress St.
(603) 766-3474
jumpinjays.com
Innovative approaches to fish and seafood, such as sole roulades and haddock piccata. Up to seven varieties of fish are on the catch-of-the-day list, with a choice of sauces, such as lobster veloute. Open daily, reservations suggested. Moderate.

The Merrimack Valley

While the seaport provided the early links that built Portsmouth and Exeter, the size and force of the Merrimack River, as it gathered waters from rivers and mountain streams in the north, provided power for manufacturing that built the valley cities. Towns sprang up around the mills, and they continued to grow together. Manchester, the state's largest city, grew with the largest cotton-mill complex ever built. Even today, long after the mighty Amoskeag Mills closed their doors, the remaining mill buildings continue to dominate the city's riverbank.

This swath up the center of the state is flatter than the land to the north or the west and is characterized by rolling hills, small lakes, and a surprising amount of open space, especially north of Manchester.

The Merrimack Valley has never been tourist country. Most visitors pass through it on their way to the pleasures of the lakes and mountains farther north. Historically home to immigrant communities, Manchester has continued to diversify and remains a multicultural city, with the school system represented by students who speak more than seventy different languages. A quick stroll downtown evidences the global culinary influences enjoyed by local residents and visitors to the area.

THE MERRIMACK VALLEY

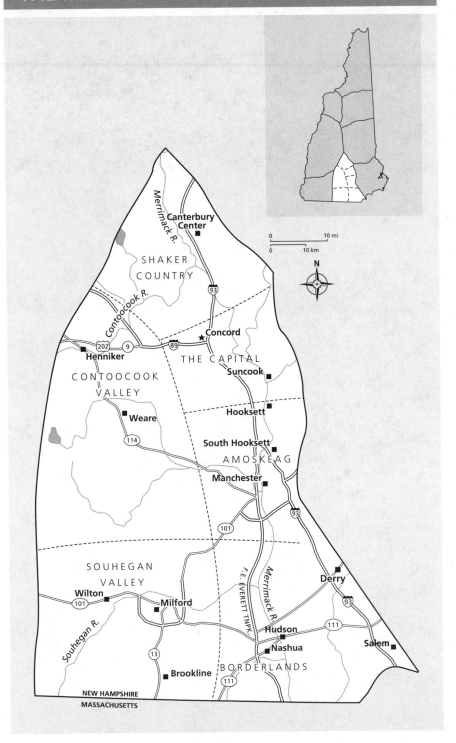

Canterbury
Center

SHAKER
COUNTRY

Merrimack R.

Contoocook R.

93

202 9
Henniker

Concord ★

89

THE CAPITAL

Suncook

CONTOOCOOK
VALLEY

Weare

Hooksett

114

South Hooksett

AMOSKEAG

Manchester

93

101

SOUHEGAN
VALLEY

F. E. EVERETT TNPK.

Merrimack R.

Derry

Wilton

101

Milford

93

111

Hudson

Salem

Souhegan R.

13

Nashua

Brookline

BORDERLANDS

111

NEW HAMPSHIRE
MASSACHUSETTS

0   10 mi
0   10 km

N

Borderlands

Although it is the state's second-largest city, **Nashua** is as rarely explored as the back roads that surround it. An early manufacturing city, it retains much of its millyard area and the canal that provided the 36-foot vertical drop needed to run the machinery. This history, as well as life in Nashua during the industrial era, is well illustrated in the museum of the **Nashua Historical Society.** Changing exhibits feature subjects ranging from the role of Nashua in wars since the Civil War (arranged with interpretive and background information, as well as artifacts) to the interior of a local dry-goods store. Children will enjoy the schoolroom and the player piano. Open year-round, Tues, Wed, and Thurs 10 a.m. to 3 p.m., subject to guide availability. The museum is at 5 Abbott St., just off Route 101A (Amherst St.), Nashua; (603) 883-0015.

Next door, and also owned by the historical society, is the elegant **Abbot-Spaulding House,** a Federal-style home built by the "Father of Nashua," Daniel Abbot. Both Daniel Webster and Franklin Pierce were frequent guests here; the furnishings were collected by the later owners and include several originals by designer Dexter Spaulding, as well as the family's collection of Sandwich glass. Although the Spauldings added some decorative details that were not there when the Abbots owned it, these are historically correct to the period and style of a leading family of the time. Open by appointment; call (603) 883-0015.

For a view of Nashua's canal, walk along the **Mine Falls Park Heritage Trail.** The path borders the river and canal, forming a loop that can be reached from Riverside Street, where there is ample parking. A put-in on Mill Pond gives canoes and small boats access to the canal. You can also reach the trail from the millyard in downtown Nashua.

A bright urban bistro, **MT's Local Kitchen and Wine Bar** is upscale, yet casual in its atmosphere, but not casual about its food. Presentation is attractive, and the dishes are a nice blend of innovation and tradition. They also feature a celebrated wine list. Open Sun through Thurs from 4 p.m. to 9 p.m. and Fri through Sat from 4 p.m. to 10 p.m. Located at 212 Main St., Nashua; (603) 595-9334; mtslocal.com. Prices are moderate. Just across the street, the same chef, Michael Buckley, operates **Surf,** specializing, as you might suspect, in the freshest of seafood, artfully prepared and presented, with hours that match MT's. Moderate pricing.

Another good choice for eating out, and significantly less formal, is **Martha's Exchange** at 185 Main St. Martha's has been there since 1932, and offers good, well-prepared food in an informal atmosphere. They also have their own mini-brewery and music and dancing Friday and Saturday nights. Open every day at 11 a.m. for lunch and dinner, closing Mon and Tues. at 9 p.m., Weds. at 9:30 p.m., Thurs at 11 p.m., and Fri and Sat at 1:00 a.m. Prices are moderate.

The **Seedling Cafe** in nearby Merrimack offers a warm and friendly atmosphere where you can get fresh, seasonal, organic foods prepared to order. Much of the produce in season is from the owners' organic gardens. The menu is heavy on wraps, but not those filled with the same old ingredients. Innovative sandwiches, such as honey-roasted turkey with tomatoes, red onions, cheddar cheese, applewood-smoked bacon, and fresh avocado on a whole wheat tortilla, are finished on the grill. Salads feature equally interesting flavor combinations. Organic and local beer and wines are also served. The Seedling Cafe is open Wed through Fri 8:30 a.m. until 2 p.m. and Sat 8 a.m. until 12 p.m., at 246 Daniel Webster Hwy., (603) 594-4002; theseedlingcafe.com.

The **Robert Frost Homestead** on Route 28 was the home of the poet for the first decade of the twentieth century. Frost credited the years that he spent at this Derry farm with shaping his future by providing him with time and seclusion. The simple 1880s farmhouse, the barn, the brook, orchards, and stone walls mentioned in his poems are all here, much as they were during his time. A nature trail labeled with lines of his poetry winds through meadow and forest. Open daily mid-June to Labor Day and weekends only Memorial Day to mid-June and Labor Day to Columbus Day. It's located at 122 Rockingham Rd., Derry; (603) 432-3091; robertfrostfarm.org.

Although sawmills are not rare in New Hampshire, the **Taylor Up and Down Sawmill** is the only up-and-down mill still operating. More than 200 years old, this sawmill is water-powered, with gears made of wood. The mill runs two Saturdays a month, May through Sept 10 a.m. to 3 p.m.; ask for dates if you are interested in seeing it. Write Ballard State Forest, Island Pond Rd., Derry 03038, or call (603) 431-6774.

On the first floor of the old fire station on West Broadway is the **Derry Fire Department Museum,** with old photos, vintage lifesaving and firefighting equipment, and an old industrial pumper from a local mill. Look for the poem Robert Frost wrote for the Derry Fire Department after he lost control

EVENTS IN THE MERRIMACK VALLEY

High Hopes Hot Air Balloon Festival
Father's Day Weekend, Hillsborough
(603) 464-0377

Hillsborough County Agricultural Fair
early Sept, New Boston
(603) 641-6060
hcafair.com

of a grass fire on his farm. Across the street at 29 West Broadway, #6 (603-434-1247), collections of the ***Derry Historical Society*** cover subjects ranging from the local witch hazel, shoe, and egg industries to native son and astronaut, Alan Shepard. Robert Frost is, of course, featured here. The museum is open Sundays from 1 p.m. to 5 p.m., and by appointment.

The village of East Derry, a short detour on the way to the Taylor Sawmill, was the original settlement in 1719; today several fine old buildings, including the village hall, make up the ***Upper Village National Historic District.*** A catalog of the buildings is available at the library, across from the village hall. A marker notes that the first white Irish potato in America was planted in the adjacent "common field."

The brunch buffet at ***The Bedford Village Inn*** has been voted the best in the state by *New Hampshire Magazine* readers, and it may be the biggest, too. Chef's stations prepare made-to-order omelets, waffles, and carved meats, and the buffet may include citrus-poached shrimp, maki rolls, steamed dumplings, or cheese blintzes with fruit compotes. The dinner menu is equally interesting, and dependent upon fresh seasonal ingredients. In the fall, for example, look for such dishes as grilled quail with red lentils and chorizo, or roasted heirloom beets mixed with horseradish, citrus aioli, and marinated cucumber. Desserts are a specialty: Consider hot chocolate potpie with White Russian ice cream and black currants. The Bedford Village Inn is at 2 Olde Bedford Way, just off Route 101 in Bedford; (603) 472-2001 or (800) 852-1166; bedfordvillageinn.com.

Amoskeag

Scouts and leaders will want to stop on the way into ***Manchester*** at one of the finest collections of Boy Scout memorabilia and books in the United States. The ***Lawrence L. Lee Scouting Museum*** is located at the headquarters of the Daniel Webster Council, where there are also picnic tables and camping facilities. Covering more than 3,000 feet of floor space, the museum houses more than 95 percent of all Scout books written in the United States, as well as historic uniforms, worldwide postage stamps commemorating Scouting, and the original paintings used for covers of *Boy's Life*. Located on 395 Blondin Rd. in Manchester; call (603) 861-2501 for more information and to confirm hours of operation (contingent on volunteer availability) or visit scoutingmuseum.org.

For more than a century, the ***Manchester Historic Association*** has preserved the history of this city. At one time the association's collection was shown in their 129 Amherst St. headquarters, but now that facility is used for research and special exhibits and the museum collections are housed in the ***Millyard Museum,*** located at 200 Bedford St., in Mill #3 at the corner of

Pleasant and Commercial Streets in Manchester (603-622-7531 or manchester-historic.org). The building housing the museum was once part of the huge Amoskeag Mill complex. The exhibit, "Woven in Time: 1,000 Years at Amoskeag Falls," tells the story of human life around the river and falls, beginning with paleo-Indians and ending with the mills and the people who manned the machines that made millions of yards of fabric. Another exhibit serves as the orientation center for the Amoskeag Millyard Scenic and Cultural Byway and includes large photomurals of the mills when they were in operation. In addition to the permanent exhibits, special exhibits are mounted frequently. The museum is open Tues. through Sat. from 10 a.m. to 4 p.m. While there, be sure to take the kids upstairs to the *Science Center* (603-669-0400; seescience center.org), where interactive exhibits allow kids to walk on the Moon and experience weightlessness, explore momentum, and even delve into chemical reactions in a real chemistry lab. Open Mon to Fri 10 a.m. to 4 p.m., Sat and Sun 10 a.m. to 5 p.m.

Book lovers and anyone who misses the independent bookstore in their town or city should check out one of downtown Manchester's newest businesses, *The Bookery* (844 Elm St.). Between an extensive selection of titles, a charming children's section, unique furniture, and a creative café, The Bookery is a great rainy day stop, or the perfect place to pop in for that beach read en route to the coast. For more information on hours and events, visit the website bookerymht.com or call (603) 836-6600.

For a no-frills meal, walk a block off Elm Street to the *Red Arrow Diner.* It will be open, whatever the time of day; it has been since 1922. Well, almost always; it does close for eight hours on Christmas Eve. The menu includes pork pie, baked beans (baked right there), chicken potpie, liver and onions, and meat loaf—you get the idea. Most entrees are priced under $6. Breakfasts are as generous as dinner and just as inexpensive. Open 24 hours, 7 days a week, all year, at 61 Lowell St. (between Chestnut and Elm Streets) in Manchester; (603) 626-1118.

Manchester has a lot of little places to eat, many of them ethnic restaurants run by people who came from the country whose cuisine is featured. *The Athens,* on Central Street (603-623-9317), is good for hearty portions of Greek food. A French-Canadian flavor is found at *Chez Vachon* at 136 Kelley St. (603-625-9660). Even if you never had a Québécois *memere* (grandmother), you could grow nostalgic over a big piece of *tourtiere* (pork pie) or the savory cretons on hot buttered toast. Locals even dip into Quebec-style *poutine,* fries topped with chicken gravy and fresh grated cheese. The atmosphere isn't fancy, nor is the food, but it's authentic, hearty, and tasty. Open for breakfast and lunch Mon through Fri 6 a.m. to 1:30 p.m., Sat and Sun 6 a.m. to 2 p.m.

A popular spot for sushi, **Mint Bistro** offers a sophisticated spin on Asian-inspired cuisine, boasting a menu designed to delight any palette. From main courses to tapas, salads, sushi, and sides, stop by for a cocktail and small plate, or make a reservation to enjoy more of the menu. Mint Bistro serves dinner Sun through Thur from 4 to 10 p.m.; Fri and Sat from 4 to 11 p.m. Located on 1105 Elm St.; (603) 625-6468; mintbistronh.com.

Just off the main drag of Elm Street, **The Crown Tavern** is a new jewel to Manchester's dining scene. Situated across the street from the historic Palace Theater, the Crown Tavern, "a fresh take on New England's 'publick houses'," specializes in delicious bites, featuring local ingredients and flavors. This is a fantastic spot to "savor the simple," and enjoy consistently creative and satisfying dishes, complemented by cocktails from a full bar, complete with an impressive beer and wine selection. The Crown is open Mon through Fri, from 11:30 a.m. to 9:30 p.m., and Sat from 4 to 9:30 p.m. The Crown is at 99 Hanover St. in Manchester; (603) 218-3132; thecrownonhanover.com.

Perhaps the success of The Crown comes as no surprise. The owners are the same proprietors behind the wildly popular **Hanover Street Chophouse,** The Crown's more upscale and refined older sibling. For a high-end dining experience devoted to steaks and seafood, check out the Chophouse menu at hanoverstreetchophouse.com; 149 Hanover St. or call (603) 644-2467 for reservations.

Those who have visited Manchester in the past might recall the popular Z Food and Drink, formerly located at 860 Elm St. Chef and owner Tom Puskarich has since branched out and opened **Restoration Café,** where healthy ingredients feature in undeniably delicious menu offerings. Stop by for a coffee, fresh-pressed juice, "snake oil" smoothie, breakfast, or lunch, Sun through Wed. 9 a.m. to 4 p.m., and Thur through Sat from 9 a.m. to 8 p.m. Look forward to brunch specials during the weekend, in addition to the weekly full menu. Restoration Café also serves beer and wine, and even offers Prosecco . . . on tap. Restoration Café is located at 235 Hanover St.; (603) 518-7260; restoration cafenh.com.

At **Matbah,** the menu is inspired by Turkish, Greek, and Middle Eastern cuisines, to the delight of locals and visitors to Manchester, alike. Open for lunch and dinner, Matbah is a can't miss spot for authentic Mediterranean staples like hummus, baba ganoush, tabbouleh, falafel, shish kebabs, moussaka, lamb,

somethingto beefabout

Before it became Manchester, the settlement of a few hardy souls at the falls of the Merrimack River was called Derryfield, and its residents subsisted largely on a diet of river eels, which became known as Derryfield beef.

and fresh fish dishes. Be sure to save room for homemade baklava. Stop by for lunch or dinner Tues through Sun. from 11 a.m. to 10 p.m., with hours extended to 11 p.m. on Sat. Matbah Mediterranean Cuisine is at 866 Elm St.; (603) 232-4066; matbahcuisine.com.

To the best of our knowledge, you'll only find one Nepalese restaurant in New Hampshire (maybe only one in New England), *Cafe Momo.* Try the *momo,* from which the name derives, a popular Nepalese appetizer of steamed dumpling, similar to the Chinese dim sum, but filled with meat or vegetables seasoned with ginger, chilis, and cumin. There's a good selection of vegetarian dishes served, but meats, including goat kebabs, are also on the menu. Cafe Momo is well outside the downtown area, located at 1065 Hanover St.; (603) 623-3733; cafemomonh.us.

The French-Canadian influence is still strong in Manchester, with a daily French-language newspaper and the *Franco-American Centre* at 100 St. Anselm Dr. (603-641-7114; facnh.com), whose library of more than 4,000 volumes centers on the development of French culture in North America. An art exhibit features French American artists' work, with regularly changing exhibits. Hours are by appointment only. The west side of town, across the river, was the French-Canadian neighborhood, dominated by the impressive *Sainte Marie's Church.* The architecture is distinctive, and the stone interior is reminiscent of the cathedrals of Quebec and Montreal.

Known for the breadth and depth of its collections, the *Currier Museum of Art* includes more than 11,000 works. Several first-floor galleries are reserved for changing exhibitions, bringing to view hundreds of items that had long languished in storage. The second floor is devoted to American art from the eighteenth and nineteenth centuries, highlighting the works of romantic artists such as Albert Bierstadt and Thomas Cole, along with works of Benjamin Champney and other artists who worked in the White Mountains. American impressionists include Childe Hassam and William Metcalf.

The museum's European collection—featuring works by Tiepolo, van Ruisdeal, Constable, and Monet—shares galleries with works dating from the late Middle Ages. Twentieth-century art occupies five galleries that include paintings by Matisse, Picasso, Rouault, and Georgia O'Keefe. An immense collection of paperweights is in a gallery devoted entirely to glass and ceramics. Tours of the *Zimmerman House,* designed by Frank Lloyd Wright, begin at the museum, by reservation only. Museum hours are Sun through Fri from 11 a.m. to 5 p.m. (closed Tues), and Sat from 10 a.m. to 5 p.m. Admission is $15 for adults, $13 for seniors, $10 for students, $5 for youth (ages 13–17); members and children under 13 years old enter for free. The Currier is located at 150 Ash St., Manchester; (603) 669-6144; currier.org.

For a modern boutique hotel experience set against a historic backdrop rich in aesthetic charm, book one of the five available rooms at Manchester's *Ash Street Inn.* This 1885 Victorian has been completely renovated to make room for up-to-date amenities, while preserving the building's original details like stained-glass and Victorian double-hung windows. Only a few blocks from the downtown area, the Ash Street Inn is located in the tree-lined, picturesque North End neighborhood of the city. Just a ten-minute drive from the airport, this is the perfect home base for your trip to New Hampshire, whether your travels are driven by business or pleasure. Depending on the season, guests love to snag a spot on the wraparound porch, although the rooms also feature beautiful furniture and cozy nooks ideal for reading and napping—no matter the weather. Given the limited number of rooms, reservations are encouraged well in advance of the busy summer and fall seasons. The Ash Street Inn provides package options for prospective guests as well, including the Frank Lloyd Wright, Love in Bloom, and Wedding Stay packages. Rates average between $169 and $229 per night, plus tax; however, these do vary according to room type and season. Visitors are encouraged to consult the website for updated prices on the availability calendar, or just give a call. 118 Ash St.; (603) 668-9908; ashstreetinn.com.

On Hanover Street between Chestnut and Pine Streets, is a nicely designed and executed wall mural depicting the mill heritage that built Manchester. Continue up Hanover Street, away from the center of the city, to see some excellent examples of Victorian architecture lining both sides of the street.

The Merrimack River, whose power once operated machinery of the Amoskeag Mills, now produces electricity at the Amoskeag Hydro Station. When salmon were restored to the river, a fish ladder was built to permit the fish to return to their spawning grounds. The Merrimack River basin can support an adult salmon population of about 3,000, and visitors to the *Amoskeag Fishway* can watch the fish make their way up a series of stepped pools in late May. Large viewing windows allow visitors to observe fish at eye level. The fish ladder is open from May to mid-June, with displays, programs, and films that illuminate the history, ecology, and wildlife of the river and of Manchester. Admission is free, and the area is wheelchair accessible. Enter at 4 Fletcher St., where parking is easily accessible on the left-hand side. The exhibit hall is open Mon through Sat 9 a.m. to 5 p.m., year-round. Contact (603) 626-FISH (3474); facebook.com/amoskeagfishways.

The only public archery ranges in New Hampshire are at *Bear Brook State Park,* northeast of Manchester. Maintained by the Fish and Game Department, each consists of fifteen targets. An additional four-target practice range is wheelchair accessible. The park includes several ponds, two marshes, and a wildlife refuge and offers swimming, tent camping, and fishing as well. Hiking trails, many of which become cross-country ski trails in the winter, cover the area.

One of the very few Civilian Conservation Corps (CCC) camps left in the Northeast is in Bear Brook State Park. The buildings house a CCC museum, a snowmobile museum, a nature center, and the *Museum of Family Camping* (603-485-3782). This unusual museum was the dream of Richmond campground owner Roy Heise, whose own collection formed the nucleus. Here you will see camping equipment from the sport's earliest years—tents, stoves, lanterns, and cooking utensils that show how camping evolved from a relatively rare means of travel to one of America's most popular summer pastimes. Much of the parkland itself was part of the CCC camp during the 1930s, and many of the picnic sites, hiking trails, recreation buildings, and roads were built by the CCC. Write Bear Brook State Park, 157 Deerfield Rd., Allenstown 03275, or call (603) 485-9874 to confirm museum hours, which are dependent upon the season.

The park is also home to the *New Hampshire Snowmobile Museum Association,* again, housed in a former CCC building. The collection is rather extensive and begins with one of the very first snow-traveling machines, an early '20s Model T Ford adapted by Virgil White of Ossipee. In addition to the well-known brands Arctic Cat and Bombardier, the collections include Lombard, Eliason, and Bolens, among others. Also at the museum is a 1992 Arctic Cat driven on a 10,252-mile trip from Alaska to Nova Scotia in 1992. The association recommends that prospective visitors call to make sure a volunteer is there. Contact the association directly at (603) 722-7069.

The *Fitts Museum* in nearby Candia is a two-story house with a low-hipped roof. Two rooms are the original 1820 dwelling, with later Federal additions. Along with its antiques-filled rooms, the museum has a special event each Saturday afternoon in the summer—the only time it's open. Children's Day features herbs, spinning and weaving, or classic cars may even be the subject; you're bound to find an interesting activity at this free community museum. Open on the third Saturday of the month, from May to Oct, 1 to 4 p.m. While admission is free, donations are always appreciated. The Fitts Museum is found on Route 27, Candia. Appointments for viewing can be made by contacting fittsmuseum.org.

A couple of miles west of the museum and also on Route 27, *Charming-fare Farm* offers hay rides and sleigh rides through their forest wildlife park, where you'll see native New Hampshire animals. Smaller sleighs and carriages for a couple or a family can be reserved ahead. In the winter, bring marshmallows to roast at the campfire, where the sleigh stops for a warm-up. In the

Oakhurst Dairy Discovery Barn, you can see miniature sheep and goats, as well as baby animals that children can feed and pat in this hands-on environment. Call (603) 483-5623 or visit charmingfare.com.

The Capital

Although it is important as the center of government for the state, ***Concord*** is not a large city. (Incidentally, if you want to immediately label yourself as an outlander, pronounce Concord as you would the usual noun. In New England, it's pronounced "conquered.") Historically, Concord's manufacturing remained small, and even now it retains the appearance of a stately

Baseball in New Hampshire

For more than a decade, the New Hampshire Fisher Cats, voted "Best New Hampshire Sports Team" by *New Hampshire Magazine,* have represented Minor League Baseball in Manchester. A member of the American Eastern League, the Fisher Cats are the Double-A affiliate of the American League's Toronto Blue Jays.

Playing on home turf at Manchester's Northeast Delta Dental Stadium, the Fisher Cats consistently win league titles and garner community accolades like "Best Sporting Event to Take Clients to," by *New Hampshire Business Review,* along with "NH's Favorite Sporting Event for Families," by *Parenting New Hampshire Magazine.* For ticket options, visit the New Hampshire Fisher Cats' official website at milb.com/new-hampshire/tickets/single-game-tickets.

The national pastime is as popular in the state as elsewhere. Nashua has its own independent minor league team named the **Nashua Silver Knights,** which plays at the city's historic Holman Stadium on Amherst Street. Call (603) 718-8883, or buy tickets online at nashuasilverknights.com/holman-stadium.

The summer games of the **New England Collegiate Baseball League** are another way to see great ball and watch future major league players. The league season is from the first week of June to the first week of August. Players from colleges all over the nation join teams in the league, living, working, and playing ball in their host communities.

Keene is hometown to the **Keene Swamp Bats,** a clever play on words, involving the little creatures that fly high over their Alumni Field home on Arch Street. In 2000 and 2003 they won the New England Conference title, and in 2001 they ended the season in second place. They are known to baseball fans for an exciting ball game and for their lovable mascot, Ribby. From Central Square take West Street about 1.75 miles and turn left onto Arch Street. Tickets at the stadium cost $5; call (603) 357-5464 or go to swampbats.pointstreaksites.com/view/swampbats.

turn-of-the-twentieth-century city, with its brick business blocks and government buildings of gray granite.

Blending into these buildings that surround the statehouse is the *New Hampshire Historical Society.* The sculpture above the columned granite facade is the work of Daniel Chester French, creator of the Minuteman statue in Concord, Massachusetts, and the seated Lincoln in Washington, DC.

Most of the society's collections are in the nearby *Museum of New Hampshire History,* opposite the front of the State House, on Main Street. You'll find the museum tucked into a little plaza, behind an unusual iron gate. As the state historical society's museum, it has collections far too vast to be displayed in their entirety, but modern gallery space allows the museum to mount special exhibits that last for a few months to a year, interpreting events, trends, and periods in the state's history. Whether the historical society is examining the works of the White Mountain artists during the era of the grand hotels or taking a closer look at the Shakers, the exhibits are arresting and informative.

Special exhibits mounted by the museum have centered on the Old Man of the Mountain, the work of prominent seacoast photographer Lewis Hine, the historic New Hampshire primary, and "Treasures of New Hampshire History." Included among the treasures are letters from George Washington, Thomas Jefferson, and Walt Whitman; a 1583 bible rescued from pirates, and the New Hampshire Constitution, which was printed six months before the Declaration of Independence.

A focal point is an original Concord coach. Splendid in decorative detail, these coaches were as strong and as well constructed as they were beautiful. They were, in fact, so perfect in their design that from the 1820s to the early 1900s, during which time more than 3,000 of them were built in Concord, almost no changes were made in their construction. It was the most perfect traveling vehicle known to its time, often called "the coach that won the West."

The small museum shop in the historical society is an excellent source of publications on New Hampshire and its history. Many of these are privately printed and hard to find elsewhere. The admission charge is $5.50 for adults, $4.50 for seniors, and $3 for children (ages 6–18); maximum family rate is $17. It's open Tues through Sat 9:30 a.m. to 5 p.m., Sun noon to 5 p.m. Open Mon. July 1 through Oct. 15 and in Dec. Just off I-93 at exit 14, Eagle Square, Concord; (603) 228-6688; nhhistory.org.

ifitain'tbroke don'tfixit

Built of New Hampshire granite (is there any other kind?), the State House in Concord is the oldest state capitol building in the nation where the legislature still meets in its original chamber. It was first occupied in 1819.

House of India is a good downtown dining choice, with a varied menu of well-prepared dishes from the Indian subcontinent. From the tandoor oven comes fresh-baked *nan, poori,* and *chapatti* as well as tandoori chicken and shrimp and chicken *tikkas.* Flavors vary from delicate and mild to a chicken vindaloo that will curl your hair. If you're not familiar with Indian foods, ask for one of the combination dishes or the mixed grill from the tandoor. House of India is just off South Main Street, at 6 Pleasant St.; (603) 227-5266; houseofindiah.com.

Concord's arts calendar is enriched by the ***Concord Community Music School,*** which brings recitals, lunch-hour concerts, free outdoor summer concerts, children's programs, and a variety of other classical and jazz performances to the area. For a complete schedule, write to the school at 23 Wall St., Concord 03301, call (603) 228-1196 or visit ccmusicschool.org.

The ***McAuliffe-Shepard Discovery Center*** opened in 2009, replacing the former Christa McAuliffe Planetarium, built to honor the New Hampshire teacher who died along with six other astronauts in the *Challenger* disaster. The air and space science center covers space exploration and allied sciences in interactive exhibits and a twenty-first-century planetarium. Visitors can try landing a space capsule on the moon, or use a flight simulator to land an airplane. Kids are engaged by Brain-Bites, short videos illustrating cool facts about space suits, using an electric screwdriver in a weightless environment, and how astronauts train to overcome motion sickness. State-of-the-art projection shows are scheduled daily, among them Dawn of the Space Age, Tonight's Sky, Oasis in Space, Black Holes, and Ice Worlds. Exhibits appeal to all ages; many are more complex and explain astronomical phenomena and the challenges of space on an adult level. The Countdown Café serves fresh-built sandwiches, salads, and snacks. The McAuliffe-Shepard Discovery Center is at 2 Institute Dr., Concord, and is open daily 10:30 a.m. to 4 p.m. Admission is $11.50 for adults, $10.50 for seniors and students (age 13 through college), $8.50 for children (ages 3–12); children 2 and younger, as well as members, receive free admission. Planetarium shows are available as an add-on to general admission for $5 per person. For information call (603) 271-7827 or visit starhop.com.

At the north end of Concord is the ***Silk Farm Wildlife Sanctuary*** and the headquarters of the New Hampshire Audubon Society. Trails traverse the forests and wetlands along the edge of Great Turkey Pond and cut across orchards, hedgerows, and fields where visitors can see rare wildflowers, as well as birds and small animals. Audubon House provides a year-round bird blind, an excellent wildlife library, and a shop featuring a variety of nature guides and gifts with a wildlife theme. The New Hampshire Audubon Society is at 84 Silk Farm Rd. in Concord, easily reached from exit 2 off I-89. Call (603) 224-9909 for more information.

Birth of the Concord Coach

Lewis Downing and Steven Abbot built an industry that made Concord the Detroit of its time. Downing started making carriages in the early nineteenth century and by the Civil War was shipping hundreds annually, most to the American West. These were the famed stagecoaches used by Wells Fargo and other companies. Buffalo Bill spread their fame, using one in his Wild West Show.

Visitors today can see these transportation heroes at the Concord Group Insurance Companies on Bouton Street in Concord, the Museum of New Hampshire History at 6 Eagle Sq., the Concord Monitor at 1 Monitor Dr., and Canterbury Shaker Village at 288 Shaker Rd. in Canterbury.

Elsewhere in the state they can be found at the general store in Moultonborough, the Flume in Franconia Notch, Six Gun City in Jefferson, at the base of the Mount Washington Auto Road in Glen, and at Old Home Days and other local events, when those owned by historical societies and private residents are rolled out to be admired.

More information on the coaches is available from the Concord Coach Society, 18 Park St. in Concord, or visit theconcordcoach.tripod.com/abbotdowning.

Silk Farm Road leads into the back entrance of **St. Paul's School,** whose chapel has a finely executed fresco in the oratory to the left of its entrance, a replica of Lorenzetti's great fresco at Assisi. Two mobiles by Alexander Calder are also on the campus; one is suspended from the ceiling in the lobby of Memorial Hall, and the other is on the grounds nearby. The outdoor mobile is stored from November through March to protect it from the harsh winter weather.

Across the river to the east, in Concord Heights, the **Society for the Protection of New Hampshire Forests** maintains several buildings powered by alternative energy sources, as well as nature trails. This organization is responsible for the preservation of huge tracts of land throughout the state by either outright ownership, purchase of development rights, or helping private and governmental bodies in their efforts to save important lands and forests. Take East Side Drive (Route 132) north from Bridge Street (Route 9) to a left turn onto Portsmouth Street (you will pass the other end of this street going to the right shortly before the turn you want). The address is 54 Portsmouth St. Call (603) 224-9945 for information about registering for events, tours, and ways to get involved.

The **Merrimack River Watershed Council** sponsors free canoe trips on rivers in all parts of the state; you can bring your own canoe or rent one. For a schedule of trips, write to them at 60 Island St., Suite 211-E, Lawrence, MA 01849; call (978) 655-4742 or visit merrimack.org.

Shaker Country

East Side Drive becomes Mountain Road, still Route 132, which leads to *Canterbury* and the beautifully maintained *Shaker Village.* Set on a hill among rolling meadows, this was once a thriving 4,000-acre farm where 300 Shakers lived and worshiped in an atmosphere of common ownership, celibacy, and a strong work ethic. In the twenty-two buildings of the village, you will see original examples of Shaker crafts in the furnishings of the houses. Skilled craftspeople are at work with wood, fiber, and plants creating baskets, boxes, brooms, and herbal crafts. Authentic lunches and dinners are re-created in the Creamery, where they use herbs from the village's garden. Guided tours begin on the hour and take about ninety minutes. A gift shop features Shaker reproductions and New Hampshire crafts. Thomas Merton once observed, "The peculiar grace of a Shaker chair is due to the fact that it was built by someone capable of believing that an angel might come and sit on it." Both that grace and its spiritual origins are evident throughout the village. Hours are seasonally dependent and visitors are encouraged to call first for updated hours and prices of admission. For information write to Canterbury Shaker Village, 288 Shaker Rd., Canterbury 03224; call (603) 783-9511 or visit shakers.org.

The Shaker Table is a fine dining restaurant at the village, specializing in lunch service exclusively. Reservations are strongly recommended and can be made by calling (603) 708-1192 or visiting shakers.org/shop-dine/the-shaker-table.

One of the things we love most about New Hampshire's is the little surprise around the next corner, and one of these is about 4 miles north of the Shaker Village, where you'll find *Fox Country Smoke House.* That's a treat, since they sell a boggling variety of their own smoked products, from garlic kielbasa and beef jerky to smoked almonds, duck, Irish bacon, rainbow trout, smoked cheeses, and even dog treats. What's more, you (and Rover) can enjoy a picnic, featuring any of these delights, at a table in their own picnic area in the woods. To find Fox Country, follow signs from I-93 to Shaker Village, then continue north about 2.5 miles and go left, following Smoke House signs for another 1.5 miles; (603) 783-4405 or (800) 339-4409.

The town of *Tilton* is inextricably linked with the Tilton family, the generous benefactors of much of the town's artistic heritage. Charles Tilton, like many cultured men of his time, believed in the importance of public statuary and began to set about ornamenting his hometown. Overlooking the town from a steep hillside on the opposite side of the river is the *Tilton Arch,* an exact replica of the Arch of Titus in Rome. Built of Concord granite, it rises 55 feet from its base, upon which lies a red granite lion. It is actually in the town of Northfield, and you can get there via the bridge at the monument on Main Street, turning left on the far side and going uphill to the Northfield Town Hall. Beside the town hall, a dirt road leads to the top of the hill and the monument.

Five of Charles Tilton's statues remain. A marble allegorical statue of America—depicted as an Indian princess—stands on Main Street, as do statues symbolizing Europe and Asia. A zinc statue of Chief Squantum now stands in a parking lot. An iron footbridge connects the town with an island, once the site of the Tilton summerhouse and now a shaded park.

Fine mansions still grace Tilton, and one of them, on West Main Street, is of particular interest. The **Black Swan** bed-and-breakfast is a beautifully preserved Victorian, filled with period architectural and decorative detail. Original wall stenciling has been uncovered during renovation. One guest room includes a huge semicircular sitting room alcove with stained-glass panels over each of its seven windows. Each room has some distinctive antique feature or furnishing, and the dining room is fully paneled in oak with built-in china cupboards and a fireplace. The gardens and lawns sweep down to the riverbanks, overhung by shade trees. It's a thoroughly enjoyable resting place at moderate prices. Write the Black Swan at 354 West Main St., Tilton 03276; (603) 286-4524; blackswaninn.net.

A number of fine craftspeople have studios in or near Tilton. The **Country Braid House** is both workshop and showroom for hand-braided wool rugs. Visitors are welcome to tour the workshop and learn about rug braiding. Those who would like to try their hand at it will find rug-braiding kits for sale. Open Mon through Fri 9 a.m. to 5 p.m., and Sat 9 a.m. to 4 p.m.; at 462 W. Main St. in Tilton; (603) 286-4511 or countrybraidhouse.com.

Affectionately called T-HOP by locals, **Tilton House of Pizza** doubles as a family restaurant and community center, thanks to the good food and friendly owners. Pizza is only the beginning of the menu, which includes Italian and Greek dishes (including baklava), as well as seafood plates. Meatball subs just don't get any better. From I-93 exit 20, head west on Route 3, which becomes the main street of downtown Tilton. Tilton House of Pizza is at 298 Main St., Tilton; call (603) 286-7181, or scope out their weekly specials online, tiltonhouseofpizza.com.

The sign with the happy cow will make you smile, but the fried clams will make the smile even wider at **Dipsy Doodle Dairy Bar,** just over the line into Northfield. Their big, fat, juicy clams taste like the sea—and are cooked just right, so they are tender and juicy inside, crisp outside, and never greasy. Warning: Once you've eaten their hot lobster roll with butter, you may never be satisfied with ho-hum mayo lobster rolls again. And of course, there is the ice cream, served in giant scoops. To find them from Route 3 in Tilton, turn south at the railway station, at the west end of the business district—that's Park Street. Open May through Oct. Dipsy Doodle Dairy Bar, 143 Park St., Northfield, just north of I-93 exit 19; call (603) 286-2100 or visit dipsydoodle.com.

Contoocook Valley

West of Concord lies an area of rolling farmlands and attractive villages. Hopkinton's wide Main Street is lined with trees and a number of homes from the colonial era. In the center of town on Main Street, the *New Hampshire Antiquarian Society* features a museum of early items including journals, diaries, maps, and a collection of music scores. The building, which is on the National Register of Historic Places, also houses a library for genealogical and historical research. Call (603) 746-3825 for current hours and inquiries.

St. Andrew's Episcopal Church, in the village center, has particularly fine stained-glass windows and, unlike most churches, has a thorough printed history of them, researched and written by retired St. Paul's teacher, John Archer. The latest of these windows was added by Tiffany, a cross-and-lilies design much simpler than most Tiffany windows. You can get a copy of Archer's book and a key to the church from the office on weekdays.

Meet farm animals up close, ride in a horse-drawn wagon to choose your own pumpkin from the field, get lost in a corn maze, or just buy a big ice-cream cone and enjoy it at the picnic tables on the front lawn of *Beech Hill Farm* in Hopkinton. Owned for generations by the Kimball family, this diverse farm also has a garden center, a small museum of antique farm tools, and a bakery, all open May through Oct. 107 Beech Hill Rd., Hopkinton; call (603) 233-0828 or visit beechhillfarm.com.

A turn off Route 9/202 onto Route 127 in West Hopkinton takes you across the Hopkinton Dam, with its Art Deco–style control building. At the foot of the hill on the other side is Rowell's Covered Bridge. The road parallels a pretty stretch of the Contoocook River and leads past *Elm Brook Park,* with a beach, playgrounds, walking trails, a shaded picnic grove, and launch for kayaking and canoeing on one of the several lakes of the dam impoundment. At the far end, airplanes often circle above the park's radio-controlled model airplane flying field. The park is open mid-May through the second weekend in Sept from 9 a.m. to 6 p.m., Mon through Fri, and 9 a.m. to 8 p.m. (7 p.m. in Sept.) on Sat and Sun. A fee of $2 per person is charged, with a minimum day use of $5 per car. Call (603) 746-3601 or visit nhstateparks.com.

The only *Henniker* on earth was named for a London merchant who was a friend of Royal Governor Benning Wentworth. New England College is in the center of town and gives it a lively air. The college offers a series of cross-country ski trails named for Marx Brothers movies. The toughest, which goes over a small mountain, is called You Bet Your Life.

Skiing is not a new pastime in Henniker. For more than thirty years, the Patnaude family has operated one of New Hampshire's southernmost ski areas, *Pats Peak.* It's not easy keeping a mountain skiable in southern New Hampshire, but even when it is brown everywhere else, Pats manages to keep the trails white. Some of the most modern snowmaking equipment in the east covers 100 percent of the trails and fires up whenever the temperature allows; that is good enough to keep skiers happy and on the slopes. About half of the twenty-two trails are rated as novice, whereas the balance is split between advanced and expert—and when they say expert, they mean it. The food in the base lodge is homemade, and it's the kind of family ski area where you don't mind your kids skiing alone. Ski school, nursery, rentals, and other facilities are offered, and ticket sales are limited to the number of people that the lifts can comfortably handle without overcrowding. Write Pats Peak, 686 Flanders Rd., Route 114, Henniker 03242; call (603) 428-3245 or (888) PATS–PEAK; patspeak.com.

Fine dining and lodging are only a bit out of town at the *Colby Hill Inn,* a rambling New England hostelry that has been updated and renovated without losing its country-inn flavor. The sixteen guest rooms, each with a private bath

Paddlers' Alert

The Merrimack River between Franklin, where the river is formed by the confluence of the Pemigewasset and the Winnipesaukee, and Concord offers gentle paddling for kayakers and canoeists, with a few stretches reaching class II status. The put-in in Franklin is below the high school, where the water can be fast moving, but below that the river slows and swings in great snakelike curves through Boscawen until it reaches a dam a little over 3 miles below the bridge where Route 4 crosses the river in Penacook.

The prettiest stretch is between Northfield, south of Franklin, and a takeout just downstream from the point where the Contoocook River joins from the west (left). In this stretch you'll see hardly any sign of humans as you paddle a very lazy river, sometimes beneath 50-foot banks. Don't expect much help from the current in the summer, when the surface is almost lakelike.

You can paddle farther, taking out above the Sewalls Falls Dam in West Concord. Or you can run a stretch of rapids below the dam and continue about 7 miles farther, past sand bluffs to a takeout south of the bridge where US 202/I-393 crosses the river.

Is It the Ghost of Ocean-Born Mary?

On Gulf Road off Route 114 in Henniker stands a house that was home to "Ocean-Born Mary." Shortly after her birth on the high seas in 1710, the ship was attacked by pirates, but their leader, on seeing the infant, promised to leave the ship unharmed if the mother would name the child Mary, after his mother. The pirate left a bolt of silk for Mary's wedding dress. Mary lived to a ripe old age in her Henniker house. After her death and until fairly recently, owners and neighbors have reported seeing a black carriage drive up to the house at night and stop, while a veiled figure descended and walked (or floated) to the well, where it appeared to drop in a parcel before leaving in the ghostly carriage. You can find Mary's tombstone, labeled "Widow Mary Wallace," in the Quaker Cemetery on Quaker Meeting House Road.

and two with working fireplaces, are decorated with antiques. Details of decor and hospitality are all here—elegant bed linens, a full cookie jar, plenty of public rooms, and spontaneous and gregarious hosts. The location is perfect, surrounded by meadows and a backyard where you can watch pheasants as you sit in the perennial garden. In the winter, part of the backyard becomes a skating rink for guests.

The dining room at Colby Hill Inn serves dinner to the public as well as to inn guests—and a fine dinner, too, with a frequently changing menu. Chicken breast stuffed with lobster is the signature dish. The salmon is cooked to perfection. This is a full-service inn, so its prices are higher than those of a typical bed-and-breakfast, but also include a full country breakfast. Call (603) 428-3281 or visit colbyhillinn.com for more information and to make reservations.

For gifts that are a little less farmhouse style and a little more farm animal, check out the **Fiber Studio.** This shop features hand-dyed yarns, beads, and supplies for spinning, weaving, and knitting, as well as hand-woven fabrics and sheep-related gifts. It's at 161 Foster Hill Rd. off Routes 202 and 9 in Henniker; (603) 428-7830.

The Souhegan Valley

Union Square, known to everyone as "The Oval," is lined with shops, among them the eclectic **Moonstone Antiques** (603-673-0303), located at 263 Union, with a quirky assortment that ranges from vintage hats to furniture and china. If a stop at Moonstone puts you in the mood for serious antiquing, continue on 101A (now Elm Street) to number 323, and the easy-to-spot **New Hampshire Antique Co-Op.** The 200-plus dealers occupy 20,000 square feet of galleries and display area, some of it in room settings. For the best bargains, investigate the Discovery Barn, or raise your sights in galleries devoted to nineteenth- and twentieth-century fine art paintings. Call (603) 673-8499 or visit nhantiquecoop .com.

If you're within reach of the Milford area in late September, you're sure to see brightly colored balloons decorating the sky. They are from the High Hopes Foundation's annual *High Hopes Balloon Festival.* In addition to popular hot-air balloon rides, the event has hayrides, skydivers, helicopter rides, live entertainment, a craft show, and food booths. The proceeds go to the foundation, which is dedicated to granting the wishes of seriously ill New Hampshire children. Contact them at High Hopes Foundation, 12 Murphy Drive, Suite 106, Nashua 03062; (603) 966-3483 or highhopesfoundation.org.

A very handy (and very good) stop on Route 101 for breakfast, lunch, or teatime is the *Black Forest Cafe* in Amherst. Classical music, the morning papers, giant scones, and huge cups of coffee make for a good way to start a day. Lunch brings grilled chicken on a bed of greens, crab cakes, or unique sandwiches at moderate prices. The bakery, also known as the marketplace, (with cafe tables) is open 8 a.m. to 6 p.m. on Mon; 8 a.m. to 8 p.m. Tues through Sat; and 8 a.m. to 5 p.m. on Sun. The dining room serves only lunch on Mon from 11 a.m. to 3 p.m.; Tues through Sat 11 a.m. until 8 p.m.; and Sun brunch 8 a.m. to 2:30 p.m. Call (603) 672-0500 or visit theblackforestcafe.com for additional information.

Sausage is the specialty of *The Dog House,* also beside Route 101 a bit farther west in Wilton, at 766 Elm St. Choose a traditional long hot dog or bratwurst on a *brochen* with sauerkraut and a side of tasty German potato salad. The House scoops up generous ice-cream cones; you can eat at the picnic tables in the tidy yard.

Water power was central to New Hampshire industry from the earliest days, and *Frye's Measure Mill* is still operated by an upright turbine driven by water from two ponds. Actively engaged in the making of fine round and oval wooden boxes, just as the first ones were made here in 1858. The mill shop sells the shaker and colonial boxes, as well as other early crafts. The mill is located at 12 Frye Mill Rd., at the junction of Davisville Road and Burton Highway in Wilton; call (603) 654-6581 for more information or visit fryes measuremill.com.

Andy's Summer Playhouse, also in Wilton, gives children stage experience and adults enjoyable summer-theater productions, from June through Aug. Call (603) 654-2613 or visit andyssummerplayhouse.org for summer shows and ticket prices.

The rambling *Birchwood Inn* is as much a part of the town of Temple as the neighboring white-spired church. Its low-ceilinged dining room is decorated with murals believed to be by Rufus Porter, an itinerant nineteenth-century painter. Now owned by a trio of Brits, there is an emphasis on all things British, such as a full English breakfast and British specialties in the dining room. Look for the likes of "A taste of Old England in New England," featured in steak-and-ale pie, fish-and-chips, bangers and mash, and shepherd's pie, in addition to the daily specials. The consistent focus in the kitchen is on the use of fresh, locally grown products when available. On Route 45, a few miles off Route 101, in Temple, the inn is open year-round and serves dinner Wed through Sat evenings from 4:30 to 9:30 p.m.; (603) 878-3285 or thebirchwoodinn.com.

Along the border west of Nashua are the quiet country towns of Hollis, Brookline, and Mason, where roads wind among fields and through forests that sometimes meet overhead. *Silver Lake State Park* is here, with a good horseshoe-shaped shallow beach that is nearly empty on weekdays (but can get very crowded on summer weekends); admission is $4 for adults, $2 for children aged 6–10; seniors and children under 5 admitted free.

Hollis Flea Market is nearby, a huge area that, on weekends, is covered with dealers and locals cleaning their barns and attics. There's no predicting what you'll find there; call (603) 465-7677 for information and dates.

On Route 123 in the town of Mason, watch for a sign on the south side of the road that announces *Uncle Sam's House,* a little red cape farmhouse that Samuel Wilson helped his father build. It was about 1780 when the family moved there in order to get away from British troops in Menotomy, Massachusetts, now Arlington Center. Sam lived in the farm in Mason from the time he was 14 until he left at the age of 23, in 1789, to establish his career in Troy, New York. Sam and his brother first established a brick kiln and then branched out into meat packing, providing food for the US Army. Sam returned to Mason

The Early Bird Gets the Surprise

It's not unusual for flea-market dealers to arrive the night before and camp in trucks so they can set up early in the morning, but Gerald St. Louis probably won't do it again, at least not at Hollis Flea Market. He and two boys who were helping him were startled one night in 1977 by an 8-foot furry creature, which left footprints over 16 inches long. Mr. St. Louis didn't wait to measure the prints; he jumped in his truck and left with the boys. Two other dealers, unaware of St. Louis's experience, described having their truck shaken by big furry hands, and they left pretty quickly, too. The tracks found by their truck matched the others.

in 1797 to marry his sweetheart, Betsey Mann, and tradition says he won out over Johnny "Appleseed" Chapman for her hand.

A popular man, Sam was called Uncle by everyone who knew him. The army required him to brand the letters US on those barrels of meat destined for government use, and when a steamboat passenger asked one of his employees what the US branded onto the barrels meant, the employee responded "Those are Uncle Sam's initials; he's feeding the whole army!" The notion stuck and word spread.

Seen as a joke, within a year everything marked with US came to be known as "Uncle Sam's," from beef to rifles and ships. Sam himself enjoyed the notoriety and rode in Fourth of July parades wearing a top hat. By 1813, a recruiting poster stated IF UNCLE SAM NEEDS, I'LL BE GLAD TO ASSIST HIM. The theme was later used in James Montgomery Flagg's well-known "I Want You" poster for the US Army in 1938. The figure of Uncle Sam we know today came from a costume first worn by George Buchanan at a parade in Amesbury, Massachusetts, in 1851. A *Leslie's Illustrated New York News* correspondent saw him, and a picture of Buchanan in costume was in the next issue. The image grabbed the public's fancy, and soon it appeared everywhere. The house in Mason, which is not open to the public, stands much as Uncle Sam and his family built it.

If you love herbs or perennial flowers, or just enjoy lovely gardens, follow the signs from Mason to **Pickity Place.** It's so far off the beaten path that you'll be sure you're lost long before you get there. Persevere and you will find, along with gardens, the cottage used by Elizabeth Orton Jones for Grandmother's House in her classic illustrations of *Little Red Riding Hood* and a shop brimming with handmade and herbal gifts. You can have an herbal luncheon in the cottage, which is open daily, but be sure to call for reservations, since a lot of people manage to find their way here. Pickity Place, 248 Nutting Hill Rd., Mason; (603) 878-1151. When you leave Pickity Place, you can go on to New Ipswich instead of backtracking—or you can approach Pickity Place by following signs from Route 31 in Greenville.

Tucked along Route 101, visitors to the Souhegan Valley are often surprised to spot the vineyard leading up to the picturesque **LaBelle Winery.** Guests are invited to stop by for a tasting (no reservations required), between the hours of 11 a.m. and 5 p.m., daily. If your schedule allows (and we suggest it should), call (603) 672-9898, ext. 1, to make a reservation for lunch or dinner at the Bistro. Reservations are especially encouraged for Sunday brunch. LaBelle Winery prides itself on participation in the Farm-to-Fork movement, meaning all produce and dairy products are either grown or raised on-site or come from local vendors. Certified local by the New Hampshire Farm to Restaurant connection, guests can dine with confidence that their meals are fresher, healthier, and created in support of New England farmers. Tours of the vineyard and grounds are offered during the weekend, between noon and 5 p.m. The vineyard is located at 345 Horace Greeley Hwy. (SR 101), in Amherst; (603) 672-9898; labellewinerynh.com. If your travels take you towards the seacoast, you can also enjoy the LaBelle labels at *LaBelle Portsmouth,* the wine and gift shop at 104 Congress St., Portsmouth; (603) 319-8035.

The *Barrett House* in New Ipswich, one of the state's most outstanding federal mansions, remained in the Barrett family from its construction in 1800, until it was given to the Society for the Preservation of New England Antiquities in 1948. Ornamented with pilasters and a central pediment, it is said to have been built as a wedding present to Charles Barrett Jr. from his father. Furnished with the best that each generation of the family could afford, including imported china and even a glass harmonica, the house interprets the life of a wealthy New England textile manufacturer and farming family over the course of several generations. Teas with guest lecturers are held throughout the summer, and special events such as a late-May antiques show highlight the schedule. It is open June 1 through Oct 15 on the second and fourth Sat of the month, with house tours hourly from 11 a.m. to 4 p.m. Admission is $8 for adults, $7 for seniors, and $4 for students. Take Route 124 to New Ipswich, then Route 123A. You can contact them at Main Street, New Ipswich 03071, or call (603) 436-3250 or visit historicnewengland.org/property/barrett-house.

Windblown Cross Country Skiing and Snowshoeing keeps 25 miles of trails well groomed for cross-country skiers. Along with their waxing shed and restaurant, the center offers a warming hut with "sleeping-bag accommodations." The views are spectacular. It's at 1180 Turnpike Rd., Routes 123 and 124, 3 miles west of the town of New Ipswich; call (603) 878-2869 for more information or visit windblownxc.com.

More Places to Stay in the Merrimack Valley

In Nashua-Manchester areas, most of the major chains have hotels, but for inns or bed-and-breakfast lodgings, you'll need to look a little farther north or west.

BEDFORD

Bedford Village Inn
2 Ole Bedford Way
(603) 472-2001
bedfordvillageinn.com
In a converted barn behind the farmhouse, stylish rooms with all the comforts. Expensive.

CONCORD

Holiday Inn
172 North Main St.
(603) 224-9534
Not the ordinary chain hotel, this hotel is stylish and immaculately maintained. Moderate rates.

HENNIKER

NOTE: Don't plan to stay near Henniker on Mother's Day weekend; it's graduation at the local college, and rooms are booked two years in advance.

Henniker House Bed and Breakfast
10 Ramsdell Rd.
(603) 428-3198 or (866) 428-3198
hennikerhouse.com
A Victorian house, with king and twin rooms. Full-course breakfasts in the solarium overlooking the river. Moderate.

MANCHESTER

Ash Street Inn
118 Ash St.
(603) 668-9908
ashstreetinn.com
The well-kept Victorian house with a wraparound porch offers guest rooms furnished in antiques and is known for its afternoon teas, served at 2 p.m. on Tues, Thurs, and Sat. Tea is also served to non-guests by reservation. High moderate; includes a full breakfast.

TEMPLE

The Birchwood Inn & London Tavern
340 NH-45
(603) 878-3285
thebirchwoodinn.com
Breakfast included. Moderate.

More Places to Eat in the Merrimack Valley

BEDFORD

Bedford Village Inn
2 Ole Bedford Way
(603) 472-2001
bedfordvillageinn.com
Choose between the old New England farmhouse dining rooms or the bright, airy sunporch; the menu puts a new spin on old favorites. Expensive.

CANDIA

Cello's Farmhouse Italian
143 Raymon Rd., Unit #1
(603) 483-2000
cellosfarmhouseitalian.com
Staffed by self-proclaimed foodies quick to serve up classic, country-style Italian specialties, with focus on the freshest ingredients and seasonal flavors. Try the pollo rosso, the chef's featured risotto, and seafood-rich cioppino. Takeout available.

CONCORD

The Barley House
132 North Main St.
(603) 228-6363
thebarleyhouse.com
Across the street from the
State House, this lively
restaurant serves hearty
soups and stews and an
internationally inspired list
of sturdy entrees that range
from Irish Whiskey Steak
and Cuban Mojito Double
Chop to jambalaya and
bratwurst braised in beer.
A variety of bands and solo
artists perform Monday
through Saturday nights.

The Common Man
25 Water St.
(603) 228-3463
thecman.com
A popular and solid
choice for meals on the
road. Seafood, prime rib,
sandwiches, or a lighter
menu. Breakfast, lunch,
and dinner.

Hermano's Cocina Mexicana
11 Hills Ave.
(1 block off Main Street)
(603) 224-5669
A wide choice of beers—
Mexican and otherwise—
accompany traditional
South-of-the-Border dishes
and some unusual ones.
Lunch Mon through Sat,
dinner every night.

DEERFIELD

The Lazy Lion
4 North Rd.
(603) 463-7374
thelazylionrestaurant.com
Serving lunch and dinner,
The Lazy Lion boasts
comfort food options made
to order, along with fun
events like live music and
trivia.

HENNIKER

Daniel's Restaurant and Pub
48 Main St.
(603) 428-7621
danielsofhenniker.com
Sandwiches, pastas, and
light and full-size entrees
in a pub atmosphere
overlooking the river.
Moderate.

HUDSON

North Side Grille
23 Derry Rd.
(603) 886-3663
hudsonnorthsidegrille.com
Comfort food and great
service in an inviting
atmosphere. Serving
breakfast, lunch, and
dinner.

MANCHESTER

Cotton
75 Arms St. (in part of the
old mill off Bridge Street)
(603) 622-5488
cottonfood.com
American bistro theme,
specializing in fresh
wood-grilled fish.
Moderate dinner entrees,
weekend reservations
recommended.

Fratello's Ristorante Italiano
155 Dow St. (in the
Amoskeag Mills complex)
(603) 624-2022
fratellos.com
Moderately priced
portabella panini or chicken
Capri are favorites at lunch,
and a delicious combo
of chicken and sausage
crema rosa or seafood
Sophia is a good choice
for dinner. Open weekdays
for lunch and dinner,
dinner only on weekends.
Wheelchair accessible.

Wild Rover
21 Kosciuszko St.
(603) 669-7722
wildroverpub.com
Irish music plays in a
traditional (almost—it's
smoke-free) pub setting
every Wed and Thurs
evening, but the menu is
more international, with
quesadillas and Bourbon
Street beef tips alongside
the lamb and Irish sausage
stew.

MASON

Parker's Maple Barn

1316 Brookline Rd.
(603) 878-2308
parkersmaplebarn.com
Maple-sugar house with a
rustic country restaurant
that serves breakfast and
lunch.

MILFORD

The Mile Away

52 Federal Hill Rd.
(603) 673-3904
mileawayrestaurant.com
The continental menu
includes a wide variety of
entrees, with rack of lamb,
fish, chicken, and several
veal specialties from veal
Marsala and picatta to
schnitzels. At least one
vegetarian dish is always
on the menu. All entree
prices ($16 to $26) include
a full four-course meal.

TILTON

Upper Crust Pizzeria

65 Laconia Rd.
(east of I-93 exit 20)
(603) 286-3191
The independently owned
pizza shop is almost
hidden behind the tangle
of malls and superstores,
but it's worth looking for.
Take out or eat in; Italian
entrees, including chicken
Marsala, join excellent pizza
and pasta dishes.

The Monadnock Region

Word has it that **Mount Monadnock** is no longer the second-most-climbed mountain in the world. With motorized access to Fujiyama's summit, fewer people are climbing it, so Monadnock may now be number one. Whichever, its rocky ledge summit on a fine summer day is definitely not off the beaten path. But its broad-shouldered cone standing alone with no other mountains for company is the focal point for an entire region. Views of it provide the backdrop for towns miles away, from Jaffrey, where most of the mountain lies, to Keene. On clear days you can see as far away as Boston and the Green Mountains of Vermont.

Geologically, the mountain is the definitive monadnock, a mass of rock more durable, hence more resistant to erosion and glacial action, than the land around it. It is this mountain for which the geological phenomenon was named. The rest of the land of this southwest corner of New Hampshire is rolling, accented with small mountains and lakes. Only one city, Keene, is located in the entire area. Both Keene and Peterborough provide the cultural and business centers, but the smaller towns are surprisingly active, with their own museums, concert series, and theater groups. The bandstands that decorate the

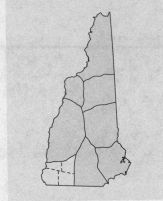

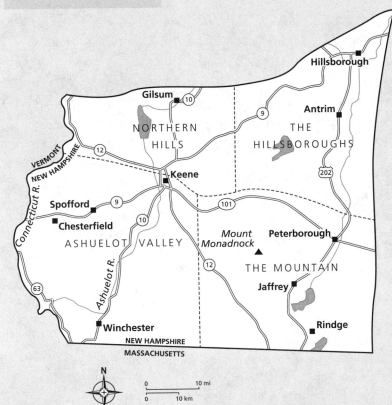

Hillsborough

Gilsum

Antrim

NORTHERN HILLS

THE HILLSBOROUGHS

VERMONT

NEW HAMPSHIRE

Keene

Connecticut R.

Spofford

Chesterfield

ASHUELOT VALLEY

Mount Monadnock

Peterborough

Ashuelot R.

THE MOUNTAIN

Jaffrey

Winchester

NEW HAMPSHIRE

MASSACHUSETTS

Rindge

N

0   10 mi

0   10 km

commons of Monadnock's towns are not there just to be photographed. Painters, writers, and musicians have found a haven in this area for more than a century, giving it a rich tradition in the arts.

The Hillsboroughs

Visitors from outside New England often comment on the apparent lack of originality displayed in the naming of towns here. In one area, town after town with the same name is prefixed by the four points of the compass, or by "Center," "Upper," or "Lower," or even suffixed by "Falls," "Mills," "Junction," "Street," or "Depot." The reason has to do with the town system of government, which was often based upon the original land grants. Large parcels of land were settled with several villages springing up within the boundaries of a town. Hillsborough is a good example. Within the limits of the town are Hillsborough, Hillsborough Center, Hillsborough Upper Village, and Hillsborough Lower Village.

Now bypassed by a new limited-access highway, travelers should not bypass the town of ***Hillsborough.*** The town offices and library on School Street (603-464-3595) are in the former Governor John B. Smith Mansion, a composite colonial revival and Queen Anne–style building that features exquisite woodwork and ornate gold arabesque ornamentation on its ceilings. It's open weekday during regular business hours. Continuing on School Street, you will eventually come to Hillsborough Center. The road itself is worth the drive, passing well-tended countryside, old homes and farms, and some of the finest stone walls in the state.

Fox Research and Demonstration Forest is a 1,448-acre area of managed forest that contains plantations of exotics (trees that do not grow here naturally) and some unusual protected natural areas as well. One of these is a black gum, or tupelo, swamp. This tree is common to the South but rarely found in New England. A ravine of mature hemlock and one of the state's rare stands of virgin forest are here, as well as a true sphagnum bog formed by a floating mat of moss filled with rare wild plants. More than 20 miles of hiking trails wind through the forest; cross-country skiers are welcome on the trails in the winter, but there are no other recreation facilities here, since this is a forest, not a park. No motorized recreational vehicles are allowed in the forest. You are welcome to picnic on the grounds (they have a few tables) as long as you respect the "carry-in, carry-out" policy. Open year-round from dawn to dusk. Look in the display box at the kiosk beside the parking lot for a trail guide. Write ***Fox State Forest,*** Hillsborough Center Rd., PO Box 1175, Hillsborough 03244, or call (603) 464-3453 for more information, or visit nhdfl.org.

Hillsborough Center is among New Hampshire's loveliest towns, its houses set around a circular road on a slight slope, with two churches. The entire center of the village is webbed with stone walls, testament to the number of rocks that northern New Englanders have had to pull out of their farmlands over the centuries. A well-preserved town pound, built to keep stray animals out of neighbors' gardens, completes this almost perfect village scene. Just outside of town, rows of nearly perfect double stone fences border the fields of two exceptionally beautiful hillside farms.

If you continue out East Washington Road, you will come to *Sage Knoll Herbs and Perennials,* a labor of love for Joan Phipps, who has collected many old herb and perennial varieties from cellar holes and roadsides, as well as by tracking them down in heritage gardens. Her plant list has more than 165 perennials and herbs for sale. She doesn't ship, so you'll just have to visit with this fascinating horticulturist between mid-May and the end of Oct, Tues through Sat 9 a.m. to 5 p.m. at 955 East Washington Rd.; (603) 478-5461.

Just west of Hillsborough on Route 31 North is the boyhood *home of Franklin Pierce,* New Hampshire's only native son to become president of the United States. The mansion is a more elegant residence than was common in rural New Hampshire when it was built in 1804, and its interior has some surprises in store for those who think of New England decor as restricted to somber puritan colors. The stenciling and decorative painting, which have been restored from remaining paint samples, are in vivid reds; the original Balfour mural wallpaper in the parlor is among the finest examples in any restored home. Hillsborough's active historical society, which maintains and staffs the house, also holds monthly programs, with speakers who explore some facet of New Hampshire history. These are usually held at the Pierce Homestead on the fourth Monday of the month at 7 p.m. You can call the house for a schedule. Open Fri through Tues 10 a.m. to 4 p.m. from late May to early Sept and 10 a.m. to 4 p.m. (weekends only) from early Sept to late Oct. The last tour is at 3:15 p.m. Admission is free for children, students, and seniors who are New Hampshire residents; adult NH residents pay $4. Nonresident adults and seniors pay $5 and nonresident children (ages 6–17) pay $3. Located at the intersection of Routes 9 and 31, the address is 301 2nd NH Turnpike, Hillsborough; (603) 478-3165; nhstateparks.org/visit/Historic-Sites.

This was Pierce's boyhood home; to see the house where he took his new bride (not open to the public), turn left from the driveway and cross Route 9. Begin counting houses at the corner, and the Pierce house is the fourth on the right. Continue on down that road, passing a small cluster of homes with a little church at Union Village, where the pavement ends. Just beyond, on the unpaved road, you'll cross a fine pair of stone arches, which you can see best from the little road that goes off to the right just after you cross them. A brochure with a self-guided walking tour of the Franklin Pierce neighborhood is available at the mansion. The walk is about a mile in length, and the brochure describes the lives, times, and structures that surrounded the future president as he grew up.

Hillsborough has five fine stone-arch bridges. The new US 202 bypasses one just west of the town of Hillsborough at its intersection with Route 9. Another is at the intersection of Shedd Jones and Beard Roads. This one stands in the open, where you can get a good view of it from both directions. From the Pierce house, turn right, then right again down the hill onto Shedd Jones Road. Follow it until you come to the intersection with Beard Road, and you'll see the double-arched bridge right ahead of you. If you turn right, Beard Road will take you back to Route 9, passing a riverside swimming hole maintained by the town, but without lifeguards.

If, however, you go left on Beard Road, you will cross another stone bridge, this one spanning *Gleason's Falls,* which you can best see by following the path downstream a few yards. The river continues to cascade from pool to pool through a jumble of moss-covered boulders for a little way below the falls; notice the long groove the water has carved in the ledge. Be careful above the upper pools, since the pine-needle floor of the forest is very slippery and the drop a substantial one. If you continue on Beard Road a very short way and turn right onto Gleason Falls Road, you'll come out just above Hillsborough Center, on the road to East Washington. A left turn onto Gleason Falls Road does not take you back to Route 31 where you began, even though maps show it. *Trust us on this one.* As you go west on Route 9, look for a double stone-arch bridge beside the road. It's worth a stop here to walk around to the upstream side for a better picture of what it looked like in the nineteenth century.

EVENTS IN THE MONADNOCK REGION

Cheshire Fair
early Aug, Keene
(603) 357-4740, (603) 271-3588
cheshirefair.org

Festival of Fireworks
late Aug, Jaffrey
(603) 532-4549
jaffreyfireworks.com

Pumpkin Festival
late Oct, Keene
pumpkinfestival.org

If you follow Route 31 instead of going right onto Shedd Jones Road, after leaving the Pierce Homestead, you will come to Windsor Road on your left, which leads to ***Stonewall Farm Bed & Breakfast.*** This 1785 farmhouse is well restored, furnished with antiques and fine reproductions, and situated on five-plus acres of gardens and meadow. More than one hundred varieties of hybrid lilacs form a rare arboretum and extend the lilac-blossom time by at least a month. They are simply spectacular at their height in late May. Rooms are priced from $120 and up in high season and include a full breakfast. They are located at 235 Windsor Rd., Hillsborough; (603) 478-1947; stonewallfarmbedandbreakfast-countryweddings.com.

In nearby ***Washington*** you'll pass by the picturesque, historic town common on your visit to ***Gibson Pewter,*** where the father-and-son team of Raymond and Jonathan Gibson produce heritage-quality, lead-free pewter in contemporary and traditional designs. Some of their work is in the Boston Museum of Fine Arts—in the museum displays, not just the gift shop. In addition to plates, bowls, tankards, and chalices, they produce candlesticks and collector-quality spoons. Their shop is open Mon through Sat 9 a.m. to 5 p.m., and Sunday's "by chance." To inquire about the repair of old pewter, write or visit at 26 North Main St., Washington 03280; (603) 495-1776.

Follow the road around to the right along the shore of the millpond, left at the meetinghouse, and up the hill. A few miles up the road, ***Eccardt Farm*** in East Washington is a real, operating dairy farm, where you can watch the milking and see an amazing collection of live birds, including peacocks and exotic chickens and ducks, as well as sheep, goats, and rabbits. Milking times are 2:30 and 7 p.m. In the spring, you can help them turn sap into syrup. They also have a fascinating collection of old farming equipment including tractors and tools. This is a multigenerational farm, a real place without glitz and a great experience for kids. The farm is open all year; (603) 495-3830; eccardtfarm.com/.

While you are passing the millpond in East Washington, it would be a shame not to visit two places that are less than a mile away, just over the line into neighboring Bradford and much easier to find from here. Follow Springs Road from the three corners by the forlorn little tumble-down building, and in less than a mile you will see a sign on your right at the entrance to ***Bradford Bog.*** It's a fine one, an Atlantic white-cedar swamp, its floor formed by an eerie tangle of sphagnum-covered cedar roots. A boardwalk provides a safe foothold over impossibly uneven "ground," and a profusion of seclusion-loving wild plants grow beside the trail. Continue into the open bog to an observation tower, which gives an overview of this flat bog ringed by low hills. You'll see tamarack, mountain holly, heather, and black spruce, along with bog rosemary and laurel. A leisurely exploration takes about half an hour.

Less than half a mile past the bog entrance, look for a lane into a grassy clearing and a sign for the site of ***Bradford Springs.*** New Hampshire had very few of these mineral springs, which were fashionable health spas in the late 1800s. But, like the White Mountain Mineral Springs (see the Eastern White Mountains chapter), this one had a rather grand hotel for guests who came to take the waters. The hotel's foundation of large granite stones is beside the road, and if you look in the woods behind it, shortly past the sign reading BRAD-FORD SPRINGS, you'll find the round stone-lined spring—or former spring. Over it once stood an octagonal springhouse, which you can now see, along with an engraving of the hotel itself, at Muster Field Farm Museum in North Sutton (see the Dartmouth-Sunapee Region chapter).

The Mountain

The white-spired meetinghouse in ***Hancock*** is said to be the most photographed church in the state, although it is hard to understand how such a statistic is determined. The entire town of Hancock invites photography with its neat rows of fine old buildings along the main street. On Saturdays from May to October, the carriage sheds behind the church house a farmers' market.

Leaf Peeping on Two Wheels

New Hampshire has hundreds of good venues for bicycling in the summer, and nearly every one of them is partially bordered by hardwoods that provide an entirely different experience in autumn. In contrast to the pine-scented rides of summer, fall's own strong earthy scents are reason enough to get out onto the road. But the visual show is even better when the foliage of the state's mixed hardwood forests bursts into red, yellow, and orange flame.

The secret to fall riding is to layer your clothing so that as you, and the day, warm up you can eliminate a layer and control the evaporation of perspiration. For long trips, begin with a wicking T-shirt and add several layers of light clothing. Also, be sure to wear a cycling helmet.

Pick a road that is not heavily traveled—like those around Bennington, Mont Vernon, Greenfield, and Francestown—or look for any road that circles a pond or lake. Remember that although back roads are less traveled than highways, they are still used by cars and trucks. Stay to the right and do not ride down the middle or side by side with others in a group. A hazard to watch for in autumn is fallen leaves and pine needles. Pine needles act like hundreds of ball bearings under your tires, and leaves—especially when they are wet—can make the road seem greased. So beware and go gingerly when you hit a patch of either.

Between 9 a.m. and 2 p.m., herbs and vegetables, baked goods, honey, hand-crafts, and other locally produced goods are sold in a friendly small-town atmosphere. For details call (603) 525-3788. The *Hancock Inn* has been welcoming travelers for more than 200 years. One of its guest rooms has wall murals painted by the itinerant artist Rufus Porter. It is at 33 Main St., Hancock; (603) 525-3318 or (800) 525-1789; hancockinn.com.

The *Harris Center,* located in Hancock, is dedicated to educating the public about environmental and conservation issues, and it sponsors a full calendar of activities, field trips, outings, and workshops throughout the year. At least one hike or program is held each weekend. Some of these activities are at the conservation center, while others show participants little-known places of natural interest throughout the area. The center's own property of about 7,000 acres in Hancock includes two small mountains and is traversed by about 7 miles of trails that lead to their summits, woods-surrounded ponds, and boulder trains. You can walk, ski, or snowshoe there, or join one of their guided walks that usually have a theme. In early November of each year, they welcome volunteers to join them for a Saturday of trail maintenance, which is a good way to repay the free use of the trails and free programs. To get to the Harris Center, follow Route 123 (King's Highway) west from the village of Hancock for about 2.5 miles, turning left at the signs. To find out what programs are scheduled, call (603) 525-3394 or visit harriscenter.org. Trail maps and schedules of all events and programs are found just inside the door.

Only a short way past the entrance to the Harris Center, on the opposite (north) side of Route 123, is the road to one of New Hampshire's most pristine lakes, where you may see loons, wood ducks, or herons. Set inside the *dePierrefeu-Willard Pond Wildlife Sanctuary,* an Audubon Society property, the pond has a nice sandy put-in for canoes, kayaks, and non-gasoline-engine boats. A series of hikes ranging from fifteen minutes to two and a half hours parallel the shore and climb to a fine view of the area from the ledges on Bald Mountain. Boulders left by retreating glaciers line the shore and tumble into the clear waters, visible below the pond's glassy surface. The pond is splendid for kayaks and canoes, with a totally undeveloped shoreline. From Route 9 in Stoddard, west of Hillsborough, turn south onto Route 123, signposted Hancock, and turn left shortly after you pass a pond alongside the road. From Hancock, take Route 123 for 3.7 miles and turn right.

Greenfield State Park reserves one sandy beach just for campers who have settled into its spacious, wooded tent sites and has another one for day-visitors and picnickers. This is one of the rare places where you can rent a boat either for fishing or to enjoy the quiet of Otter Lake. One of the smaller of New Hampshire's state parks and one of the least known, it is a perfect retreat for nature lovers, swimmers, and those who seek a place to paddle their canoes in peace. Write the park at PO Box 203, Route 136, Greenfield 03047, or call (603) 547-3497. For reservations call (603) 271-3628 or visit nhstateparks.org/visit/state-parks.

Only a few years ago, New Hampshire regained a ski area everyone though was lost forever, and the skill and energy that the new owners brought to the mountain has quickly made it a top choice for skiers and boarders. *Crotched Mountain,* in Bennington, has come back to life, and with snowmaking and grooming added to its short distance from the Nashua-Manchester-Concord corridor, it draws skiers who only a short while ago were traveling to Vermont. The vertical drop is 875 feet, but the terrain is interesting and challenging. In fact, that is the fun of the place—each trail has a little something extra. The all-new, fan-gun snowmaking can produce up to 2 feet of snow in twenty-four hours and it covers 100 percent of the trails. And the groomers know what to do with it, producing some of the best-groomed trails in the east. Even the lodge is new, big, bright, and friendly. The ski rental shop also has boards and the ski school is as good as the grooming. Crotched Mountain has taken night skiing to new levels, with Friday and Saturday night lighted trails open until 3 a.m. Follow Route 101 to *Peterborough,* then Route 202 north to Bennington and Route 47 to Crotched Mountain. The address is 615 Francestown Rd. (Route 47), Bennington; (603) 588-3668; crotchedmountain.com.

Historical societies perform several valuable services to their towns, such as storing and preserving records of long-closed schools and businesses; providing a safe home for old photographs, maps, and books that would otherwise be lost; and offering a clearinghouse for historical and genealogical information. A few maintain museums based on purchases or gifts of local artifacts, furnishings, and property.

The *Monadnock Center for History and Culture* is one of the finest historical museums of any society in the state. Along with exhibition rooms featuring early tools and antiques, they have in the several buildings of their complex a complete Victorian parlor, a replica of a country store, a colonial-era kitchen, and a restored mill house. You can get a walking tour map of Peterborough here, too. Open year-round, Wed through Sat 10 a.m. to 4 p.m. Admission is $3 for adults; free for members and children 12 and under. Group tours are available and can be scheduled by calling (603) 924-3235. The museum is at 19 Grove St. (PO Box 58), Peterborough; (603) 924-3235; monadnockcenter.org.

The *Mariposa Museum* is a colorful celebration of the world's variety of cultures. Costumes, toys, musical instruments, puppets, and artifacts are used to present differences and similarities of life around the planet. Many exhibits are hands-on, including musical instruments, puppets, and a costume corner for kids. There are frequent presentations of dance, food, and music, designed for all ages, and a large library of children's books provides stories set in cultures all over the world. Call or see the website for current hours. Admission is $8 adults, $6 for seniors, and $5 for children (ages 3–16). The museum is wheelchair accessible. The location is 26 Main St., Peterborough; (603) 924-4555; mariposamuseum.org.

Peterborough has maintained a lively downtown, whose specialty shops and eateries cluster just off Main Street on Depot Square. Here you will find the upbeat food center called *Twelve Pine,* where you can have lunch in the cafe, buy a full-blown picnic, or stock up on locally produced specialty foods. It is open 9 a.m. to 7 p.m. weekdays, 9 a.m. to 5 p.m. Sat, and 9 a.m. to 4 p.m. Sun. Although you might expect it to be at 12 Pine St., it's actually at 11 School St.; (603) 924-6140; twelvepine.com.

Behind Twelve Pine, art glass and other handwork by local artists is shown and sold at the *Sharon Arts Center* shop, open Mon through Sat, 10 a.m. to 6 p.m., and Sun 11 a.m. to 4 p.m.; (603) 836-2591; nhia.edu/campus-life/sharon-arts-center.

Touted as Peterborough's only Hungarian, German, Italian, Mexican, Asian, English, and Portuguese–inspired bar and restaurant, *Harlow's* surely has something to offer everyone. Offering sixteen beers on tap, including microbrews and fan favorites, Harlow's serves up lunch, dinner, a kid's menu, and plenty of opportunities to hear live music and enjoy special events. Harlow's Pub and Restaurant is located at 3 School St., Peterborough; (603) 924-6365; harlowspub.com.

Considered upscale, but casual, the *Bantam Grill* is among the newest restaurant offerings in Peterborough. Focused on a fusion of American and Italian dishes, the Bantam Grill serves dinner Tues through Sun, and lunch Tues through Sat. Although reservations are welcome, the Bantam Grill is also able to accommodate walk-ins. The restaurant's extensive lunch, dinner, and dessert menus also offer patrons gluten-free options. Located at 1 Jaffrey Rd., Peterborough; (603) 924-6633; bantam-peterborough.com.

The entire Contoocook Valley is sprinkled with antiques shops. Featuring farmhouse style furnishings, the collection at *Bowerbird & Friends Antiques* (16 Depot Square, Suite 60, in Peterborough; 603-924-2550; bowerbirdfriends .com) includes vendors with various specialties, but all combine to present a changing collection of remarkable finds from the eighteenth through twentieth centuries. Housed in an 1800s farmhouse and barn, *Twin Elm Farm* (133 Wilton Rd., Peterborough; 603-784-5341; twinelmfarm.com) houses a treasure trove of antique and vintage furnishings curated from more than thirty dealers.

Alice Blue Antiques is well worth a stop for a nostalgic bauble or perhaps a romantic bit of fine antique European needlework or French lace. Among the antique textiles (one of the owners travels to France frequently in search of outstanding examples), the shop mixes stylish modern designer wear, a combination that makes the shop even more appealing. It is open Mon through Sat 10 a.m. to 5:30 p.m., Sun 11 a.m. to 4 p.m. Alice Blue Antiques, 10 School St., Peterborough; call 603 924-6520.

Just opposite, in the *Toadstool Bookshop,* is *Aesop's Tables,* a lively cafe open Mon through Fri from 7 a.m. to 4 p.m., and Sat 9 a.m. to 4 p.m. for sandwiches, soups, muffins, and cappuccino; (603) 924-1612. Across School Street is *Joseph's Coat,* with quality folk art and clothing; (603) 924-6683; jocoat.com.

Peterborough's community tradition as a center for the arts is also demonstrated in the *First Friday* evenings of music, open shops, galleries, and other free programs. Various town groups, including the MacDowell Colony and the Peterborough Folk Music Society, participate in this celebration on the first Friday of each month.

One of the state's largest organic farms, *Rosaly's Garden and Farm Stand* is worth visiting for its produce stand and for the herb gardens, which include a tea garden and water garden. A full acre is bright with flowers you can pick yourself, and in each season are pick-your-own berries. More than 120 varieties of organic vegetables are grown here and sold at the farm stand, which is open every day from 9 a.m. to 6 p.m., mid-May until Columbus Day. Rosaly's Garden and Farm stand, Route 123 (just south of Route 101), Peterborough; (603) 924-7774; rosalysgarden.com.

thethirteenthwife

Joseph Smith, founder and leader of the Church of Jesus Christ of Latter-Day Saints, died suddenly in the 1840s, while Brigham Young was conducting a revival meeting in Peterborough. While still in Peterborough, Young was chosen to replace him as the Mormons' leader, and when he left for Utah, some time later, 136 "leading citizens" of the town followed him, including one young woman who became his thirteenth wife.

Also on the road to Sharon, Route 123, which leaves Peterborough from Route 101 just as 101 begins the long climb over Temple Mountain, you'll pass *Apple Gate Bed and Breakfast.* Rooms, each named for an apple variety, are nicely decorated. We like Granny Smith, an airy corner room in pale green, but Crispin has a view over the neighboring apple orchard and would be our choice in the spring, when the trees are a cloud of white blossoms. Full breakfasts are bountiful and always feature one apple dish—perhaps muffins or baked apples. Even the inn's friendly dog is named McIntosh, but the apple theme isn't carried to the point of being tiresome. Rates are inexpensive to moderate, and the inn is not suitable for children under 12. It is on the corner of Route 123 at 199 Upland Farm Rd., Peterborough; (603) 924-6543.

The **Sheiling Forest** provides pleasant walking through fields and forests, following stone walls built by farmers of long ago trying to clear their fields of the oversupply of granite boulders with which New Hampshire was blessed. These are easy, level walks. On Saturday there are programs for small-woodlot owners on the care and management of woodlands. Open daily dawn to dusk year-round on Old Street Road in Peterborough.

Although not as well-known as its sister mountain, **Pack Monadnock** in **Miller State Park** offers easy access to mountaintop views extending from Boston to the White Mountains and Vermont. A fee is charged for use of the auto road to the summit, or you can climb it on foot by any of three hiking trails, each about 1.5 miles long. Picnic areas and an observation tower are at the open summit. The entrance is on Route 101 as the highway crests the hill. Only a few miles from Peterborough on Route 202, **Jaffrey** is a fine old mill town with its attractive nineteenth-century mill complex still intact and in good repair. Route 124, in front of the mill, leads to Jaffrey Center, a beautiful collection of nineteenth- and early-twentieth-century homes set around a common.

The **Melville Academy Museum** (jcvis.org/Melville.php) is housed in a building that was a private academy from 1833 to 1857 and then a town school until World War I. Nicely restored, it has a local history museum on its first floor and the original classroom on the top floor. The classroom will make you acutely aware of how far education has come. Downstairs are reminders of life in small rural communities: kitchen implements, tools, straw hats, and handwork. What makes it particularly appealing, however, is the large collection of Hannah Davis hatboxes. This nineteenth-century woman established her own industry making boxes from especially thin-sawn boards. Once assembled, they were covered in attractive printed paper and sold from her wagon all over New England. The boxes have become highly collectable, and the Smithsonian covets this collection. The museum is open Sat and Sun from 2 to 4 p.m. in, July and Aug, or by appointment from May through Oct. Melville Academy is one of several historic buildings in Jaffrey Center's Historic District, which also features an outstanding church and a one-room schoolhouse, along with the burying ground. Near the wooded edge of the cemetery is the gravestone of the author Willa Cather, who first visited Jaffrey in 1917 and returned to rent rooms at the old Shattuck Inn for two summers and in the fall of the following years. She wrote in a tent, pitched in a meadow behind a friend's summer home, and it was here that much of *My Antonia* was written. She left instructions to be buried in the Old Burying Ground.

And Then There Were None

Looking at the rocky peak today, it is hard to believe that Mount Monadnock was once covered to its top in forest. The entire summit and its ledges, except for Bald Rock, are described by early accounts as covered in red spruce. However, farmers clearing land on the lower slopes often set fires to make their work easier and faster. These fires spread quickly, fanned by the winds to which mountains are exposed, and spread unchecked to consume forests on the upper slopes and summit. In 1800, one of these blazes continued unchecked for two weeks as a ground fire burned the thick layer of needles and organic soil in which the trees were rooted. Giant spruces toppled, leaving a massive tangle that was made even more impenetrable by further blowdown from storms.

This entanglement provided a safe refuge for wolves between their forays into sheep pastures and pens on the lower-slope farms, so farmers banded together to burn it. Of course, the fire got away from them, and in two weeks of burning it consumed everything that was left growing on the top of the mountain. Contemporary reports describe a fire so hot that it caused rocks to split and explode.

The ***Monadnock Inn*** sits opposite the academy, across the wide village green, anchoring the idyllic village scene. Its rooms are individually decorated, many with antiques and each with a pleasant flair all its own. Although it has plenty of country inn warmth and charm, don't expect a same-old "ye olde country inne" menu in the dining room. Instead look for a creative menu of dishes, such as pan-seared duck breast with dried plums soaked in Cassis or chicken rubbed in lavender and fennel seed, as well as new takes on traditional New England ingredients such as sweet potatoes, green apples, cranberries, and cider. These may be interpreted in styles borrowed from Venice, Japan, Provence, California, or Jamaica to create dishes that are like nothing that ever came out of grandma's kitchen. If you're lucky, the chef's signature Savory Sweet Potato Flan will appear on the appetizer menu—a surprising non-dessert twist, with soy sauce added to the maple glaze. Chicken-and-fig sausage is another specialty, and pork roast may be encrusted in almonds and sauced with Amaretto.

The Sunday brunch is served from the menu, not the ubiquitous buffet, and is divided into "The Breakfast Side" and "The Lunch Side." On the breakfast list are not only eggs Benedict, but also the chef's own variations between the English muffin and the egg/hollandaise layer: Eggs Atlantis (smoked salmon and sliced tomato with capers) and Eggs Godiva (baked ham, spinach, Swiss cheese, and cream), plus steak-and-eggs, a breakfast club, and the usual French toast and egg dishes. The other side of the menu offers Asiago Tortellini Carbonara among the lunch dishes. The dining room is open Mon through Sat for dinner and for brunch on Sun. The Monadnock Inn is on Route 124, 2 miles west of downtown Jaffrey; (603) 532-7800; monadnockinn.com.

Sunflowers, once occupied by Aylmer's Grille, now fills the space at 21 Main St. in Jaffrey. This welcoming place spices the flavors of fresh seasonal dishes with music—smooth jazz piano sounds on Sunday evening and a changing program of country, bluegrass, acoustic folk, jazz improv, and folk rock on Friday evenings. The bright dining room provides an easy, comfortable place for lunch or a light dinner—or one of chef/owner Carolyn Edwards's sumptuous desserts. Cakes are her specialty; they were always the hit of all the local parties she catered before opening the restaurant. Chef Edwards shares the secrets of these and other specialties in her cooking classes. The Café is open Mon through Thurs from 11 a.m. to 2 p.m. for lunch and again for dinner from 5 to 8 p.m., with evening hours extended to 9 p.m. on Fri and Sat. Sunflowers is open on Sun from 9 a.m. to 3 p.m. Call (603) 593-3303 or visit sunflowers catering.com for additional information.

West of Jaffrey, in *Rindge, Cathedral of the Pines* is an outdoor church, as well as a national memorial to those who lost their lives in wartime military service. People of all faiths hold services here, using the various altars and wooded "chapels." The Memorial Tower holds a peal of Sheffield bells and a set of four Norman Rockwell bas-reliefs in memory of women who served in the military. Even when Cathedral of the Pines is not open for services, you can walk through the grounds, a forest of tall pines atop a hillside, with views of Monadnock, Kearsarge, and southern Vermont. Off Routes 202 and 119 in Rindge; call (603) 899-3300 for more information or visit cathedralof thepines.org.

Those with fond memories of the *Woodbound Inn* or of Aylmer's Grille, the popular Jaffrey restaurant, will be happy to hear that the two have been united. The newly renovated inn has a variety of rooms, some with double tubs. One- and two-bedroom cabins along the shores of Lake Contoocook have sitting areas, fireplaces, and refrigerators. In the winter guests can relax by the inn's fireplace after cross-country skiing through the inn's snow-covered meadows and woods. The inn is now the home of *Aylmer's Grille,* with a creative American menu that changes seasonally. Expect to find entrees such as "pan-kissed" pepper-crusted tuna, coated in fresh-crushed peppercorns, with a buttery sashimi interior. Aylmer shines at grilling fish, which he often serves with a salsa over micro-greens. Roasted tomato tart is a favorite starter, but more adventurous palettes should begin with an example of his playful combinations of cuisines, the Cajun chowder. Perhaps end the meal with profiteroles with their own fudge sauce. Aylmer's Grille at Woodbound Inn, 247 Woodbound Rd., Rindge; (603) 532-8341; woodbound.com.

The *Friendly Farm* sits at the edge of the woods near Dublin Lake, where kids and adults can meet, pet, and get to know farm animals. Baby animals predominate and love to be fed. Wander about the tree-shaded farm and have close encounters of the good kind with baby chickens, hens, roosters, ducks, and geese. In one building are some of the strangest-looking fowl you have ever met. Also at the farm are sheep, goats, piglets, rabbits, and even a baby cow or two. Handy dispensers, like the old-time peanut machines, let you buy feed so kids (of any age) can get up close and personal. Open 10 a.m. to 5 p.m. daily from late April through Labor Day and weekends until mid-Oct, weather permitting. Half a mile west of the lake, 716 Main St. (Route 101), Dublin; (603) 563-8444; friendlyfarm.com.

Across Dublin Lake, just east of the Friendly Farm, is a beautiful view of Mount Monadnock. It's worth circling the lakeshore for a look at some of the fine homes that are more visible when the leaves are off the trees. Dublin was home to the *Dublin Art Colony* (dublinartcolony.org), a group that included Abbott Thayer, Frank Benson, George de Forest Brush, and Rockwell Kent. These and writers including Mark Twain, Rudyard Kipling, and Amy Lowell were frequent visitors at these lakeside "cottages."

Del Rossi's Trattoria does a good job with the unlikely combination of a real Italian restaurant and a first-rate folk, world, and jazz music venue. Neither is ever compromised for the other. Get their schedule and reserve early for big names, or go on a weeknight just for the food, which includes fettuccine with shiitake mushrooms, peas, and Marsala, or a breast of chicken stuffed with basil and fresh tomatoes in a Gorgonzola sauce. About twenty entree choices tempt you. The wine list is also excellent. It's open for dinner only, Tues through Sun, on Route 137 in Dublin, at 73 Bush Brook Rd. just north of Route 101; (603) 563-7195.

Since opening in 1996, *Audrey's Cafe* (13 Main St., Dublin; 603-876-3316; audreyscafe.com) has featured mouth-watering specials every week, like vanilla walnut and strawberry stuffed French toast, along with the can't miss breakfast favorites in the form of puffy pancakes, perfectly cooked bacon, and fresh eggs. Audrey's Café is the destination for "diner fare reimagined."

The beautiful little brick village of *Harrisville* clusters at the head of its millpond, north of Dublin and Route 101. It is a rare nineteenth-century textile town that remains almost unchanged. Original small, brick mill buildings are in good repair and are still used by *Harrisville Designs,* where textile arts thrive in the Weaving Center. Knitting and weaving supplies sold there include high-quality yarns, original patterns, and looms. Weeklong (and occasionally shorter) workshops, taught by leading textile artists, concentrate on basic instruction and specific skills, such as Navajo weaving, rag rugs, or Estonian knitting. For updated information, regarding class schedules and times, please call the HD Retail Store at (603) 827-3996 or consult the website. The yarns sold in the shop are spun at the adjacent spinning mills. The shop is open Tues through Sat from 9 a.m. to 5 p.m., in Center Village, Harrisville; (603) 827-3996; harrisville.com.

While other towns may be "postcard towns," Fitzwilliam is a "Christmas-card town." Its white town hall and stately homes set around the snow-covered common make it a favorite for artists and photographers creating greeting cards. One building on the common is the **Amos J. Blake House,** a museum maintained by the Fitzwilliam Historical Society. Built in 1837, this was the home and law office of a well-respected community leader. His law office is intact, and other rooms are furnished in period antiques. A kitchen, parlor, music room, and reconstructed schoolroom are part of the museum, as are displays of military and firefighting memorabilia. A small shop, filled with local crafts, New England food specialties, soaps, and gifts, uses original country-store counters, furnishings, and cash register. Admission is free. Open year-round, Thurs from 9 a.m. to 11 a.m. and Sat from 1 p.m. to 4 p.m. Write the Blake House, On the Common (PO Box 87), 66 Route 19, Fitzwilliam 03447; or visit fitzwilliam.org/fhs.

Fitzwilliam has a number of antiques shops, several of them gathered picturesquely around the village green. **MacReay Landy Antiques** (603-585-9581; fitzwilliam.org/maclandy; open Thurs through Mon 10 a.m. to 5:30 p.m.) and **Bloomin' Antiques** (603-585-6688; bloominantiques.com); open Thurs through Sat 10 a.m. to 5 p.m., Sun noon to 5 p.m.) face each other at one end of the green. A few steps away, behind the Fitzwilliam Inn, is **Brian Luddy American Country Antiques** (603-585-9180; open Wed through Sun 10 a.m. to 4 p.m.).

One of the largest stands of wild rhododendron north of the Allegheny Mountains is in Fitzwilliam at **Rhododendron State Park.** The 15 acres of large shrubs bloom by mid-July in a riot of huge flower clusters against glossy, deep-green leaves. At any time of year, the trails through this park are bordered by masses of broad evergreen leaves and the thick tangle of trunks and branches that support them. The Fitzwilliam Garden Club created an adjoining wildflower trail. Native plants are labeled in the open woodland that borders the path. It is a lovely, quiet, and cool spot, with 1 mile of easy walking. Follow the signs off Route 119.

A back road that branches off Route 12, not far north of the rock ledges south of Keene, gives more views of Monadnock, as well as a stone bridge.

It brings you to Route 124 and into Marlborough, where you can satisfy your hunger after a day of hiking or antiquing.

For the ultimate Chinese and Japanese food fix, check out ***Lee & Mt. Fuji*** (314 Main St., Marlborough; 603-876-3388; leeandmtfuji.com). Whether you prefer General Tso's Chicken, moo goo gai pan, or something from the sushi bar, you'll have plenty to choose from during lunch and dinner service. Be sure to check out their lunch specials for new twists! Craving cocktails? Check out ***Piedra Fina Latin Restaurant*** (288 Main St., Marlborough; piedrafina.com). Designed almost like a choose-your-own-culinary-adventure, the Cuban and Venezuelan dishes at Piedra Fina are served on small and medium plates—the perfect portions to allow you to try more than one menu offering. Pair your plates, or tapas, with a beverage from the considerable cocktail menu and enjoy a little piece of Latin culture, right here in New Hampshire.

Ashuelot Valley

Keene's main street is lined for several blocks by beautifully cared-for private residences covering all architectural periods since the mid-eighteenth century. In the 1750s, the founders of ***Keene*** laid out all of the main lots so that the buildings would be set well back from the center of the highway. That decision set the tone for the development of downtown. At the north end of Main Street stands a large white church with a wedding-cake spire. This is one of the most beautiful of New England's churches, and its location at the head of Central Square gives it a commanding presence.

On the west side of Main Street is the ochre-colored, eighteenth-century ***Wyman Tavern.*** It was from this tavern that a contingent of Keene minutemen departed to join in the Revolution on April 23, 1775, four days after the battle at Concord, Massachusetts. Prior to that, the first trustees' meeting of Dartmouth College was held here. The tavern is now a museum, furnished in the 1770–1820 period. It is open June 1 to Aug 25, and admission is $5 for adults and $3 for children. Contact the Historical Society of Cheshire County up the street at 246 Main St. for hours, or see their website at hsccnh.org. You'll find the Wyman Tavern at 339 Main St. in Keene (603-357-3855, summer only).

Keene was the home to the nationally known muralist and artist Barry Faulkner, whose works decorate public buildings in Washington, DC, and elsewhere. Several sites in Keene display individual pieces, and there are two full-scale murals. Elliot Hall, at Keene State College, is a large brick mansion near the corner of Main Street and Wyman Way that serves as the admissions office for the college. In the front hallway a large ***Faulkner mural*** depicting Central Square fills the winding staircase. In the main hall of Fleet Bank at the head of Central Square, his mural series *Men of Monadnock* fills the back wall, and at the Keene Public Library on nearby Winter Street a number of sketches he did for murals elsewhere are exhibited.

The **Archive Center of the Historical Society of Cheshire County** has a number of Faulkner works in its Barry Faulkner Room, to the left of the main entry. On display are an oil self-portrait, a rare 1930s lithograph of work done on the National Archives, and several drawings and sketches completed over his lifetime. The newest accession is a full-color painting of the mosaic mural that Faulkner did for Radio City Music Hall in 1939.

Other exhibit rooms in the society's headquarters highlight the prominent role of local glass and pottery manufacture, with large collections on display. The society has acquired all of the metal toy collection of the Kingsbury Corporation dating back to the nineteenth century. Consisting of more than 250 items, the collection is a boon for antique toy lovers and includes cast iron and sheet metal items. Horse and wagon, fire engine, classic auto, zeppelin, and racecar forms are among the toys included. Items of historical interest from the society's collection are also exhibited, with special exhibits mounted several times each year showcasing particular aspects of local history. The reference library contains extensive genealogical material and histories of the region and the state. The archive is open Tues through Fri from 9 a.m. to 4 p.m. and Sat from 9 a.m. to noon at 246 Main St., Keene; (603) 352-1895; hsccnh.org.

The **Arboretum and Gardens** at Keene State College are well described in a brochure that you can get for free at the Mason Library on Apian Way, the pedestrian street that cuts through the center of the campus from Main Street. For some years, tree plantings have been planned to create a collection of specimen trees, and now include a wide variety of exotics, several of which are at the far northern edge of their range. The booklet includes a map of the campus and silhouettes of leaf shapes to help you identify the species you'll see on a tour of the campus. For more

parrishthe thought

As you drive around Central Square in Keene, you may notice an advertisement for Parrish Shoes painted on the side of a brick building and featuring a picture of an old-fashioned shoe. It's all that's left of the sets for *Jumanji*, starring Robin Williams, which was filmed in Keene. For the movie, the brick business buildings surrounding the leafy park were transformed back to their appearance of many years ago, then trashed for the later scenes—their signs hanging, their paint peeling, and their facades unkempt. After filming, Keene was restored to its 1990s appearance, with only this painted sign as a reminder of Robin's time travels there.

information about the arboretum, call the Plant Sciences Department at (603) 358-2544.

Also on the Keene State College campus, the free ***Thorne-Sagendorph Memorial Art Gallery*** shows traveling exhibits and an impressive permanent collection of well-known nineteenth-century artists who painted in the shadow of Mount Monadnock. The gallery is open Sun through Wed from noon to 5 p.m., Thurs and Fri from noon to 7 p.m., with hours extended to 8 p.m. on Sat. Thorne-Sagendorph Memorial Art Gallery, Wyman Way (off Main St.), Keene; (603) 358-2720; keene.edu. One of the state's most unusual "old house" museums is in this same neighborhood, next to St. Bernard's Church on Main Street. The ***Horatio Colony House Museum*** is not a home restored to one particular period, but the residence of a twentieth-century heir to a fortune that allowed him to live the life of a nineteenth-century gentleman of leisure. He traveled all over the world, collecting as he went, with a fine eye and highly cultivated tastes. The Oriental art he brought back with him is at home in the 1806 Federal mansion, amid fine eighteenth- and nineteenth-century furnishings. Some of his collections are in glass cases in the ell, while other items are displayed as he lived with them. You will leave feeling that you have known this well-read, well-traveled, and generous gentleman who left his estate for others to enjoy. Open May 1 to Oct 15, Wed through Sun 11 a.m. to 4 p.m., and in winter by appointment. Admission is free; park behind the church. The address is 199 Main St. in Keene; (603) 352-0460; horatiocolonymuseum.org.

Observe life farther up Main Street at the big windows of ***Thai Garden*** while dining on some of the best and most authentic Thai dishes in the state. Helpful family members, who know the menu, staff the bright and pleasant dining room. Dishes marked with hot pepper symbols will curl your hair; others are delicate blends of exotic and fresh local ingredients. The restaurant is open daily for lunch 11:30 a.m. to 3 p.m. and for dinner 5 to 10 p.m. It is located at 118 Main St., Keene; (603) 357-4567.

On Main Street, just below Central Square, look for ***Hannah Grimes Marketplace,*** an excellent craft boutique carrying works of many local craftspersons. The crafts and locally made food products you'll find there include pottery, candles, fiber work, woodenware, herbal sachets and cooking blends, jams, jellies, and even New Hampshire–made muffin mixes and stone-ground flours. We never know what new items will be on their shelves. They also carry stained glass, fine prints by local artists, photography, and cards. You can buy a cup of herbal or China tea there to drink as you browse, or you can sit down to drink it with a fresh scone or cookies from their bakery shelf. Hannah Grimes Marketplace is situated at 42 Main St., Keene; (603) 352-6862; hannahgrimesmarketplace.com.

Just up the street is the new *Fairfield Inn & Suites by Marriott,* formerly the E. F. Lane Hotel. Keene had not had a downtown hotel for decades, which makes this attractive place especially welcome. An air of calm and comfort begins in the lobby, with its stylish tones of tan and cream with dark green carpeting. Each room is decorated with quality classic and contemporary furniture. Some have king or queen beds, some offer whirlpool tubs, and all rooms have desks with computer and high-speed Internet hookups. The creators of the inn have used detail work in the door facings and elsewhere that brings back the nineteenth-century flavor of this converted downtown office and commercial space. Rooms vary from the very large and high-ceilinged Classic room to the super-large Executive and a two-floor Chairman's Suite, all of them handsome and comfortable. Rates for double occupancy are high-moderate, and special rates for a two-night stay are available for college graduation, parents, and homecoming weekends and for foliage and Pumpkin Festival weekends. Rates include a light breakfast. The Fairfield Inn & Suites is at 30 Main St., Keene; (603) 357-7070; (888) 300-5056.

Celebrating Food

While some states have a trademark food product or dish—such as Maine lobster, Vermont cheddar, or Rhode Island johnnycakes—New Hampshire has a little of everything. Its boats harvest lobsters and fish from the sea, and its farms and orchards produce an abundance of apples, berries, and field-fresh vegetables. In the spring its hillsides run with sap that is boiled into maple syrup.

Although it produces an abundance of native foods, from farm cheeses to pumpkins, no one harvest is its trademark. However, the state does celebrate each season with a splendid cornucopia of food festivals. In the southwest corner (the Monadnock region) alone are a strawberry festival in Fitzwilliam, an apple festival in Walpole, and a gingerbread festival in Charlestown.

The granddaddy of them all is Keene's Pumpkin Festival, held just before Halloween each October. In 2003, the tree-canopied square and main street were lined with 28,952 jack-o'-lanterns, each with a lighted candle inside. Keene holds the Guinness World Record for the most carved pumpkins in one place, a category it originated and defends with an increasing number each year. All day Saturday you can see the collection grow while you feast on harvest goodies, including cider and homemade pumpkin pies and cookies.

A week earlier, in nearby Winchester, is one of our favorite local homegrown celebrations: the Pickle Festival. In 1999, more than 4,000 pickles were eaten in one day—not to break a record but because they taste good. The day begins with a parade and ends with a barn dance. In between are sports competitions, an antique car show, a field full of scarecrows, barbecues, and, of course, pickle judging.

On the opposite side of the street is the ***Colonial Theatre.*** Thornton Wilder read his plays, Amelia Earhart lectured, and a Metropolitan opera star once sang four encores of *"O Sole Mio"* in this theater, opened in 1924, as a state-of-the-art stage and movie house. Its interior had deteriorated badly by 1991, when its restoration began. Today, it retains part of its original Art Deco frieze and its other elegant details have been restored. It also hosts art films and traveling performers (Joan Baez and The Kingston Trio have performed here since its restoration). Watch the marquis at 95 Main St., or contact the box office at (603) 352-2033; thecolonial.org.

Next to the theater is ***Brewbakers,*** a coffeehouse with a laid-back atmosphere. Grab a paper or one of their many novels and curl up with a cup of coffee and a homemade scone or muffin. There is a booth, too, and ice-cream tables; in the summer a few tables spill out onto Main Street. In addition to coffees and biscotti, they also have a lunch menu. Located at 97 Main St., Keene; (603) 355-4844.

On West Street (it's the street heading west from Central Square, but it was named for a person, not for its direction), ***Ashuelot River Park*** is a pleasant place to stop, sit on a bench, and enjoy the sunshine. The river here was once part of a millpond feeding the factory across the street (now the Colony Mill Marketplace). Today, the pond is smaller and bound by a garden with a footbridge over to an island. On the north side a trail leads through the woods along the banks of the slow-flowing river. The shaded path is a good place to see wildlife, especially waterfowl. Several species of ducks are common visitors. At its north end, the path connects to a paved bike/walking path that, if you go west, will take you to the city's ***Wheelock Park,*** where you will find athletic facilities, including tennis courts, and a city-operated camping area. The path allows campers to get to the center of the city without traveling on a public street. For camping information contact the Parks and Recreation Department, 312 Washington St., Keene 03431; (603) 357-9829.

Not long ago, people in Keene used to go across the river to Brattleboro, Vermont, for a fine dinner; now Brattleboro people travel to Keene, especially since Italian-born chef Nicola Bencivenga has opened ***Nicola's Trattoria,*** with a menu of classic and innovative dishes based on impeccably fresh, high-quality ingredients. No shortcuts here: The polenta is real, light in texture, and made the long, slow way instead of the quick-fix, heavy cornmeal mush served as polenta in too many places. The whole menu is enticing, but we usually order the specials just to see what he's created that day. Go on Saturday night for osso bucco or any night for the cioppino. The Risotto alla Milanese is superb—or choose any risotto special. It may be blended with perfectly cooked shrimp and pesto or another equally delicious combination.

Nicola added the Tuscan Room, open later than the restaurant and the perfect place for light meals, dessert, or a late-night chocolate ricotta torte, *tartufo,* or a crisp, freshly filled cannoli after a show at the Colonial. This is the time of night when Nicola can escape the kitchen and meet his guests. Keene's our hometown, and Nicola's is our favorite place for dinner; it's at 51 Railroad St., but you enter from Winter Street, beside the elegant 1858 brick courthouse (you can park behind the courthouse); (603) 355-5242. They're open for dinner Tues through Sun from 5 p.m.

Keene's favorite place for a quick breakfast or lunch is **Timoleon's,** on Main Street, just south of Central Square. This is the sort of place where everyone calls the waitresses by their first names, and the menu has all of the old favorites. They are noted for chicken croquettes, meat loaf, and, on Friday, codfish cakes. The breakfast pastries are all baked right there and have earned a "Best of New Hampshire" award. Located at 27 Main St., Keene; (603) 357-4230.

The Redfern Arts Center on Brickyard Pond at Keene State College has an active performance schedule (603-358-2168; keene.edu/arts/redfern), and Keene supports its own choral group, the **Keene Chorale.** Their professional-quality concerts are held in the spring and before Christmas and may include sacred works, such as masses and oratorios, or operatic choral selections. For a schedule of concerts, call (603) 357-1534. During the summer, concerts featuring popular bands are held on Wednesday evenings at the bandstand in the common on Central Square from 7 to 8:30 p.m. (603-357-9829).

Colony House B&B is located a block from Keene's thriving Main Street. It is in a lovingly restored 1819 home that at one time belonged to the owner's great-grandfather. Guest rooms all have private baths and guests have a living room, a butler's pantry with microwave and toaster, and a study as public rooms. Computer access, a fax and copier, and a computer are all available. Entry to the guest rooms is through a private entrance. All of the attractions of the city, including the Colony Mill Marketplace, Colonial Theater, historical society museums, and shopping are within easy walking distance. Located at 104 West St., Keene 03431; (603) 352-0215; colonyhouse104.com.

Goose Pond is a recreational nature reserve 4 miles from Central Square on East Surry Road, accessed from Court Street. You will see a sign for the parking area. A trail leads along a stone wall to the undeveloped pond, which once served to power several mills downstream. The trail then circles the pond, close to the shore through woodlands. In one spot it forms a tunnel through overhanging hemlock boughs, but the woods are mostly mixed, with birch, white pine, and maple. Watch for signs of beaver activity here, including their lodge built against the shore, close to the path. The total distance around

Goose Pond is about 3 miles, including the short walk from the parking area to the pond.

Just east of Keene, ***Granite Gorge*** serves as a perfect entry for beginners to the sports of skiing and snowboarding. Granite's specialty is snowboarding, with terrain parks that are noted for their challenges. But they also have alpine and cross-country trails. Granite Gorge, Route 9, Keene; call (603) 358-5000 or visit facebook.com/granitegorge.skiarea.

Stonewall Farm, off Route 9 just west of Keene, is a demonstration farm with an active dairy herd. If you go between 4:30 and 6:30 p.m., you can watch the milking session, especially popular with children. Youngsters also enjoy the other animals that are kept close to the education center—a flock of chickens, a sow with a brood of piglets, goats, sheep, and a calf. The farm's two teams of Belgian draft horses can be seen grazing in the pasture or working on the farm as they plow, hay, or haul sap in the spring for the farm's sugarhouse. Stonewall Farm maple products are sold at the small gift shop in the education center. A 1.2-mile nature walk is self-guided, with the help of a sixteen-page booklet available at the trailhead. Special events include an Annual Art Auction and Gala in early May and a Thanksgiving Farm Fare in mid-November. For a complete schedule of events and programs, contact Stonewall Farm, 242 Chesterfield Rd., Keene 03431; (603) 357-7278; stonewallfarm.org.

Swanzey, directly south of Keene, has maintained and preserved three covered bridges over the Ashuelot River, as well as built one brand new. The following route will show you all of them. Leave Keene on Route 10 (Winchester Street) and turn left onto Matthews Road just past the veterinary clinic. Go left at the end and through the first of the bridges. When that road ends, go left again and shortly join Route 32 at the ***Potash Bowl*** (remember where this is—we'll get back to it later). All this sounds complicated, but it's a distance of only 3 to 4 miles. Go south on Route 32 to Carleton Road, where you will find another bridge in a few hundred yards. If it's early spring and the water is high, the bridge may be closed, but you can drive down to watch the river lapping at its floorboards. Return to Route 32 and continue south to Swanzey Lake Road on your right. Follow this winding road until it ends at a T. Go right, and you'll come to West Swanzey. The third bridge is to your left when you reach the crossroads at the top of the hill. Go through it, then turn right, and you will come to Route 10. At Route 10, turn left (south). You will pass auto dealerships, shopping centers, and antiques dealers before coming to a Y intersection. The main road goes to the right, but you should follow the left-hand road to reach the state's newest covered bridge, the ***Slate Covered Bridge.*** In the late 1990s, an arsonist burned the historic nineteenth-century covered bridge that stood here. Through the hard work of townspeople, a new bridge was built, replicating exactly the one that was lost. In the summer of 2001, it finally opened to traffic. After enjoying this beautiful new/old bridge you can backtrack to Route 10, following it north back toward Keene.

Covered bridges did not originate in New England—they were a common sight in the Alpine regions of Europe for the same reasons early New Englanders built them. The roof protected floorboards and support timbers from the harsh weather and snow buildup that would weaken or break the bridge under its weight. Snow falling on the sloping roof would slide off, as it does on a house roof. The biggest job for road agents was shoveling snow *onto* the bridge so that sleigh runners could slide over them in the time of year when the sleighs replaced carriages and wagons for transport. (In New England the term *road agent* means a person whose job is to maintain roads. It does not refer to a highwayman, as it does in many other places.)

On the east side of Route 10 is the ***Swanzey Historical Museum,*** which features some interesting exhibits. Here you will find an operational Amoskeag steam fire pumper made in Manchester and a stagecoach. The museum is wheelchair accessible and is open June through Oct, Mon, Thurs, and Fri from 1 to 4 p.m.; Sat and Sun 10 a.m. to 4 p.m. on Route 12 in Swanzey; (603) 352-4579.

Close to the Potash Bowl, and to two of the covered bridges, is a newly opened bed-and-breakfast, the ***Inn of the Tartan Fox.*** In an early 1900s Arts and Crafts–style stone "cottage," smartly renovated to provide private baths (with heated marble floors) for each room and to make one wheelchair accessible, the inn is the essence of comfort. Antiques highlight rooms, which are light and airy, using Scottish tartans in the decoration. Full breakfasts include a main course, as well as freshly baked scones or muffins. Rates are moderate to expensive. The inn is on Route 32, about a mile past the entrance to the airport (follow airport signs from lower Main Street/Route 12) at 350 Old Homestead Hwy., Swanzey; (603) 357-9308; (877) 836-4319; tartanfox.com.

Almost to the Connecticut River (and Vermont), a left turn from Route 9 leads up ***Welcome Hill Road,*** where residents have created a beautiful place in the spring, which they generously share with total strangers. As you begin to ascend the hill, you see little patches of yellow daffodils beside the road, then a banking of them, and then an entire yard full. And just past the crest of the hill, the road widens enough for a few cars to park, overlooking a beautiful little vale simply yellow with flowers.

A trail winds down through this sea of daffodils, and there is a bench at road level for those who prefer to enjoy the picture from above. As the season progresses, the daffodils are joined by a colorful scattering of tulips; at about the same time, the tree above the bench bursts into bloom.

Chesterfield Gorge shows the power of persistence. A relatively small brook has worn a deep gorge through the rocks here as it cascades from pool to pool for a distance of about 0.25 mile. It is an easy hike, just over 0.5 mile, through a forest of beech and hemlock of unusual size. A small pavilion at the head of the trail contains information on the geologic history of the gorge's formation. A shady grove provides a good place for a picnic. The gorge is on Route 9, west of Keene.

keene'sfireproof house

Fred Sharby was afraid of fire. Two of the theaters he owned burned flat, and he had a terror of dying in a fire. So he tore down his house on the north side of Roxbury Street in Keene and built a new one, all of fireproof materials. Steel girders, stucco, plaster, fireproof floor tiles, doors of solid metal, and a furnace enclosed in cement walls have indeed lasted to this day without a fire. Fred wasn't so lucky. He chose the night of November 28, 1942, to go to the Coconut Grove in Boston and died in that fire.

Farther west, Route 63 crosses Route 9 and leads south to *Chesterfield* and the entrance to *Pisgah* (pronounced "Piz-gee") *State Park.* The road to this wilderness preserve winds along the edge of a hill through mixed hardwood forests. There are no facilities in the 13,000 acres of this park, and camping is not allowed. Twenty miles of hiking and ski trails crisscross the area, which is a favorite with anglers and hunters. Some of the trails connect with *Road's End Farm Horsemanship Camp* on Jackson Hill Road, and you're welcome to hike on these trails as well. For ten weeks in the summer, the camp is filled with girls sharing the experience of riding and caring for the camp's horses. In other seasons, experienced riders can call for reservations to enjoy these same trails and the views of Pisgah Park, Mount Monadnock, and even Mount Snow in Vermont. The farm's hilltop setting is unparalleled. The location is Jackson Hill Rd., Chesterfield; (603) 363-4900; roadsendfarm.com.

More trails into Pisgah lead from Route 119 in Ashuelot, at the southern end of the park. This village, part of the town of Winchester, has the elegant and freshly restored 160-foot *Ashuelot Covered Bridge.* Built in the town lattice-truss style, with walking corridors along each side, between 1853 and 1858 (not in 1864 as the sign indicates), the bridge is one of New England's best examples of the American Gothic style of architecture translated to bridge design.

Just across the bridge, on the left, is the *Winchester Historical Society Museum* in the Sheriden House. This home of the local gentry has been rescued from oblivion and is in the slow process of restoration. The two finest rooms, with richly inlaid floors, have been restored and furnished to the late 1800s; others are in various states, which makes it fun to watch the progress. In the barn is a series of very nice horse stalls, and a Sunday "barn sale" helps raise money for the restoration. Admission is free, and the museum is open May through Oct on Sun afternoons from 2 to 4 p.m. and Wed from 9 a.m. to noon. You can see it at other times by appointment; (603) 239-4211; winchester nhhistoricalsociety.net.

If you follow it northward, Route 63 winds along the shore of Spofford Lake and into Westmoreland (with the accent on *west*) and on through the settlement of *Park Hill,* a cluster of noteworthy early buildings, the likes of which are rare outside of Portsmouth or Exeter. *The Meeting House* is one of the state's earliest, built in 1762 with a facade and spire considered among the finest in that period of architectural design. The Paul Revere bell was placed there in 1827. Around the church are several homes dating from as early as 1774.

Follow the signs off Route 63 in Park Hill to the Cheshire County Complex, a county-operated farm, where you can park at the top of the hill to enjoy one of the few walking trails along the banks of the Connecticut River. The *River Trail* overlooks steep banks in places, so you can actually look down onto the canopy of trees, a prime vantage for bird watching. The trail is being extended, with signage pointing out natural features of the flora along the way.

Back at the farm, stop at the *Master Gardeners Demonstration Garden,* a joint project of the farm and the Cheshire County Extension Service, where you can get ideas for your own garden from their 1-acre plot, complete with arbor, pathways, and a small greenhouse.

Cheshire County's Extension Service is a very active one, with innovative programs to promote agriculture in the region and draw the public into farm activities. Check local-events listings (on Friday the *Keene Sentinel* has a calendar for the coming week) for *Open Farm Days* during the summer, when a local farm is featured, and activities are planned for both adults and children. A popular attraction is the appearance of a van from the Granite State Dairy Promotion Board, dispensing unlimited quantities of free ice cream. The highlight of the agricultural year is the *Cheshire Fair* in early August. Although it has a midway with rides, it is still largely an agricultural event, with 4-H members showing their sheep and calves at the southern end of the fairgrounds, while the lunch counter in the 4-H building serves up old-fashioned homemade pies.

To learn more about the wide variety of farm-related products in the area, you can get a copy of the free booklet *"Monadnock Region Product Directory."* Listing dozens of farms where you can buy everything from llama wool to Christmas trees or sign up for classes in soap making, the book is available from Stonewall Farm, 242 Chesterfield Rd., Keene 03431; (603) 357-7278; stone wallfarm.org.

Route 63 winds past some of New Hampshire's finest and most fertile farmland, with meadows full of grazing cattle and views across the Connecticut River Valley into Vermont. From mid-February until mid-April and from mid-September until the end of November, you can stop for breakfast, lunch, or a snack at **Stuart and John's Sugar House.** It's best in late February and into March, when the sap is running and the back room is filled with steam from the evaporators. The corn fritters and homemade doughnuts are delicious, and syrup comes in a full-size milk pitcher that the waitress plunks on the table when she brings the menu. All you need to decide is what to pour it over. If it's not time for breakfast or lunch when you are passing by, try a maple sundae, frappé, or maple apple pie (in the fall). This place isn't fancy; you sit on folding chairs at church supper–style tables. It's family style, family run, and a favorite low-cost Sunday outing for local families. Open weekends 7 a.m. to 3 p.m. (Feb through May) and Thurs through Sun from 7 a.m. to 8 p.m. (from Memorial Day through Labor Day), on Route 63 at Route 12 in Westmoreland; (603) 399-4486; stuartandjohn.com.

Northern Hills

Walpole looks down onto Route 12, and this picture-perfect village is a good place to stroll around and admire the beautifully preserved and maintained eighteenth- and nineteenth-century homes that encircle the green. On Sunday evenings during July and August, band concerts fill this grassy common with music and people.

The prosperity that built the many homes and public buildings in Walpole resulted from the building of a canal around the Great Falls of the Connecticut River in 1790. The canal allowed river traffic (water was the main means of moving goods in those days) to proceed past here to the North Country. The heirlooms of many of these early families have found their way to the **Old Academy Museum.** Silk dresses with the kind of needlework that only prosperous women had the time to pursue have been preserved here along with furniture, tools, utensils and kitchenware, and a completely restored schoolroom from the original academy. Shaker furniture, and the original piano mentioned in *Little Women,* a gift to the Alcott sisters when they were living in Walpole, are just a few of the treasures that have been presented to the museum. Open from 2 to 4 p.m. Wed and Sat, June through Sept, or by appointment. On Main Street in Walpole; call (603) 756-3449 or visit walpolehistory.org for more information.

ALSO WORTH SEEING IN THE MONADNOCK REGION

Colony Mill Marketplace,
222 West St., Keene
(603) 622-6223
Not the usual mall with chain stores, this carefully renovated historic mill building is filled with locally owned specialty shops and eateries.

The chocolates made at **_L.A. Burdick_** by Swiss-trained Larry Burdick are tops. Be sure to try one of their dark, white, or milk chocolate mice. The cafe at the shop serves hot chocolate, tea, espresso, and tempting pastry. Open Tues through Sat 7 a.m. to 9 p.m.; Sun 9 a.m. to 5 p.m.; and Mon 7 a.m. to 5 p.m. at 47 Main St., Walpole; (603) 756-2882 or (800) 229-2419 (to order chocolates by mail); burdickchocolate.com.

Few dairy farms in New Hampshire produce cheese, but a happy exception is **_Boggy Meadow Farm_** in Walpole, north of the intersection of Route 63 and Route 12. They sell Swiss and smoked Swiss cheeses under their label Fanny Mason Cheese in a small retail shop right at the farm where they are made on River Road. The shop is open daily 8 a.m. to 5 p.m. You'll find the farm from Route 12 by its discreet FARMSTEAD CHEESE sign; (603) 756-3300; (877) 541-3953; boggymeadowfarm.com.

Overlooking the wide Connecticut River valley not far from Boggy Meadow, **_Alyson's Orchard_** is easy to spot alongside Route 12 because of the beautifully crafted metal apple tree that sprouts green leaves and red apples even in midwinter. This is just a tantalizing hint of the surprises that Alyson's has in store. Bronze cranes and herons fool the eye as they stand in the pond. The orchard grows more varieties of apples than the common Macs and Cortlands—many of the forty-odd varieties are nearly lost heritage strains—and there are more than a dozen types each of pears and peaches. The hilltop grounds are a popular wedding venue, with sweeping views of the Connecticut River. Alyson's is at 57 Alyson's Lane in Walpole; (800) 856-0549 or (603) 756-9800; alysonsorchard.com.

If you have a spare day and a sense of adventure, you could take any road out of Walpole and follow it until it ends in the dooryard of a farmhouse or bumps into Route 12A. The hillsides are covered with well-kept farms and are separated by lovely little hollows. The views over the valley are beautiful when you reach the hillcrests, most of which have been cleared for pastureland. North of Walpole, Route 123 heads into more hills, following the Cold River (all rivers here are cold; one wonders who decided that this one should be so honestly named). From the village of Drewsville, a road heads north toward Langdon, and in about a mile it passes New Hampshire's shortest covered bridge, only 36 feet long.

More Places to Stay in the Monadnock Region

ANTRIM

Maplehurst Inn
67 Main St.
(603) 588-8000
A comfortable country inn.
Inexpensive.

CHESTERFIELD

Chesterfield Inn
20 Cross St.
(603) 256-3211
chesterfieldinn.com
Classy, pricey rooms in a fine, old home overlooking the Connecticut River Valley.

KEENE

The Carriage Barn Bed and Breakfast
358 Main St.
(603) 357-3812
keenebnb.com
A block from downtown shops, with three museums and an arts center within a five-minute walk, its location matches the quality of its rooms. Moderate.

RINDGE

The Grove at the Woodbound Inn
247 Woodbound Rd.
(603) 532-8341
woodbound.com
Operating since 1892; the current owners offer accommodations that blend the best of the inn's nostalgic past with modern amenities and conveniences.

TO LEARN MORE ABOUT THE MONADNOCK REGION

Greater Peterborough Chamber of Commerce
10 Wilton Rd.
Peterborough 03458
(603) 924-7234
peterboroughchamber.com

WEST SWANZEY

Bridges Inn at Whitcomb House
27 Main St.
(603) 357-6624
bridgesinn.com
An attractive B&B within sight of the historic Slate Covered Bridge, with moderate rates.

More Places to Eat in the Monadnock Region

HANCOCK

Fiddleheads Cafe & Catering
28 Main St.
(603) 525-4432
fiddleheadscatering.net
Opposite the inn, the friendly cafe serves excellent custom-built sandwiches.

HILLSBOROUGH

High Tide Take Out
239 Henniker St.
(603) 464-4202
Well-prepared fast-fried seafood, burgers, hot dogs, ice cream. Inexpensive.

KEENE

Ocean Harvest Seafood Restaurant
433 Winchester St.
(603) 357-3553
Skip the chain-brand seafood restaurants to have the area's tastiest (and never greasy) fried clams and shrimp, broiled scallops, and fish sandwiches.

Papagallos
9 Monadnock Hwy.
(603) 352-9400
papagallos.com
Very popular with locals, family dining with an emphasis on Italian but a good mix of other options and interesting wood-fired pizzas. Inexpensive.

PETERBOROUGH

Peterborough Diner
10 Depot St.
(603) 924-6202
It's the real thing, been there half a century. Inexpensive.

RINDGE

Emma's 321 Pub & Kitchen
377 US-202
(603) 899-3322
emmas321.com
Ideal place to grab a bite before or after fall foliage leaf-peeping. Offers a range of fan favorites like house-made chicken fingers, crispy fried wings, and other fare to enjoy while watching a game or in between rounds of pool. Enjoy some discounted pricing with happy hour, running from 3 to 6 p.m. every day, and all day on Thursdays.

The Grove at the Woodbound Inn
247 Woodbound Rd.
(603) 532-8341
woodbound.com
Elevated pub fare. See website for dining hours.

Hometown Diner
1421 Route 119
(603) 889-3200
hometowndinernh.com
Serving breakfast and lunch Sun, Mon, and Wed (closed Tues); breakfast, lunch, and dinner served Thurs through Sat until 8 p.m. Free coffee refills and you can now order a beer or wine with your New England Yankee pot roast, liver and onions, or hand-breaded chicken breast platter.

WALPOLE

Bellows Walpole Inn
297 Main St.
(603) 756-3320
walpoleinn.com
This beautifully restored 1762 inn has an up-to-the-minute dining room, with a frequently changing menu offering such dishes as smoked pork ribs with sweet potato fries. Moderate.

The Dartmouth-Sunapee Region

The **Connecticut River** flows through a broad, flat valley as it forms the border between New Hampshire and neighboring Vermont. Along its shores and up the hillsides that overlook it are sprawling farmlands: fields of corn, herds of cattle, truck farms, and family farms. Their massive barns and tall, round silos punctuate the landscape. These venerable homes were built by some of the earliest settlers in the valley.

The farms were not always so serene. The river was the major artery of travel for Native Americans, as well as settlers, and the French and Indian Wars were fought along its banks. It was to educate Native Americans that Eleazer Wheelock founded a school that is now Dartmouth College. Its cultural influence and that of Colby-Sawyer College in nearby New London on the entire Upper Valley are significant, especially in the performing and fine arts.

To the east of the Connecticut River Valley rise the gentle slopes of Mounts Sunapee, Kearsarge, and Cardigan—each about 3,000 feet in altitude—and other smaller mountains. The Appalachian Trail crosses the river on its way south, and nearly every mountain in the region, however small, has a trail to its summit.

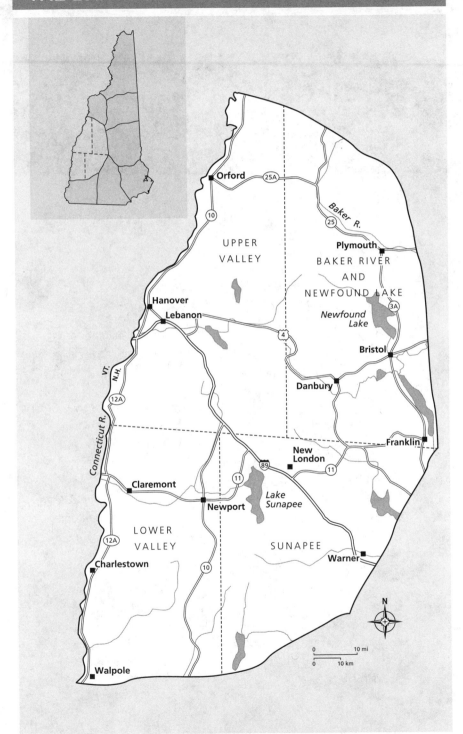

Lakes dot the landscape. This region is a quiet part of the state, and even the interstate that bisects it hasn't changed that. In fact, from the point where I-89 leaves Concord until it arrives in Lebanon, at the Vermont border, there is almost no commercial activity visible along its sides, only miles of forest and farmland backed by mountain vistas.

The Lower Valley

The *Fort at No. 4* was once the northwesternmost English-speaking village in the New World. This museum is an authentic reconstruction of the settlement founded there in 1740. It is New England's only living-history museum of the period of the French and Indian Wars. Within its log stockade are furnished province houses and shops where costumed interpreters carry on the daily work of an isolated colonial village. Dinner is prepared in a huge open fireplace, candles are hand dipped, and wool and flax spun and woven. From the lookout tower, sentries kept watch over the river and valley for signs of attack by the Native Americans or the French. The skirmishes that took place here in those early years are re-created in full costume each year, and a cloud of smoke from musket fire hangs over the river as it did two and a half centuries ago when, in 1747, the fort was besieged by a force of 400, but withstood the attack. This success resulted in the withdrawal of French forces to Canada and the beginning of English supremacy in northern New England. Of particular interest here is a working blacksmith shop, where a master smith creates the tools and utensils necessary for daily life and work on the frontier. A museum shop carries items of the period at extraordinarily reasonable prices.

Prior to making a special trip to Fort No. 4, call for the current opening information and hours. Admission is $10 for adults, $8 for seniors and youths (ages 13–17) and $6 for children (ages 6–12). Children under 5 are admitted free. The Fort at No. 4 is at 267 Springfield Rd. (Route 11), Charlestown 03603; (603) 826-5700; fortat4.org/visitor.php.

the river's ours 'til it floods

New Hampshire's northern border wasn't established until 1842's Webster-Ashburton Treaty, which finally set the international boundary with Canada. But the Vermont–New Hampshire line wasn't clear until a 1934 Supreme Court decision set it at the low-water mark on the Connecticut River.

Charlestown's *Main Street National Historic District* is lined with distinguished homes, many dating from the early 1800s. It is almost a mile long, and fifty-two of its sixty-three buildings are historically important; ten of them

If This Is Africa, Where Are the Lions?

Continental plates are great travelers, but they don't tend to follow the admonition of today's eco-travelers to tread softly and leave no tracks. When these giant pieces of the earth's crust move, they leave lots of tracks; in fact, they leave pieces of themselves hanging about after they've left, which is what the African Plate did after it bumped into Vermont. It left New Hampshire behind.

This accounts for the obvious differences in landscape and the wholly different geologies of the two states. The Connecticut River covers the seam, except in one place, where you can actually see where Africa and North America meet. If you go to North Walpole, where the bridge crosses over a deep gorge and into Bellows Falls, Vermont, you can see the two different rocks join in the riverbank below you.

date from the 1700s. Stephen Hassam, great-grandfather of the impressionist painter Childe Hassam, who often painted the Isles of Shoals, designed the Unitarian Church and two of the houses. St. Catherine's Church has four signed Tiffany stained-glass windows. Stop at the office of the town clerk for an inexpensive booklet describing the history of each building.

Known as one of the nation's premier flight centers, *Morningside Flight Park* in Charlestown teaches hang gliding and paragliding to all people at all levels of expertise or interest, from the cautiously curious to those with many hours of airtime in their logs. For a thrilling sightseeing ride and a new perspective on the Connecticut River Valley, you can choose a Tandem Aerotow, a two-person hang glider. With an instructor at the "controls," you can ride as the glider is towed to a 2,500-foot altitude. On release, you'll have a ten- to twenty-minute scenic glide over the river and valley. Morningside Flight Park is on Route 12 in North Charlestown; (603) 542-4416; flymorningside.com.

Claremont's early settlers quickly saw the potential of the waterfalls in the Sugar River as it flows from Lake Sunapee to the Connecticut River. The first dam was built in 1767 for a gristmill and sawmill, and other plants soon followed, their machinery powered by the force from the 300-foot drop in the river as it passes through town. Mill buildings still dominate the center of Claremont, and you can learn how they once operated by following a walking tour of *Claremont Village Industrial District.* A free brochure available from the chamber of commerce on Tremont Square describes the original uses and evolution of various buildings, including millworkers' housing, owners' residences, shops, the foundry, a weave shed, and other structures, each of which is marked on an accompanying map.

The manufacturing that created the massive mills along the Sugar River also created the wealth to build Claremont's imposing new city hall in 1897, with its tall, prominent clock tower. Its third floor boasted an opera house with one of the largest stages north of Boston. Although the ***Claremont Opera House and Atrium*** now has a separate wheelchair-accessible entry, those who enter through the old building can enjoy the carved archway and oak paneling of the lower lobbies and public areas. The large opera house has a curved balcony and cast-iron-based seats open one to see its unique reclining back. This outstanding example of public architecture of the past hundred years still hosts varied performances on a regular basis. It is open for performances and from 9 a.m. to 5 p.m. on weekdays. Call (603) 542-4433 for a schedule of events or visit claremontoperahouse.com.

About 3 miles west on Route 103 is the settlement of ***West Claremont*** and two historic churches. Union Church, a large, white clapboard building with curved windows, is the oldest Episcopal church building in New Hampshire. It is a surprise to see the oldest one this far inland—and this far from any present-day settlement. Its only neighbor, directly across the street, is St. Mary's Church, the first Roman Catholic church in the state, built between 1823 and 1825 and an outpost mission of St. Bernard's in Keene. The priest who established St. Mary's parish was the son of the Episcopal rector of Union Church across the street. The son had converted to Catholicism. The two men conducted a school for the children of West Claremont millworkers on the second floor of St. Mary's. Today, these vanguard churches stand alone, surrounded only by the West Part Burying Ground, the settlement they once served long gone.

EVENTS IN THE DARTMOUTH-SUNAPEE REGION

Dartmouth Winter Carnival
mid-Feb, Hanover
students.dartmouth.edu/collis/
traditions-events/winter-carnival

League of New Hampshire Craftsmen's Fair
early Aug, Sunapee
(603) 224-3375
discovernewengland.org/
annual-league-nh-craftsmens-fair

Farm Days
late Aug, Muster Field Farm Museum,
North Sutton
(603) 927-4276
musterfieldfarm.com

Fall Foliage Festival
early Oct, Warner
wfff.org

The Knights of Columbus have restored the little brick St. Mary's Church, and it is used for small weddings. During the summer it is open on Sunday afternoons and is staffed by volunteers from the Knights. Be sure to go to the third floor to see the bright and sunny classroom where the founder, Father Barber, had a school for boys. The white clapboarded Episcopal church across the street is not open at this time, but does hold Sunday morning services.

To get there from downtown Claremont, follow Route 12/103 west. About 3 miles out of town look for a historic marker on the left. Take the left over the river and another left turn, just after the bridge (this is where the original mills stood). Bear right at the next fork. The churches stand on either side of the road, just ahead. You can also reach the churches from Route 12A, south of the Route 103 intersection. This intersection is also marked with a historic marker.

The bridge across the Connecticut at Cornish is the longest covered bridge in the United States. (The longest in New Hampshire is at Bath; this one doesn't count since its other end is in Vermont.) Built in 1886, it traverses the river in two spans and has an unusual timber lattice-truss construction.

At the turn of the twentieth century, Cornish was the home of a thriving colony of artists, writers, poets, and patrons who built or purchased summer homes around the studio of Augustus Saint-Gaudens. Italian terraced gardens surrounded old farmhouses, and the summer season's social life was one of wealthy bohemia.

The artists are gone, but the genius of the sculptor who attracted them to this retreat lives on in his beautifully situated home. His sculptures are displayed in the studios and galleries and throughout the grounds of the *Saint-Gaudens National Historic Site.* The gardens and grounds, lined with tall pine and hemlock hedges and delicate birch trees, are worth a visit in their own right. The original Stanford White bluestone base for the statue of Admiral David Farragut has recently been moved here from New York City, where it was being damaged by pollution. The house, just as Mrs. Saint-Gaudens left it, is filled with artworks, each piece with some personal significance. A spirited house tour brings the family to life and lifts this site above the usual "home of a famous person" category. Sunday afternoon (2 p.m.) concerts in the summer bring musicians of all styles, along with music lovers carrying picnic baskets to the estate's shaded lawns. The house is open 9 a.m. to 4:30 p.m. daily from Memorial Day through late Oct; the grounds remain open until dusk. Admission is $10, but free for children under 15. Write to Saint-Gaudens National Historic Site, 139 Saint Gaudens Rd., Cornish 03745; call (603) 675-2175 or visit nps.gov/saga.

Beginning with the settlement of Augustus Saint-Gaudens, the other artists, architects, and writers also established summer or even year-round residences.

One of these was **Maxfield Parrish,** an illustrator and painter whose work is regaining the popularity it had a century ago. While Parrish's home was destroyed by fire, and his studio is now a private residence, a strong sense of his presence lingers here.

Possibly the most stunning of his work here is in the **Plainfield Town Hall** (plainfieldnh.org/about.htm). In 1916, Parrish and his friends decided to stage a play, *The Woodland Princess,* written by Louise Saunders, the author of *The Knave of Hearts,* which Parrish had illustrated. The stage set was designed by Parrish and quite likely was painted by him.

The backdrop curtains show a mountain (said by locals to be Mount Ascutney) rising behind a lake. Along the shore are granite boulders; the side curtains are painted with pine, birch, and maple trees and frame a woodland glen. Above, a gossamer header curtain of colored leaves completes the illusion of autumn. Between 1992 and 1994, the town came together to raise funds to have the sets professionally cleaned and the damages of time repaired. An ingenious lighting system, dating from 1916, allows the set to change from full noon to sunset to evening and back through a beautiful dawn. The effect of the slowly changing light on the colors is astounding.

Parrish Blue, a video examining Parrish's life, is shown in the small auditorium. Several original Parrish works are for sale along one wall, and reproductions and publications, including Parrish postcards, are on the other wall. The profits go to maintain the stage set.

The town hall is open Sunday afternoons 1 to 5 p.m. from July through Labor Day weekend, or by reservation. Admission is $1. To schedule an appointment, contact Phillip Read Memorial Library at (603) 675-6866, e-mail the director@plainfieldnhlibrary.org, or visit plainfieldnhlibrary.org. They hold the annual Maxfield Parrish Vintage Print and Collectibles Sale at the town hall on the first weekend of October. Those particularly interested in the artist can

Who Actually Painted It?

While most local people believe Parrish did actually paint the set at Plainfield Town Hall, at least one local art collector doubts it. Parrish did not have students or assistants in his Plainfield studio, and it would seem unlikely that local amateurs could have executed such a major work, using the placement, colors, and shading that are so definitively Parrish's. One letter written contemporaneously refers to his creation of the work, but his own records fail to mention it at all. Most locals are satisfied that it is his painting, as well as his design (about which there is no question), but without definitive historical proof, it remains a mystery.

inquire at the Town Hall, when it's open, or at the public library across the street for directions to his grave in a nearby cemetery.

A busy rail line once connected Newport and Claremont, crossing the Sugar River twice on its way. The route is now a walking trail, level and smooth, covering 9.7 miles along the river. En route, it passes through two rare covered railroad bridges, the Chandler Station and Wrights. The former is clearly visible, and both are accessible from Sugar River Drive, which parallels the south bank of the river. You can reach the path from Broad Street beyond the Chestnut Street intersection if you want to walk or bike the whole distance, or you can pick up the path at any of several points where it crosses Sugar River Drive.

A cool place to while away a hot summer afternoon is ***Pollard's Mills Falls.*** Actually a long series of small falls on the South Branch of the Sugar River, the cascades work their way through several hundred feet of a granite chasm lined with boulders. A path through the trees at the top of the embankment brings you to the site of the old mills, their rough stone foundations very evident along the shore of the stream. Be sure to find the large square cut into the bedrock to anchor the machinery of the mill. To get to the falls, follow Route 11 west of Newport about 0.5 mile and take a left onto Unity Road. Follow this for about a mile and then take a left onto Pollard's Mills Road. About 0.4 miles farther, turn right at a Y in the road. Just around that corner is a parking area overlooking the falls. The path is to the left.

We like to find worthy and significant old buildings that have been preserved for other uses when they were no longer needed, so we were happy when ***The Old Courthouse Restaurant*** opened in Newport's former Superior Court building. The 1826 brick building with its white tower sits behind the ***Newport Opera House*** (see below), part of a small cityscape that has remained relatively unchanged for the past century. It is listed on the National Register of Historic Places. The restaurant's menu changes weekly, with dishes such as lamb chops stuffed with olives, grilled salmon served over spiced lentils, or seared jumbo scallops paired with braised veal and served with saffron orzo and roasted vegetables. All entrees are reasonably priced; lunch and dinner are served Wed through Sat., with a brunch buffet served Sun from 9 a.m. to 1:30 p.m. The Old Courthouse is at 30 Main St.; (603) 863-8360; eatatthecourthouse.com.

The Newport Opera House, reopened in 1896 after a fire, was once one of the largest stages north of Boston and hosted many of the twentieth century's major performers before it dipped into a period of neglect. Restored in the 1970s, it again hosts traveling and local performances; (603) 863-2412; newport operahouse.com.

Sunapee

We have no intention of entering the historical dispute over the original mean-ing of *sunapee* in the Native American languages. It's a lovely region, in any language, with the mountain and lakes of the same name and the succession of smaller lakes between Mount Sunapee and **Mount Kearsarge.**

To the south lies Warner, with its **Mt. Kearsarge Indian Museum.** The museum's spirit is probably best summed up in the words of Chief Seattle in the late 1800s: "Every part of the earth is sacred to my people . . . every shin-ing pine needle, every sandy shore, every light mist in the dark forest . . . we are part of the earth and it is part of us." The purpose of the museum is not so much to show the incomparable artifacts as to interpret the lifestyle through art and culture and to renew in all of us the positive relationship the Native Americans experienced between the earth and its people. It succeeds. The exhibits are the lifetime collection of Charles (Bud) and Nancy Thompson, who didn't want to have "a mausoleum of pickled artifacts" but rather a museum with a voice.

The voice is that of Native Americans. Except for the quotations, there are no written labels or signs in this beautifully displayed collection. Instead, a docent conducts hourly tours, explaining the displays and focusing on those things that catch the visitors' interest. A museum shop sells authentic Indian handiwork, such as rugs, beadwork, and pottery, as well as books about vari-ous Indian tribes. Outdoors, a self-guided walk leads through 2 acres of native plants and trees used for medicine and food. Open May 1 through Oct 31, Mon through Sat 10 a.m. to 5 p.m. and Sun noon to 5 p.m.; weekends, Nov to April, noon to 5 p.m. or by appointment for groups of three or more. Admission is $9 for adults, $8 for youths (ages 13–18) and seniors, $7 for children (ages 6–12); no charge for children under 6; family rate (two adults and children under 18) is $26. Write Mt. Kearsarge Indian Museum, 18 Highlawn Rd., Warner 03278; (603) 456-2600; indianmuseum.org.

Warner is a town with an air of prosperity, and it has attracted a number of artists and writers. To sample the works of both, stop in at **MainStreet BookEnds,** a combination of art gallery and bookstore, open daily 9 a.m. to 6 p.m. Prominent in the front of the store is an entire cabinet of books by local authors, and the large art gallery in the back not only shows works of Warner artists in all media (including fine woodworking and pottery), but is also the venue of programs every Friday evening. Most are free, many are by authors, and the subjects include everything from the writing life, nature, and the arts to musical performances. The shop/gallery is at 16 East Main St.; (603) 456-2700; mainstreetbookends.com.

To see the works of three talented Warner artists, one of whom is also a naturalist and writer, stop at **Carroll Studio,** east of the bookshop in Lower Village. Laurette Carroll paints in the studio, where her work is shown along with that of her son, Sean, and the nature prints of her husband, the much-acclaimed naturalist/artist, David Carroll. His latest book, *Swamp-walker's Journal,* is a beautifully illustrated guide to the life and seasons of New England wetlands. Many of the prints from this book and his previous work on turtles are sold in the shop, as are these same images imprinted on T-shirts—an above-average souvenir of New Hampshire. The studio is open all year, Sat and Sun 10 a.m. to 3 p.m., or by chance or appointment, at 237 East Main St. (Route 103), Warner Lower Village; (603) 456-3947; carrollstudio gallery.com.

One of the more unusual buildings in Warner is **Clark's Cider Mill,** on Pumpkin Hill Road. This wooden building appears from the road to be a barn, but what you see is actually the upper part of a four-story (or maybe five, depending on what you count) mill, built into the steep banks of a ravine. The mill was built in 1886 and used as a threshing, shingle, and cider mill, as well as an icehouse. Its current owners plan to restore it and are using it as an antiques shop (where we found prices amazingly low).

The village of **South Sutton** looks as though it had been dropped there overnight from a previous century. Around its green is an ensemble of notable early buildings crowned by an 1839 meetinghouse with double doors and a curved gallery (you can get a good look inside through the side windows). Behind it is a schoolhouse (note the collection of vintage lunch boxes), and below are several homes, one built in 1756.

In an arrangement somewhat more logical than you often find with New England village names, North Sutton lies north of South Sutton, also along Route 114. Its tidy crossroads are marked by the blue (or frozen) waters of Kezar Lake and by the large, white-clapboard **Follansbee Inn.** This is an old-fashioned, warmhearted inn with its own beachfront on the lake and canoes, rowboats, bikes, and snowshoes for guests. Its spacious, bright rooms have hand-pieced coverlets, and each morning begins with a full breakfast that guests choose for themselves in the kitchen. This moderately priced inn is open year-round and adjoins the ski and snowshoe trails of Wadleigh State Park. Follansbee Inn is in North Sutton; (603) 927-4221 or (800) 626-4221; follansbeeinn.com.

Kezar Lake has an island perfect for picnics, and if you are not staying at the inn you can launch your own canoe or kayak from the town beach at the crossroads. Last time we were there, we met a charming gentleman, Dr. Robert Breed from Lynn, Massachusetts, who told us that between him and his father, they had come to Follansbee Inn for 117 summers. The innkeepers have changed over the years, but the hospitality has not, he assured us. He also told us about a rare Native American site across the lake.

Very few tangible sights remain in New Hampshire to show its aboriginal heritage. The Penacook tribe summered in the area and gathered at the lakeshore to roast the abundant mussels they found there, in a spot where they had a view of Mount Kearsarge, which they revered. The ***Penacooks' stone-lined cooking pit*** is still there. Follow signs to Wadleigh State Park and continue on the road around the lake for 0.5 mile. As the pavement ends, you will see a pull-off and a stone wall. Toward the far end of the stone wall is the pit.

Wadleigh State Park, on Route 114 (603-927-4724 or nhstateparks.org) receives few visitors—which is a shame, since its lakefront beach is beautiful and shaded in tall red and white pines interspersed with birch and hemlock. Abundant picnic tables and fire pits are well spaced in a shaded grove, and there are changing facilities and a lifeguard. Admission, as to all day-use parks, is $4 for adults; $2 for children (ages 6-11); children under 6 and New Hampshire residents over 65 are admitted free. From the park or from any point along the lake you can walk around the shore, a 3-mile flat walk mostly along unpaved roads with nice views. The park is open 9 a.m. to 6 p.m., mid-May to mid-June, then daily until Labor Day.

If you turn left from the park entrance and then right onto Wadleigh Hill Road, you will climb a well-surfaced, but unpaved road. At just over 1.5 miles is an excellent cellar hole on the right; then you will pass a mill overhanging a ravine. This is one of eighteen that once lined the roaring little brook that drops (along with the road) into ***Sutton Mills.*** Nearly all these were destroyed in the flood of 1936, but you can see dams and stone foundations along the brook in the village below.

The road past Follansbee Inn leads, after a right turn, into the center of the ***Muster Field Farm Museum.*** This unique collection of historic buildings surrounds the ***Matthew Harvey Homestead,*** an excellent example of rural architecture of the late 1700s. Basically Georgian, it was updated with a few Federal-style touches about 200 years ago. In beautiful condition, most of its hand-shaved clapboards are original, and its windows are glazed in original hand-poured glass. The ballroom on the second floor indicates its use as a center for community activities, such as celebrations following musters of the Thirtieth New Hampshire Regiment, which took place in the adjoining fields.

But the house is only the beginning of the museum. The last owner of the 250-acre property, Robert Stannard Bristol, began collecting historic farm buildings and other structures that were threatened with destruction and placing them in the fields along the ridge on which the house stands. He left the property as a museum and working farm to preserve New Hampshire's agricultural heritage. These buildings, which surround cultivated fields of flowers and vegetables that will make any gardener green with envy, include barns, a schoolhouse, corn cribs, two blacksmith shops, the springhouse from Bradford Springs (see the Monadnock Region chapter), and an icehouse, which in midsummer still has firmly frozen blocks of ice cut from Kezar Lake in January.

You can tour these buildings and see the collections of old farm equipment free any day year-round, or go on Sunday in July, August, and September, when the homestead is open from 1 to 4 p.m. and also free. Demonstrations of early crafts and rural skills accompany these summer Sundays. For even more demonstrations and activities, come for one of the several special events, which include late-August Farm Days, an entire weekend that features an encampment and muster, as well as crafts, an engine show, and a chance to try your own hand at several old-time skills. Admission to these special events is $5 for adults and free for children under 6 years of age. For a full schedule of events, visit the farm or call (603) 927-4276, or visit musterfieldfarm.com. The farm stand sells high-quality fresh vegetables, herbs, flowers, and preserves daily from noon to 6 p.m., mid-June through Oct.

Located just a hair over 10 miles from Ragged Mountain Ski Resort, the *Highland Lake Inn* provides a boutique hotel experience in a tranquil setting. Offering plenty of activities on-site, and a variety of packages and tours, adventure is available around every corner. Check room availability online or call to speak with the inn keeper about specials, discounts, and planning the details of your trip. The inn is located at 32 Maple St., Andover; (603) 735-6426; highlandlakeinn.com.

In the Victorian-era railroad station at the village of Potter Place, the *Andover Historical Society Museum* has interesting collections, including an original Western Union Telegraph office. The building itself is intact, a fine example of the ornamented stations that once lined the tracks throughout New England. One of the highlights of the museum is a dugout canoe that is in very good condition; outside on the tracks are a caboose and a plow car used to clear the tracks during snowstorms. Open Sat 10 a.m. to 3 p.m. and Sun 12:30 to 3 p.m. Memorial to Columbus Day; free. There is no phone, but you can visit the museum's website, andoverhistory.org.

Nearby in Andover is the workshop of young woodworking artist Trip Stiles, who crafts fine, individually made furniture from top-grade hardwoods. His pieces include harvest tables, writing tables, a pencil-post four-poster bed, an early dressing cabinet, blanket chests, and Shaker reproductions. Although he works mostly in cherry, he will make pieces in other woods as requested. All joinery is done with hand-made mortise-and-tenon and dovetail joints, and pieces are finished with four coats of hand-rubbed oil. These are museum pieces of the future, and you can visit the shop to see works in process. *Ragged Mountain Woodworks* is at 7 Pleasant St., Andover; (603) 735-6100; fax (603) 735-6594. Open by chance or appointment.

If you follow Kearsarge Valley Road south from Route 11, turning left onto Kearsarge Mountain Road, you will climb (and climb and climb) until you reach *Winslow State Park* (603-526-6168 or nhstateparks.org). Few picnic areas offer better views—180 degrees of valley, lakes, and mountains. Barlow Trail leads into a 1.7-mile loop, and Winslow Trail is 1.1 miles along the upper slopes of Mount Kearsarge. There is a $4 day-use fee for the park for adults, $2 for children (ages 6–11); children under 11 and New Hampshire residents over 65 are admitted free. Neighboring Elkins borders the shore of Pleasant Lake, where there is a boat put-in. If you stop to enjoy the lake and browse in the antiques shop in the nearby garage in the late afternoon, you may hear the meetinghouse chimes that play at 6 p.m. each day.

New London is the home of *Colby-Sawyer College,* whose stately campus dominates the southern end of the town's main street. Throughout the school year, theater and musical performances keep the local arts scene lively, and then a summer theater takes over the job with Broadway musicals. The town is a good center for hiking and skiing; hikers and walkers can choose from among eight or nine trails leading to or past such varied attractions as a cave, a quarry, cascades, a beaver pond, abandoned farms, and lovely mountain views.

New London Barn Playhouse really is in a barn, converted into a theater that has been performing Broadway musicals since 1934. The barn itself is moving toward its second century, built of a sturdy hand-hewn timber frame and sheathed in the original boards that were sawed at the old water-powered up-and-down sawmill at nearby Hominy Pot. The backstage section was added only in 1962. Before then, actors had to climb ladders for stage-left entrances— pretty awkward in certain costumes. From late June until late August, Broadway actors and interns alike enjoy roles in a repertoire of popular shows, as well as their Monday morning children's shows. The theater is on Main St.; (603) 526-6710 or (800) 633-BARN (2276); nlbarn.com.

The *New London Historical Society* maintains a museum that incorporates an entire village of nineteenth-century buildings, plus more than two dozen horse-drawn vehicles. The village is made up of a farmhouse with attached barn, an herb garden, carriage sheds, a blacksmith shop, a schoolhouse, a country store, a violin shop, a firehouse, a hearse house, and a meetinghouse. From Memorial Day until Columbus Day, the village is open with docent-led tours Sun from 1 to 4 p.m., and on first Saturdays in June and July. Admission is $5 for adults, with children ages 12 and under admitted free. A Holiday Open House in early December features hearthside cooking, crafts, and period music. New London Historical Society, Little Sunapee Rd. (Route 114), New London; (603) 526-6564; newlondonhistorical society.org.

By this time, you've probably caught onto the fact that we like bogs, but this is one you must experience—a real quaking bog, where you could fall in and be swallowed up, as several animals have been, if you wander off the boardwalk. So pay attention as you walk through ***Philbrick-Cricenti Bog,*** or you won't get to see the North Country. The bog was formed over a pond of glacial meltwater. About 10,000 years ago, arctic tundra plants began to grow, and their roots created a mat over the surface. Peat formed in the acid waters, made of accumulated plant debris, and the tundra plants continued to thrive in this acidic environment. Part of the old bog has become solid enough to support forests of spruce and, eventually, red maple within the original shoreline.

You can see all of these environments on a forty-five-minute walk, or just go for the dramatic part, which is on the "quaking loop," where you can feel the unstable mat jiggle under your feet. Believe the trail map when it tells you that those light-green "grassy" patches are only thin layers of moss and sedge. Under them lie cows, deer, and a horse that couldn't read the warnings. To find the bog, bear left onto Newport Road when Main Street forms a Y, following signs to Georges Mills. The trail leaves the left side of the road 0.3 mile from Cricenti's Market. The sign for the bog is not visible from the road, but you will see a small pull-out for parking.

Several restaurants offer dinner in New London, but for a unique dining experience, reserve a table at ***Oak & Grain*** inside ***The Inn at Pleasant Lake.*** Arrive by 6:15 p.m., when all guests gather for a detailed preview of the evening's menu by the good-humored Chef Leary. (Be sure to order dinner wine before this presentation, or it will not arrive until after your first course.) The menu and price are fixed, with a choice of a fish or meat entree each evening. Little details of preparation and presentation make up for the lack of choice and the timing problems created by having to serve each course to everyone at once. Entrees for this candlelit dinner might be rack of lamb, pan-seared mahi-mahi with exotic mushrooms, wood-smoked duck breast with lingonberries, or roasted veal tenderloin in Madeira. Salads get the same careful attention as entrees, with dressings designed to suit the greens; breads are excellent as well.

The wine list is well chosen. The restaurant is closed Mon and Tues. Reservations are required.

Guest rooms upstairs have woodland or lake views to Mount Kearsarge; some have whirlpool baths. The gabled inn is thought to be where the song "When the Moon Comes Over the Mountain" was composed, and it certainly could be, since the moonrise views are near perfect, reflected in Pleasant Lake below. The inn keeps a canoe and rowboat for the use of guests. Or you can admire the lake from the porch over afternoon tea with fresh-baked sweets, served to inn guests daily. For current rates and seasonal specials, call (603) 873-4833 or (800) 626-4907; innatpleasantlake.com.

The restaurant at the **New London Inn** is all about fine dining, with creative combinations and elegant presentations. Everything is inspired by the season and the availability of fresh ingredients, and the chef revels in little surprises, pairing ingredients you wouldn't expect to find together or rethinking old favorites. Silky, seared sea scallops are served with a salad of diced watermelon and celeriac, and grilled fresh tuna replaces the usual canned in a *salade Niçoise*, whose ingredients are not tossed, but served more like an antipasto on a bed of baby greens. Entrees keep up the pace, with choices that have included thick-cut and juicy pork chops with chorizo, tiny potatoes, and steamed mahogany clams; striped bass with roasted fresh corn in a creamy sauce; and skillet-roasted loin of venison with sweet potato puree and parsleyed shallots. We don't usually order desserts, but these were irresistible: rich chocolate terrine, creamy cheesecake, fresh strawberry sorbet, or lemon-lavender ice cream. The restaurant is open for dinner only, Tues through Sat. The New London Inn is at 353 Main St.; (603) 526-2791 or (800) 526-2791; thenewlondoninn.com.

Although New Hampshire's granite bedrock does not form true caves, such as those found in limestone, glacial scouring produced boulder caves and deeply undercut cliffs. One of the best examples of the latter is the **Royal Arch Hill Cave,** overlooking the town of Georges Mills north of New London. The best way to find it is from Georges Mills, from the road that leads from Route 11 in Georges Mills to exit 12A off I-89. Follow this road, under I-89, until it comes to a T. Go right, heading south toward New London, then take your first left, just at the top of a short hill. Just when you see the PRIVATE PROPERTY sign ahead, park and look for the small sign on an old woods road to the left.

The trail is marked to the right, a short way down that woods road. After about half a mile through the woods and a rocky area, the trail begins to climb steeply up Royal Arch Hill, soon arriving at the cave. The trail continues along the ledge in front of the cave and up the ridge behind it, where it angles off to the left and into Giles State Forest, a large tract of wild land that reaches all the way to Route 4A. From above the cave, which is large enough to shelter a small group of people, the view stretches from the town of Georges Mills to Little Sunapee Lake, on the northern boundary of New London.

Although spring-fed *Lake Sunapee* was a very popular resort area in the late 1800s, its shores have never been scoured by bulldozers or scarred by development. The only way to see the fine Victorian cottages nestled among the trees here is from the water. The *MV* **Mount Sunapee II** takes passengers on an hour-and-a-half-long cruise along the 10-mile length of the lake, a tour made even more interesting by the intelligent and good-humored narration about the lake's history and lore. From the boat you can see Sunapee's three lighthouses, said to be the only ones on a New England lake. From mid-May to Columbus Day, the boat sails Sat and Sun at 2 p.m.; in addition, between mid-June and Labor Day, it sails daily at 10 a.m. and 2:30 p.m. from Sunapee Harbor. For reservations call (603) 938-6465 or visit sunapeecruises.com.

For a taste of the days of the grand hotels, dine aboard the *MV* **Kearsarge,** a replica of the early lake steamers that brought guests from the train station to their lodgings. The *Kearsarge*'s Victorian interior sets the stage for a buffet supper served during the summer sailings from Sunapee Harbor. For reservations call (603) 938-6465 or check mvkearsarge.com.

Until the 1930s, the Woodsum family operated a fleet of steam passenger ships on Lake Sunapee. The *Sunapee Historical Museum* displays the pilot-house of one of these, rescued when the 70-foot SS *Kearsarge,* built in 1897, sank in 1935. Memorabilia of that golden age, including the handmade steam engine of a horseless carriage made in Newport in 1869, a milk delivery wagon, an 1824 fire pumper, an intact eighteenth-century dugout canoe, shop signs, and even a wooden water pipe, fill the museum. Plans are underway to restore the Woodsum Brothers machine shop. The museum is open 1 to 4 p.m. Tues through Sun and 7 to 9 p.m. Wed during July and Aug; open weekends only in the spring and fall. It is at the landing in Sunapee Harbor; (603) 763-9872; sunapeehistoricalsociety.org/museum-hours.

Along with its lake, Sunapee is known for its mountain, where Mount Sunapee State Park offers camping and a chairlift that operates in the summer, as well as for skiers at the ski area in the winter. Now among the best ski areas in New England, *Mount Sunapee* has come a long way since it was an indifferently funded, state-owned ski area. Some of the best snow-making and grooming in the northeast have turned this ugly stepsister into a princess. We like the range of challenges here and the fact that those just starting out have an appropriate and separate area where they can gain confidence. Skiers will seldom see such perfectly cared-for trails; even when there is no snow elsewhere, they manage to make and groom it at Mount Sunapee. While it has no on-premises lodging of its own, more than 20 local inns and hotels have packages available. The **Sunapee Express Chairlift** offers rides on weekends during foliage season and when there are special events at the mountain, as well as for skiers in the winter. The views are spectacular, 360 degrees of lakes, hills, and mountains, clad in orange maples and green pines in the fall. The ride is just over a mile long, climbing 1,402 vertical feet to Mount Sunapee's summit. From there you can see Lake Sunapee and views across New Hampshire to Vermont's Green Mountains. The ski area is located on Route 103, Newbury (close to I-89); (603) 763-3500; mountsunapee.com.

New England Handicapped Sports Association at Mount Sunapee offers a unique opportunity for people who may have thought it was impossible for them to enjoy the ski slopes, as well as a chance for active skiers to share their sport with people of all ages and with any number of physical abilities. Mount Sunapee offers lift tickets, and the association provides adaptive equipment and expertise. Volunteers act as instructors, guides, and blockers (e.g., to alert other skiers to the approach of a blind skier) or simply greet newcomers and get them started. NEHSA has its own wheelchair-accessible lodge, and new skiers will enjoy learning on their own private slope. To learn more, to become a volunteer, or to join the program, call NEHSA at (800) 628-4484 or (603) 763-9158; nehsa.org.

Not far from the cultural attractions of Sunapee and Hanover is a state park that is possibly the least known of any in New Hampshire. *Pillsbury State Park,* on Route 31, in the tiny town of Washington, is the perfect place for a getaway camping trip, especially if you are a paddler or hiker. The thirty-nine camping sites here are large and well spaced, with several right on the water, each carved out of the woods and providing maximum privacy.

There are four ponds in the park. Butterfield and May Ponds are the largest, and sites on these are mostly accessible by car. Two other smaller ponds (North Pond and Baker Pond) also have remote sites where campers have to paddle in. Because of their remote location, no fires are allowed in these campsites. On the east end, sites 26, 36, 37, and 40 are walk-in sites.

The real draw of Pillsbury for us is the paddling. We like to have a site on Butterfield Pond, a bit marshy, but great for exploring in our kayaks. In this part you will find a profusion of reeds, sedges, and water lilies to examine and even a few fish lurking beneath them. On the far side, one arm of the pond reaches down to Route 31, where there is a put-in near the dam, which is not on the park lands. At the other end, a narrow passage leads out into the much larger

May Pond. We love being out there at dusk as the autumn sun sets behind the hills across the water. Look for waterfowl in this pond, especially along the east end. Along the shore all that we could see were a few scattered camp lanterns; there is no development at all anywhere around the lake, other than the campground. While we haven't fished here, we are told it's pretty good. Canoe rentals are available at the park.

For hikers there are hiking trails on the east end of the park worth exploring. One of the trails starts at a point near campsite 27, crossing over the small stream below the dam of Mill Pond. Another two trails begin close to the bar gate at sites 34 and 35. The one on the left goes to Balancing Rock along a forest trail. The other option, straight ahead, will lead to the Five Summers Trail to the North Pond campsites (numbers 36 and 37). For long-distance hikes, the Monadnock-Sunapee Greenway, a 51-mile trail between the two New Hampshire mountains, passes through the park.

There is a day-use fee of $5, children (ages 6–11) $2; under 6 and New Hampshire residents over 65 are admitted free. Camping is $21 per site (two adults and dependents under 18) per night, $10 additional per person per night above allotted number. Swimming at Sunapee State Beach is included in the camping pass. Reservations can be made up to seven days in advance by calling (603) 271-3628, Mon through Fri, Jan through early Oct, or by visiting nhstateparks.org. The park's number is (603) 763-5561.

Late in the nineteenth century, New Hampshire promoted the reuse of abandoned farms as summer homes for the wealthy. John Hay, secretary to Abraham Lincoln, acquired *The Fells* in Newbury, at the southern tip of Lake Sunapee, in 1888. After his death, his son, Clarence, and his wife created extensive gardens on the property overlooking the lake. The rock garden covers both sides of a gently falling ravine and includes a stone Japanese lantern presented to Hay for his role in the Treaty of Portsmouth in 1905; a small stream flows through the ravine into a rock-lined lily pond before continuing

Yesterday's News

If the little details of local history fascinate you and bring a place to life, you'll enjoy a small, local magazine called *Soo Nipi*. Each issue is filled with old photos of everything from extinct grand hotels to tiny stations on long-gone rail lines that once brought summer visitors to Lake Sunapee towns. Some articles discuss historic items such as the Cornish colony of artists and writers or the old churches of Claremont. Other articles explore walking trails or places to paddle. Look for the magazine locally or call (603) 763-2441 or (800) 339-6094.

into the forest below. The rose and perennial beds are in more formal terraced gardens, and an easy trail to the lake features placards with nature notes. A 5-mile trail network offers views and wildlife, and the gatehouse has a tiny orientation exhibit. On Route 103A between New London and Newbury, The Fells is open 9 a.m. to 4 p.m. weekends from late May through Labor Day; Wed through Sun mid-June through Labor Day. Call (603) 763-4789 or visit thefells.org to arrange a group tour and confirm seasonal times and prices of admission.

Newbury's *Center Meeting House* was originally built about 1821, but was disassembled and rebuilt on its present site in 1832. It is now located at the intersection of Routes 103 and 103A. A Bulfinch-inspired design, it has a unique interior arrangement; the box pews of the congregation face the entry doors (which would surely discourage late arrivals). The finely executed woodwork of the pulpit is supported by four columns and reached by a double staircase. Sunday services during July and Aug are at 11 a.m. Visit centermeetinghouse .org for information on planning special events.

Railroads were important to the future of small towns when the line to Newbury was built in 1871. To complete it, the engineers had to excavate a massive trench, the *Newbury Cut,* through a solid granite hilltop, using nitroglycerin to blast and strong backs to move the rubble, a process that took a year. Although the trains haven't run since 1961, you can get to the still-impressive cut in a leisurely twenty-minute walk along the old rail bed, now a level, birch-lined path alongside a marsh. Park at the town landing, just across the Route 103 intersection from the Center Meeting House, and look for the wide trail behind the small shopping center.

Few people passing through Bradford, just south of Newbury on Route 103, realize how close they are to one of New England's rare stands of virgin pine. Near the intersection with Main Street is *Tall Pines Scenic Area,* accessible by a 0.25-mile trail from the rest area, where you can park. Fourteen trees over 200 years old are among the state's tallest white pines. Such stands of the virgin timber that once covered the state are few and are usually far from roads or on steep and hard-to-reach mountainsides.

Upper Valley

The town of Hanover and *Dartmouth College* are clustered around a large green, decorated in winter by a giant ice sculpture if the weather cooperates. Overlooking this from a slight hill are the white buildings of the original college. Two of the remaining sides are lined with redbrick college buildings, among them Baker Library. The south side is divided between the *Hanover*

Inn and the *Hopkins Center for the Performing Arts.* In and around that quadrangle lies an amazing wealth of art.

In the basement of *Baker Memorial Library* is a series of frescoes completed in 1934 by the Mexican artist José Clemente Orozco. A free brochure describing the frescoes is available at the central desk. They are powerful and, following their recent cleaning and restoration, true to their original brilliant colors. They were quite controversial in the 1930s, but are now appreciated as a rare art treasure. Even less well known is the *Hickmott Shakespeare Collection,* also housed at Baker Library in the special-collections room, open 8 a.m. to 4:30 p.m. Mon through Fri. The collection includes all four of the folio editions, close to forty quarto editions, all of the pre-1700 editions of *Macbeth,* and many other early editions. In the library's treasure room is Daniel Webster's set of John James Audubon's *Birds of America* in a folio first edition, more than 150 titles of incunabula (works printed before 1501), a 1439 Bible, and a collection of more than 200 volumes illustrating the art of fine bookbinding.

Adjoining the Hopkins Center is the new *Hood Museum of Art,* containing galleries for collections of American, European, African, Indian, and ancient art. The collection of Assyrian reliefs from the ninth century BC is rivaled in New England by only one other series. At the other end of history, the Hood is one of the very few American museums to own the entire suite of Picasso's Vollard etchings. There are Roman mosaics; paintings of the Italian Renaissance and baroque periods; landscapes of the Hudson River school; and representative pieces from every major style and period. Traveling exhibits often incorporate pieces from Dartmouth's own collections.

In 1991, the museum acquired the most comprehensive collection of Melanesian art in the country. Nearly 1,000 objects from Papua New Guinea and Vanuatu, ranging in size from miniatures to monumental works more than 8 feet tall, form a collection both comprehensive and rich in detail. Even with its new building, the museum cannot display everything; so, do inquire if you are interested in a particular subject. Temporary special exhibitions change twice each Dartmouth term. Open all year, Tues through Sat 10 a.m. to 5 p.m. (open to 9 p.m. on Wed) and Sun noon to 5 p.m. Free. You can write for information to the Hood Museum, On the Green, Hanover 03755; call (603) 646-2808 or visit hoodmuseum.dartmouth.edu for links to a schedule.

The Hopkins Center is as broad in its offerings of performing arts as the Hood is in the fine arts. Call (603) 646-3493 or visit hop.dartmouth.edu for a schedule.

The *Hanover Inn* is an institution almost as revered as Dartmouth College itself. Whenever the inn changes so much as a carpet, some old grad notices and comments. That has not stopped the inn from undertaking renovations to keep it up to date, with modern amenities, such as phones with modem ports. As the oldest continuously operated business in New Hampshire, the inn treads a careful balance between maintaining its historical flavor and providing luxurious accommodations and service that anticipates every need. Rooms are elegant, some with real marble baths. The inn is on The Green in Hanover; (800) 443-7024 or (603) 643-4300; hanoverinn.com.

If you are a celebrity watcher, you can get the autograph of those performing or speaking at the Hopkins Center by waiting in the corridor that connects it with the inn. They all stay at the inn and use this private lower-level passageway before and after appearances.

In nearby Lebanon, a former bank building is the venue for ***Alliance for the Visual Arts*** (AVA), where New Hampshire and Vermont artists have their studios and show their work in changing exhibitions. Shown there is a wide variety of styles and media, from very traditional to experimental art. Exhibition gallery hours are Tues through Sat 11 a.m. to 5 p.m. The AVA Gallery and Art Center is at 11 Bank St., Lebanon; (603) 448-3117; avagallery.org.

The ***Lebanon Opera House,*** like so many others, had been locked up and left to decay until the 1960s, when the local music teacher began a campaign to clean it up and attract performers to its stage. A decade later the city took a hand and restored it, so it now features top performances and Broadway musicals. 51 North Park St., Lebanon 03766; (603) 448-0400. You can find its current schedule at lebanonoperahouse.org.

High on the hill overlooking the airport is the largest cider-apple orchard in America. Yup, right here in little Lebanon. Not only the 100 acres of apple trees, but the cider house where they are transformed from wild-looking little apples with forgotten names like Calville and Brown Snout, into world-class ciders that stand proudly beside the finest from Normandy, Britain, and Spain's Basque country. ***Poverty Lane Orchards*** grows varieties that were once grown on farms across the eastern United States on trees planted by Johnny Appleseed. Choosing the right apples for their nuances of flavor, sweetness, and acidity is the secret of their ***Farnum Hill Ciders.*** Forget the cloying, grocery store hard ciders and think instead of a fine dry wine for comparison. You can visit the cider house for a tasting anytime by calling ahead, or in Sept and Oct from 8 a.m. until 6 p.m. on weekdays and 10 a.m. to 5 p.m. Sat and Sun. Farnham Hill Ciders is on Poverty Lane, off Route 4 between Lebanon and West Lebanon; (603) 448-1511; farnumhillciders.com.

Lower Shaker Village in ***Enfield,*** while not as extensive as the one at Canterbury, is of special interest for its stone architecture. "The Chosen Vale" (as the Shakers called their lakeside village) is not preserved in its entirety, but many of the stone buildings still stand. Inside the former dairy building is a museum, well stocked with Shaker artifacts interpreted to help visitors understand Shaker beliefs and their way of life. An informative booklet suggests a handy tour of the village and leads to the Shakers' Feast Ground on the hill above. A ***small shop in the museum*** and another in the adjoining inn feature fine reproductions of Shaker crafts, books on the Shakers and their design philosophy, and even kits to teach the many skills these remarkable people developed. Towering above the vale is the largest Shaker dwelling house built in any of their communities. Four and one half stories tall, it is made of solid granite blocks and the interiors remain much as they were when the Shaker brothers and sisters occupied them. Large windows light the rooms and on the walls are examples of the pegs and cabinetry that made Shakers famous. On the lower floor the dining rooms are notable for the stark simplicity that marks Shaker art. The museum is open from late May to Oct, Mon through Sat 10 a.m. to 5 p.m. and noon to 5 p.m. on Sun. Admission is $12 for adults, $8 for youth (ages 11–17), $3 for children (ages 6–10); children under 6 are admitted free. Call (603) 632-4346 or visit the website at shakermuseum.org to plan the details of your visit.

Northwest from the village of ***Canaan*** is the unusual settlement of ***Canaan Street.*** The main, and only, street is lined on both www.atsides with a mile of distinguished white homes and churches. These date from as early as 1794. Behind the single row of homes on the east is a lake, and in the

Two for Brew

With the slogan "A little out of the way, a lot out of the ordinary," this is the destination brewery for those committed to finding those off-the-beaten-path gems. Celebrated for its innovative spirit, ***Canterbury Aleworks*** features a one barrel, water-powered and wood-fired nano-brewery at its best. Sustainability is central to what's on tap at Canterbury Aleworks, and patrons are encouraged to BYO snacks . . . the ***Fox County Smoke House*** is a stone's throw away and perfect for picking out cheeses, nuts, jerky, and other bits to go with your beer. Visit the brewery at 305 Baptist Hill Rd., Caterbury; (603) 491-4539; canterburyaleworks.com.

In New London's ***Flying Goose Brew Pub,*** the menu is more all-American, with burgers, baby back ribs, and crab cakes to accompany their English-style ales. Golden-colored Split Rock Ale and a hoppy IPA, along with Honey Ale, are among their fifteen brews. Look for the pub, which is open for lunch and dinner, at the Four Corners Grille at the intersection of Routes 114 and 11, just south of town; (603) 526-6899; flyinggoose.com.

other direction is a sweeping view over the valley to the Green Mountains of Vermont. Wide lawns surround the homes, and the broad street is lined with maples and stone walls. The entire scene, so unexpectedly encountered, seems to have been dropped there from the nineteenth century.

One of New Hampshire's first ski lodges, *Cardigan Lodge* is set on the Appalachian Mountain Club's 1,200-acre Cardigan Reservation, on Cardigan Mountain in Alexandria. The AMC property is surrounded by 5,000-acre Mount Cardigan State Forest. Accessible from the lodge are ski trails cut in 1934, still enjoyed by backcountry skiers today. In the summer the lodge is a favorite for hikers, with 360-degree views from the bald summit of nearby Mount Cardigan only half a mile away. Along with casual accommodations, the lodge has a swimming pond, nature trail, and family programs in the summer. The lodge is open year-round, serving meals daily from late June through late Oct and on weekends Jan through Mar and during Feb school vacation week. During the full-service season, linens are provided for the two private lodge rooms and the bunkrooms, but in other seasons guests need to bring a sleeping bag and towels. The rate includes dinner, breakfast, and a trail lunch. Rates are inexpensive, even less expensive for AMC members. For reservations and seasonal rates, contact the AMC Cardigan Lodge, 774 Shem Valley Rd., Bristol; (603) 744-8011 or (603) 466-2727; outdoors.org/lodging-camping/Lodges/cardigan.

Baker River and Newfound Lake

New Hampshire is filled with stone profiles, and although none rivaled the fame of the Old Man of the Mountain in Franconia Notch, each has its degree of local renown. Some require a great deal of imagination or at least a view from the right spot to distinguish. *Profile Falls,* 2.5 miles south of Bristol on Route 3A, demands both imagination and the right view, but even without spotting the profile, the falls themselves are well worth the short walk. Turn off Route 3A to the east (left if you're traveling south) just before the bridge with the small sign for the falls. A short distance down that road is another small sign and a pull-out area on the right, but it is steep and slippery, so we suggest parking along the road just before the sign. Follow the road to the trail or follow the snowmobile trail, which also leads to the base of the falls. The drop is about 40 feet over a broad ledge, and the profile is supposed to be at the foot of the falls in silhouette against the white water. On hot days, local kids can often be found jumping from the high rocks into the pool at the base of the falls. *We don't recommend that you try this.*

The ***Mill Ice Cream Cafe & Fudge Factory,*** in the center of ***Bristol,*** is like stepping into an old-fashioned ice-cream parlor, and the ice cream and fudge are made right there. They also serve organic, fair-trade coffee, hot chocolate, and light meals, as well as vegetarian soups. There is live music on most Saturday nights. The Mill Ice Cream Cafe & Fudge Factory, 2 Central St., Bristol; (603) 744-0405; themillfudgefactory.com.

North of Bristol on Route 3A is a picnic area, maintained by the Rotary Club, in a grove of pines. Shortly past this, a road leads to West Shore Road, which hugs the shore of Newfound Lake and offers lovely views of the lake and mountains. Along the road, on a point of land surrounded by the unusually clear waters of the lake, is one of New Hampshire's finest and, perhaps, least-known beaches. ***Wellington State Park*** has a fine sandy beach under tall pines, so you can choose sun or shade and still be at the water's edge. You can't launch boats from the park, but you can put in canoes or small sailing craft easily. It is a busy, friendly park with plenty of beach and water, so it never seems crowded. It's open June through Columbus Day, 9 a.m. to 6 p.m. daily. Admission is $5 for adults, $2 for children (ages 6–11); children 5 and younger and New Hampshire citizens 65 and older are free. Call (603) 744-2197 or visit nhstateparks.org/visit/state-parks to better plan your visit.

At the northern end of the lake, between the attractive village of ***Hebron*** and Route 3A, is the ***Hebron Marsh Wildlife Sanctuary.*** You can park down the dirt road just before the red cottage while you visit the diverse wildlife habitats of freshwater marsh, open fields, and the banks of the Cockermouth River. Follow signs to the southwest corner of the field to find the short trail leading to the observation tower. From here you can look out over the marsh and see wood ducks, buffleheads, pied-billed grebes, great blue herons, ospreys, beavers, and, perhaps, moose and loons. Songbirds abound, and the trail through the fields gives a closer view of the wildflowers.

Only 1.25 miles down the road is the ***Paradise Point Nature Center*** (look sharp to find its sign on the downhill side of the road next to the driveway). In addition to the trails through an unspoiled lakeshore of coniferous forest, the center includes hands-on exhibits, a library, bird-viewing area, and a fascinating audio-aided exhibit demonstrating the various calls of the loon. A full schedule of naturalist programs is offered, including a sunrise canoe trip. Before walking the trails, be sure to pick up the free visitors guide, with descriptions of the natural history and inhabitants of the area. Try to spot the tupelo tree, rarely found in New England, as you walk alongside the swamp on the Elwell Trail. Its horizontal branches are covered in brilliant red leaves in the fall. Trails are open year-round. There is no admission fee, but the Audubon Society, which operates the center, is always grateful for donations to help them continue their work of acquiring and protecting natural habitats. Write Audubon Society of New Hampshire, North Shore Rd., East Hebron 03232; call (603) 744-3516 in July and Aug; (603) 224-9909 Sept through June; nhaudubon .org/sanctuaries.

Going west from Hebron through **Groton,** a road leads to **Sculptured Rocks.** About a mile from the turnoff, watch for a signpost; however, the sign may not be there during the off-season. You'll see a parking area on the left, and the chasm is on the right side of the road. The river here has carved its way under granite boulders, leaving only the crowns of some and forming giant potholes in others that appear to have been the work of a giant ice-cream scoop. Below the bridge, a trail leads past falls, pools, and huge moss-covered boulders, culminating in a sheer rock cliff on one side. Notice the full-grown trees on the sidewalls with their roots gripping the walls like fingers.

If you'd like to stay in the area, you should reserve a room at **The Inn on Newfound Lake,** which, as the name suggests, overlooks the lake. This vintage inn has been restored to add modern amenities without losing its charm. Speaking of which, everyone remembers the owners, whose personal attention shows in every detail. The dining room is excellent, with creative dishes inspired by a world of cuisines. Dinner may begin with a spicy black bean and tomato soup and move on to veal with prosciutto and aged provolone.

Ski Trails

Along with the well-known Mount Sunapee, the region has several smaller ski slopes favored by locals and others who shun long lift lines. *Ragged Mountain*, in Danbury, has six lifts and thirty-two trails that serve all skill levels. The longest trail is 1.75 miles. Low rates make it attractive to families—not to mention the available lifts on weekends or a full package, including a lesson, rental, and lift. Contact (603) 768-3600 or visit the website at raggedmountainresort.com.

You would expect a sports- and outdoors-oriented college such as Dartmouth to have its own ski slope, and it does. *Dartmouth Skiway* is where many of the school's racers practice for the Olympics and other events, but it's a popular area for local families as well. Expect some very challenging trails on this surprisingly steep mountain in Lyme, north of Hanover; (603) 795-2143; skiway.dartmouth.edu.

Perfect for kids, but challenging enough for the Kimball Union School team's training and meets, *Whaleback* is on Whaleback Mountain Road in Enfield; (603) 448-5500; whaleback.com. *Eastman Cross Country Ski Center,* close to exit 13 off I-89 in Grantham, has eight trails covering about 16 miles. It also has a small alpine center for telemark skiing, served by a chairlift; (603) 863-4500; eastmannh.org/ski.

Filet of salmon tops baby carrots and green beans in a semi-architectural presentation, sauced with avocado. Desserts are dramatic: A lemon mascarpone tart is scrolled in raspberry syrup, and crème brûlée will be highlighted with melon liqueur. Vegetables are given serious attention. The chef is dedicated to using locally grown and produced ingredients, so expect to find cheeses from local farms and fresh-picked seasonal vegetables. On Sunday mornings a buffet brunch includes wonderful waffles and enough other choices to keep you fueled all day. The Inn on Newfound Lake is on Route 3A at 1030 Mayhew Turnpike, Bridgewater; (603) 744-9111 or (800) 745-7990; newfoundlake.com. It's open year-round.

Quincy Road, which goes off the far end of **Rumney**'s village green, will take you to the **Quincy Bog**. Exactly 2 miles from the village green you will see stone pillars on either side of a small road to the left. Down this road 0.1 mile there is another left, which ends shortly at the bog entrance. Nature trails and a viewing deck offer a look at rare bog plants and a wetland ecosystem different from those of shores and marshes. The best months to see the bog plants in bloom are May and June.

On the way to the Quincy Bog you will pass the most unusual town pound in the state. While pounds were usually made of four sturdy stone walls, forming a square with a gate on one side, the townspeople of old Rumney took advantage of a geological feature as interesting as the pound itself. Huge boulders, which appear to have fallen from the cliffs above, lie in a great tumble. Two of them form protected cave-like areas, and two others form straight walls. By adding only one and a half sides and a gate, the town created a fine enclosure for stray animals, one that even offered shelter from rain and wind. Climb through the space in the center of the back, and you'll find a trail through an arch formed by two huge boulders. You can climb farther and wander amid these granite giants. The pound is a fascinating combination of natural and

New Hampshire's Place in Baseball's Hall of Fame

The first baseball glove was designed and made in Plymouth, New Hampshire. Jason Draper and John Maynard founded the Draper & Maynard Company in 1881 as a deerskin glove making factory. A year later, their collaboration with Arthur "Doc" Irwin, the shortstop for the Providence Grays, would result in the design of the first baseball glove. D&M began producing these gloves for the Red Sox, and by the twentieth century, the company had expanded to make baseballs and softballs, as well as the gloves to catch them.

human history. You'll see one wall of the pound directly across the road from the immense boulder that sits almost in the road.

Along the way to Stinson Lake is the **Mary Baker Eddy House** (800-277-8493, ext. 100). The founder of the Christian Science faith lived here in the early 1860s. The house, located at 58 Stinson Lake Rd., is open May through Oct, by appointment, with 48-hours notice suggested. While there is no official admission cost, a suggested donation is $7, which covers admission to both the Rumney and North Groton (see below) houses; however, children under 12 are admitted free; longyear.org.

From here a guide will also take you to another Eddy home in **North Groton**. The road, which turns to gravel, continues to climb through the woods. Watch for a waterfall to the left just as you cross a bridge. Farther on, as you top the ridge, you will have sweeping views into the **White Mountain National Forest**, just a teaser for the views you will have as you continue north.

The area around **Franklin**, just a bit north and west of Concord, lies in the valleys of the Pemigewasset and Winnipesaukee Rivers, beautiful winding valleys where the rivers flow through countryside and past small towns and cities. Route 3 through this region is named the Daniel Webster Highway for its favorite native son. The best and easiest way into the Franklin area is via Route 3. Take exit 17 (Route 4) from I-93 and follow signs for Boscawen and Franklin.

Few New Hampshire residents know of its **State Forest Nursery** on the west side of Route 3 in **Boscawen.** The forestry nursery was established in 1911 after the state had been largely denuded of its forests by decades of over-harvesting. Since then, more than 72 million seedling trees and shrubs have been distributed from these lands, and today it sells about a half-million trees and shrubs annually. Species grown include white and red pine; white, blue, and Norway spruce; balsam, Fraser, and Douglas fir; red oak; black walnut; butternut; and many varieties of shrubs and bushes that provide food for song-birds and other wildlife. There is no visitor center (we wish the state would build one here), but the friendly staff members welcome visitors to look around and are happy to tell anyone about their mission. One of their nursery beds is right along the road, but if that one is empty, follow the dirt road up the hill to see their other acreage. Any resident of the state may purchase trees and shrubs from the nursery, which is open weekdays 8 a.m. to 4 p.m. Hiking trails and the trout pond are open year-round. A catalogue and price list of species is available. Contact State Forest Nursery, 405 Daniel Webster Hwy. (Route 3), Boscawen; (603) 796-2323; nhnursery.com. For information or their catalogue, write Nursery Mailing List, P.O. Box 1856, Concord 03302.

North of the nursery, cross the Pemigewasset River on Route 3 to get to the main part of Franklin, once a thriving factory town, as the many small, brick mills along the rivers bear testimony. Look to see what is playing at the newly restored **Opera House** in the city hall. Even though restoration continues, they offer a schedule of events from musical concerts to theater performances, featuring such names as the Shaw Brothers, Randy Avrus, and Susie Burke. Many performances feature local performers, both adults and youth. The Opera House is at 316 Central Ave. (PO Box 172), Franklin 03235; (603) 934-1901; franklinoperahouse.org.

Starting right in town, opposite the Grevior Furniture store, is the **Winnipesaukee River Trail,** a walking and bike trail that follows closely along the banks of the Winnipesaukee River. The trail follows the route of the sewer line from Meriden to the Franklin waste-treatment facility, but the line is buried and doesn't detract from the walk. About a quarter-mile from the beginning, walkers will see the 180-foot-long **Sulphite Covered Bridge,** built in 1886. It is the only decked covered bridge remaining in the United States. Farther along, the trail runs along the edge of the river gorge as it drops 80 feet over a distance of 4,000 feet. On New Year's Day, an annual whitewater run travels this section of the river. The trail is about 3 miles long and requires a return hike, unless another car has been left at the other end.

Another reason for staying at the inn is its proximity to the **Heritage Trail,** which starts a short distance north on Route 3A. The walking trail goes from **Franklin Falls Dam** and follows along the Pemigewasset Valley. Look for the sign for the parking area on the east side of Route 3A north of Franklin. Continue to the end of the road (don't mistake the factory lot for the public lot). There is a nice view here of the dam and the river valley. The dam was

ALSO WORTH SEEING IN THE DARTMOUTH-SUNAPEE REGION

Polar Caves
Route 25, Plymouth
(603) 536-1888 or (800) 273-1886
polarcaves.com
Open daily mid-May to mid-Oct.
Chambers and passages formed by a tumble of giant boulders dislodged by glaciers. Deep inside, natural ice remains into late summer.

The area abounds in **antiques shops,** some of which are open year-round, all of which are open summer and fall.

built in 1943 to prevent the disastrous periodic flooding that had devastated the valley regularly before its construction. The route of the trail crosses part of the floodplain for the dam, so spring is not a good time to walk here. Along the way, the trail goes through the site of the original town of Hill, destroyed when the dam was built. For more information contact US Army Corps of Engineers at (603) 934-2116. The trail leaves from the northwest corner of the parking lot and requires a return along the same path. In winter it is a snowmobile trail.

For an affordable breakfast or a sandwich at lunch—as well as scoops of locally made Annabelle's ice cream—stop at *Ariana's Cafe.* Sandwiches are delicious and affordable, and there is seating indoors or, in the summer, outdoors. Stop here to pick up a picnic lunch to carry on the Heritage Trail. Ariana's Café is located at 421 N. Main St., Franklin; (603) 934-5577.

West of Franklin, off Route 127, is the little house in which New Hampshire's most famous native son was born. The *Daniel Webster Birthplace* is typical of the first homes built by farmers who settled here when New Hampshire was still a frontier. Webster was born here in 1782, while his father was still serving in George Washington's army. Webster became a lawyer and great orator, was secretary of state under three presidents, congressman from two states, and a leader known for his sense of justice and his ability to find agreement between differing points of view. He was regarded as the greatest statesman of his day. Nearly fifty years after his death, at the turn of the twentieth century, a national poll was taken to determine America's most important historical figures; Webster tied with Lincoln for second place, after George Washington and ahead of all other presidents. His birthplace is brought to life by a Living History Project, with costumed interpreters demonstrating and explaining daily life during Webster's childhood era. You may find them cooking on the open hearth, spinning, tending the herb garden, or playing an early game (which you can join). Admission to the site, which includes the house, museum displays, and a nature trail, is free. Open Sat and Sun, from mid-June to Labor Day, 9 a.m. to 5 p.m. Off Route 127, between Franklin and Salisbury; (603) 934-5057 summer; (603) 485-2034 off-season; nhstateparks .org/visit/Historic-Sites.

Near the turnoff to the Webster Birthplace, about 2 miles from Route 3, is *Tarbin Gardens,* a little paradise of formal and informal gardens, where afternoon tea is served amid flowering shrubs and plants. A formal garden room is enclosed in tall hedges, and a landscape park drops to a scenic pool. Among others are gardens devoted to alpine plants and a bog garden, as well as a sensory garden of plants especially rewarding to sniff and touch. You can wander through on your own or join a guided tour, beginning at 11 a.m. and

2 p.m. daily. The process of turning this forest hillside into expansive English-style gardens is as interesting as the gardens themselves. You are welcome to bring your own picnic to eat in the gardens. Most are accessible to motorized scooters, and all can be seen from wheelchair-accessible paths. Admission is $9 for adults, and the gardens are open Tues through Sun, 10 a.m. to 6 p.m., from May through Sept, and closed on Mon with the exception of Memorial Day and Labor Day. Tarbin Gardens, 321 Salisbury Rd., Franklin; (603) 934-3518; tarbingardens.com.

More Places to Stay in the Dartmouth-Sunapee Region

BRISTOL

Henry Whipple House
75 Summer St.
(Route 104E)
(603) 744-6157
thewhipplehouse.com
Moderate.

CLAREMONT

Common Man Inn
21 Water St.
(603) 542-0647
thecmaninnclaremont.com
A former textile mill, guests will find plenty of historic details and hints of its productive past. Features thirty rooms, including stone-walled suites.

HANOVER

The Trumbull House Bed & Breakfast
40 Etna Rd.
(603) 643-2370 or
(800) 651-5141
trumbullhouse.com
Five guest rooms and a cottage with private deck on 16 acres.

LYME

Loch Lyme Lodge
70 Orford Rd.
(603) 795-2141
lochlymelodge.com
Old-fashioned family summer camp, with cabins on a pond and canoeing. High moderate.

NEW LONDON

New London Inn
353 Main St.
(603) 526-2791
thenewlondoninn.com
Nicely restored rooms overlooking the center of town and the Colby-Sawyer college campus. High moderate.

NEWBURY

The Lake Inn at Mt. Sunapee
1349 Route 103
(603) 823-3186
lakeinnsunapee.com
Featuring a variety of modern amenities, along with available specials like Ski & Stay Packages, The Lake Inn at Mt. Sunapee provides a range of rates, depending on length of stay, as well as a limited number of pet-friendly rooms.

NEWPORT

Newport Motel
467 Sunapee St.
(Routes 11 and 103)
(603) 863-1440
newportnhmotel.com
A tidy, well-managed motel with air-conditioning, pool, and wireless Internet. Inexpensive.

More Places to Eat in the Dartmouth-Sunapee Region

GRANTHAM

Bistro Nouveau
6 Clubhouse Lane
(603) 863-8000
bistronouveau.com
Well-thought-out and well-prepared dining in a club atmosphere. Large selection of wines offered by the glass.

HANOVER

Molly's
43 South Main St.
(603) 643-2570
mollysrestaurant.com
Put plenty of quarters in the parking meter, because service is slow and lunch plates overflow with food. Pizzas are creative and cooked on a wood fire.

LEBANON

Three Tomatoes Trattoria
1 Court St. #100
(603) 448-1711
Possibly the best meal for the money. The wood-fired oven produces pizzas and grilled dishes with panache and they are made using the freshest ingredients. The ambience is very European; the food very good.

NEW LONDON

Tucker's New London
207 Main St.
(603) 526-2488
tuckersnh.com
Consistently ranked among the "Best of NH," Tucker's features five locations across the state, where they offer breakfast 7 to 11 a.m. Mon through Sat (all day on Sun). Lunch runs daily from 11 a.m. to 2 p.m. Locally sourced ingredients; menu is kid-friendly.

PLYMOUTH

The Italian Farmhouse
337 Daniel Webster Hwy.
(603) 536-4536
thecman.com/restaurants
-and-menus/italian
-farmhouse.aspx
It's really a New Hampshire farmhouse, with a kitchen and parlor transformed into dining rooms, but the restaurant in it is decidedly Italian. Interesting pasta dishes are budget priced.

The Main Street Station
105 Main St.
(603) 536-7577
themainstreetstationnh.com
Local residents like its traditional menu and moderate prices for breakfast and lunch.

TO LEARN MORE ABOUT THE DARTMOUTH-SUNAPEE REGION

Hanover Area Chamber of Commerce
55 S. Main St., Hanover 03755
(603) 643-3115
hanoverchamber.org

Lake Sunapee Region Chamber of Commerce
328 Main St. (P.O. Box 532)
New London 03257
(603) 526-6575
lakesunapeeregionchamber.com

Annie's Overflow Restaurant

138 NH-175A
(603) 536-4062
overflowrestaurantplymouth
.com

Annie's overflows with hospitality—the entire staff greets you as you enter this cheerful spot that's open daily for breakfast and lunch. Eggs are cooked exactly as ordered, and the home fries are superior. Check the board for daily specials. It's easy to miss the little building near the bridge as you enter town from I-93.

SUNAPEE

The Anchorage

71 Main St.
Sunapee Harbor
(603) 763-3334
anchoragesunapee.com

An informal place for breakfast or lunch, overlooking the lake. This is the place where the band Aerosmith began—all because the fries were so delicious. Slips available if you arrive by boat.

The Lakes and Foothills

North of the Merrimack Valley and the seacoast region lies an area of rolling farmlands and small mountains. The northern-most of these are the foothills of the White Mountains.

In the center lies Lake Winnipesaukee, an enormous body of water surrounded by several other sizable lakes. The southern shores of Winnipesaukee are covered with popular tourist paths and filled with man-made "attractions" and cheek-by-jowl resorts. While there are some lovely, quiet pockets in this area, it is generally too well known and too heavily trodden to be of interest in this book.

Instead, we shall explore the eastern shore of Lake Winnipesaukee and other lakes east of I-93, as well as the mountains and forests that border them. Ossipee, Wentworth, Squam, Silver, and Province Lakes are joined by innumerable smaller ones, providing reflecting pools for some of the state's prettiest villages. We won't name or take you past all of them, so you should explore the back roads to discover some of them for yourself. Country inns, covered bridges, rock-lined brooks, and old farms lie along back roads here, and at the crossroads are villages that date from the earliest days of the colony.

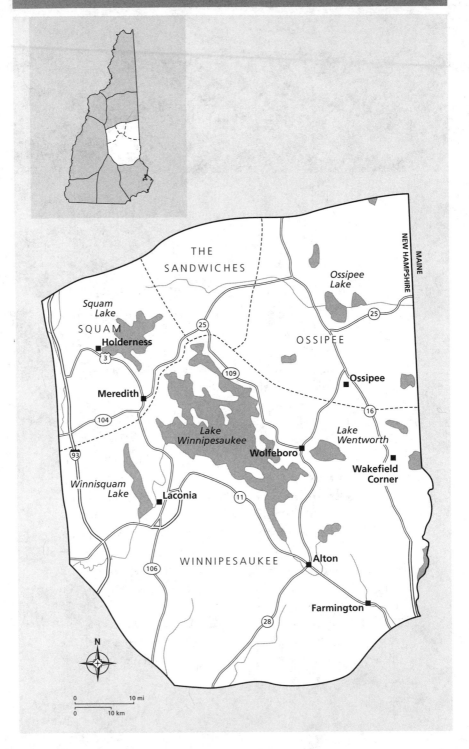

THE
SANDWICHES

Ossipee
Lake

NEW HAMPSHIRE

MAINE

Squam
Lake

SQUAM

Holderness

25

OSSIPEE

3

109

Ossipee

Meredith

104

16

93

Lake
Winnipesaukee

Lake
Wentworth

Wolfeboro

Wakefield
Corner

Winnisquam
Lake

Laconia

11

N

WINNIPESAUKEE

Alton

106

Farmington

28

0   10 mi
0   10 km

Winnipesaukee

For most of the nineteenth century, **Wakefield Corner** was an important stop on the route north, but then it lost its position to Sanbornville's rail junction. Since then, it has stayed so close to its nineteenth-century appearance that the entire village has been named a historic district. Its white wooden houses sit in gracious, fence-encircled yards, and features such as the hay scales and horse trough are still standing. A Rails-to-Trails project is in progress, converting the former rail bed into a hiking and biking path from Wakefield to Wolfeboro.

The **Wakefield Inn** is a three-and-a-half-story Federal-style inn. The rooms are large, airy, and beautifully decorated, all with private baths. Historical features such as original window glass, a three-sided fireplace, and Indian shutters make the inn as interesting as it is hospitable. John Greenleaf Whittier was a guest in 1891. Full-course dinners are served by reservation Thurs, Fri, Sat, and Sun evenings; room rates are moderate. Write the inn at 2723 Wakefield Rd., Sanbornville 03872; (603) 522-8272 or (800) 245-0841; wakefieldinn.com.

At the intersection of the village's main street with Route 16 is **Wakefield Marketplace,** a farmers' and crafts market, which opens each May. For information, check out wakefieldmarketplace.org. En route, you'll see the big tent beside the road. If you're heading south, take this turn into the village and continue on the recently designated scenic byway, along country roads shunpiking busy Route 16 from the farmers' market all the way to Milton.

Route 153 heads toward the Maine border, but just before reaching it at the shores of **Province Lake**, it passes through the settlement of **Woodman**, where **Woodman's Forge & Stove Museum** features antique woodstoves. If you're missing the lid-lifter or some other part for your own Glenwood or other antique stove, you're likely to find an original one for sale here, or you can browse among the latest technology in wood-burning in the large stove shop. Woodman's Forge & Stove Museum, Route 153, East Wakefield; (603) 522-8216; woodmanspartsplus.com.

Despite all the lakes around, finding a public place to swim can be difficult. **Wentworth Park** on Route 109 between Wakefield and Wolfeboro is a small beach with bathhouses and a picnic area along its sandy shorefront. Nearby is the stone foundation and well of the summer estate of Benning Wentworth, first of New Hampshire's royal governors. This 100-by-40-foot structure, with stories 18 feet high and windows 6 feet tall, is thought to have been the first summer vacation "cottage" in America, built in 1768. Unfortunately, the estate burned not long after the Revolution. The focal point of this 96-acre site, open daily during summer, is Wentworth House's 40-by-101-foot cellar hole.

Across the street from the beach, there is a small granite marker at the beginning of *Ellie's Woodland Walk at Ryefield Marsh,* one of several walking trails and conservation areas of the Wolfeboro Conservation Commission. Five markers identify important environmental sites along the path, including a birch grove, meadow, beaver marsh, and the animals and plants that inhabit them. This is an easy, flat walk through a lowland area. The trail is open every day year-round. Close by the granite marker on Route 109 there is a black mailbox where you can pick up a map of the trail and an explanation of the markers.

For a short but beautiful side trip from Route 28 south of *South Wolfeboro*, take Robert's Cove Road west. The road passes between a handsome set of heavily built, new stone walls and provides a nice view of an arm of the lake. Wolfeboro's Main Street is busy in the summer, but there is a leisurely air here, with no traffic jams. Be sure to walk down Railroad Street and take a look at the restored railroad station where summer visitors once detrained. There's a parking lot here and, just beyond, the *Bridge Falls Walking Trail* follows the former rail bed to the falls section of town. Running 200 yards along the shore of Back Bay, this short and level walk leads to an area that was once used by water-powered mills. After crossing Route 109 (Center Street), the trail continues along the track as far as Sanbornville, but the track and ties have not been removed from a lot of the route, and the going on that side can get difficult.

thewentworth wives

It's easy to confuse the three Wentworths, all of them royal governors and all with a habit of marrying each others' widows, which muddies the waters even more. But Benning, the best known of them, married his housekeeper, much to the shocked surprise of his guests, at a dinner party celebrating his sixtieth birthday. He chose this occasion to announce his intentions, introduce his new love to New England society, and celebrate the wedding itself, catching the rector of St. John's Church, one of the dinner guests, quite by surprise as well.

At the falls, the *Wright Museum* brings memories of World War II to life for those who lived through it and puts flesh on the bones of history for those who don't remember it. The war's effect on the home front is shown through vehicles, magazines, and even a soda fountain and a dentist's office, while another section exhibits military hardware, including tanks and half-tracks. They even have a Norden bombsight, one of the most secret devices of the war. A special section highlights the role of women in the military, including their little-known role as bomber ferry pilots. Open May through Oct, Mon to Sat 10 a.m. to 4 p.m. and Sun noon to 4 p.m. Admission is

$10 for adults, $6 for students (ages 5–17); children under 4 are free. The museum is at 77 Center St. (Routes 28 and 109), Wolfeboro; (603) 569-1212; wrightmuseum.org.

Close to the Wright Museum is the ***"Klickety Klack" Model Railroad,*** a labor-of-love exhibit of model-train enthusiast Richard Peasley and friends. There are more than 1,000 feet of HO- and N-gauge track, with twenty-two trains coursing over the track, through the tunnels, and over the bridges. The track passes through realistic villages, over mountains, and through quarry and industrial sites both day and night. You can run eleven of the trains yourself, and signs point out special things in the layout. From Memorial Day to July 1 and from Labor Day through Dec, it's open Thurs, Fri, and Sat 10 a.m. to 5 p.m.; from July 1 to Labor Day, it's open Mon through Sat from 10 a.m. to 5:30 p.m. The museum sometimes also opens by appointment, and Richard says it's okay to call him at home. Admission is charged. From Route 109, take Route 109A (Elm Street) a few hundred feet; it's on the left at 8 Elm St., Wolfeboro; (603) 569-5384 or (603) 569-1275; Visit the website at klicketyklackrailroad.com to discover more details in preparation for your trip.

Farther down Center Street is a spot that preserves the state's long boating heritage, with sleek mahogany Chris-Crafts from the fifties and other classic craft, such as Garwoods, Penn Yans, and others from earlier and later periods. On display at the ***New Hampshire Boat Museum*** are examples of small pleasure boats powered by the wind and gas engines, as well as models of watercraft. Many of the craft on display are on loan from their owners so the craft on exhibit provide a changing view of boating history. In addition to displays of recreational craft, a section devoted to boat racing has photographs and trophies from the heyday of lake racing. During the season they host an old boat regatta, a heritage boat auction, an antique car rally, and other activities. The museum shop is a good source of books on boating. Check the website for vintage boats for sale on the Trading Dock page. The museum also conducts youth, adult, and family boat building classes; women's kayak building classes, and even model sailboat building. Open Memorial Day through Columbus Day, Mon through Sat 10 a.m. to 4 p.m., Sun noon to 4 p.m. Admission is charged, discounts for seniors and kids. The museum is at 397 Center St. (Route 28), Wolfeboro; (602) 569-4554; nhbm.org.

Close to the museum is the entrance to another place for swimming, the ***Allen A. Albee Town Beach,*** on ***Lake Wentworth***. You'll find the entrance road on the east side of Route 28 (109) just after the ***Allen A. Motor Inn.***

Wolfeboro has a lot of opportunities for active recreation. If you like fishing, or think that you want to try it in a serious way, consider ***Gadabout Golder,*** which provides guided fishing trips around ***Lake Winnipesaukee***

and on the Pemigewasset, Little Swift, Bear Camp, and Connecticut Rivers. Their trips follow the season and may concentrate on salmon, pike, bass, trout, or any of the many other native species. They take experienced people and amateurs and offer fly fishing as well. The rates fluctuate with the program, destination, and species. They also do canoe trips, guided snowshoeing, nature walks, guided tracking trips, and ice fishing on the lake. A 1.5-hour dawn lake cruise costs only $90 for up to three people. The company is at 79 Middleton Rd., Wolfeboro. Call (603) 569-6426 for details on rates and specials.

The lakes region also offers lots of bicycling opportunities over terrain that can be hilly or hug the level shorelines. *Nordic Skier Sports* has good, recent-model bikes for rent at reasonable prices. They are at 19 North Main St., Wolfeboro; (603) 569-3151; nordicskiersports.com. In winter they offer 20 kilometers of well-groomed and tracked cross-country trails with lake views. This complete center also has lessons and equipment rentals, starting at $25 a day for mountain bikes.

There are a number of choices for hiking and walking in the area. The *Knight's Pond Conservation Area* features a 1.7-mile main trail, with a 0.3-mile option to the end of a peninsula. Along the way it passes around the sides of a beaver marsh and a 31-acre pond that has not had any development. From the trail are views of Caverly Mountain, Rines Hill, and Mount Longstack. A trail map and directions are available at the information center at the intersection of Main Street and Routes 109 and 28. The center also has a sheet of information on more than a dozen hiking trails in the greater Wolfeboro area suitable for family outings.

The town also has an active musical-arts program that runs from the spring through the fall. Past programs have included choral works, ragtime, jazz, Gilbert and Sullivan, the New England Brass, and much more. There is at least one program a month. For information and reservations, write *Wolfeboro Friends of Music,* PO Box 2056, Wolfeboro 03894; (603) 569-2151; wfriendsofmusic.org.

For a "lobster shack" feeling without traveling to the coast, seek out *Wolfetrap Grill and Raw Bar,* overlooking Back Bay, the lake, and the Belknap Range on the opposite shore. The long copper bar and the lobster tank provide most of the decor, but it's the fresh seafood you go there for. You can arrive on their vintage boat, which will transport you for free from Wolfeboro's town dock. Open June through Labor Day only, Wolfetrap Grill and Raw Bar is at 19 Bay St.; (603) 569-1047; wolfetrapgrillandrawbar.com.

If you follow Main Street north along the shore of the lake, you will come to the *Libby Museum* (Route 109; 603-569-1035). The focus of the museum is natural history, and its exhibits include examples of many of the birds and animals native to the area. There is also a collection of Native American artifacts and items uncovered at excavations at the Wentworth mansion site. In addition to the exhibits, it conducts an Enviro-Arts Summer Program and periodic art exhibits in keeping with the museum's mission. It's open Tues through Sat 10 a.m. to 4 p.m. and Sun noon to 4 p.m. June to mid-Sept. Admission is $5 for adults, free for children under 12; thelibbymuseum.org.

The Wolfeboro Historical Society operates the *Clark House Museum Complex,* which includes a replica of a mid-nineteenth-century firehouse, an 1805 schoolhouse, and an eighteenth-century farmhouse. Open Wed through Fri 10 a.m. to 4 p.m. and Sat 10 a.m. to 2 p.m. in July and Aug. It's on 233 South Main St.,Wolfeboro; (603) 569-4997; wolfeborohistoricalsociety.org.

An interesting two-hour cruise of the islands on the east side of Lake Winnipesaukee stops at Wolfeboro on Tues, Wed, Fri, and Sat at 11:15 a.m. The captain of the *MV Doris E* points out interesting features on shore and enlivens the cruise with local stories and history. Light refreshments are available. For details call (603) 366-5531 or visit cruisenh.com.

The *Abenaki Tower,* a little farther along Route 109 in *Melvin Village*, gives no clue to its origin except the date of its construction. This sturdy wooden structure puts you above the treetops for a 180-degree view over Lake Winnipesaukee and its wooded islands and bays. The Belknap Mountains back it to the south, and the Squam Range to the north. It's a short, easy walk, followed by a stiff climb, but the view is spectacular, especially at sunset. Notice the unusual raised lines on the boulder near the trail.

Overlooking Lake Winnipesaukee on the west side, *Gunstock Recreation Area* offers activities any time of year. In summer, the campground is very popular because campers (as well as day visitors) can hike, ride horses, and enjoy archery, skateboarding, mountain boarding, mountain biking, paddleboats, or tubing. They even have dedicated skateboard and terrain parks.

Gunstock Mountain Resort is at the same time one of the oldest ski areas in the state and one of the newest. Back in the 1930s, it came together as a project of the New Deal WPA at the urging of Belknap County officials. Over the years it has continually modernized, adding higher capacity lifts and improved snowmaking and grooming so that it is now one of the best-run ski areas. Its location, only a short ride from the Tilton exit off I-93, makes it a natural destination for skiers from the Boston and eastern Massachusetts markets and for south-central New Hampshire and southern Maine skiers. Since the beginning, however, there has been a close local connection leading to a strong commitment to ski education, ultimately producing one of the best ski schools.

In winter, you'll find some of the nicest, friendliest skiing anywhere. The mountain has 1,400 feet of vertical rise, not the tallest but still challenging. It is hardly ever crowded, and its variety of slopes and the great old CCC lodge make it a good family area. Night skiing is offered on sixteen trails, and tubing is also open at night. Gunstock also has 50 kilometers of cross-country and snowshoe trails, and they offer a full rental and instruction facility, located separate from the alpine area. From I-93 use exit 20 and follow Route 3 (also Route 11) east, turning right onto the Route 11 Bypass. Follow the signs to Route 11A and Gunstock. For information call (800) GUNSTOCK or visit gunstock.com.

Lyons' Den, overlooking the Glendale marina, offers lake views and a changing menu with continental and New England influences. We like to share the appetizer sampler of grilled shrimp, stuffed mushroom caps, and crab cakes, but the fried calamari is a good option, delicately crisp on the outside, tender and flavorful inside. The chef's signature dish is boneless stuffed duck, slow roasted and juicy tender, but he also treats veal very well. The dessert menu is tempting, especially the tiramisu cake, alternating thin layers of fine white cake with tiramisu, served with whipped cream and rum sauce. Lyons' Den is a little hard to find, but ask for directions to the Glendale Docks to locate 26 Dock Rd., Gilford; (603) 293-8833; lyonsdenrestaurant.com.

Also on the west side of the lake you will find some of the best ice cream in the state. Call ahead to reserve a table for teatime at **The Topiary at Owl's Rest Farm** in **Sanbornton** (603-934-3221). Freshly baked scones include lemon poppy seed, apricot almond, and orange cranberry and are served with Devonshire cream; tea sandwiches are in traditional combinations. Fine china and the floral works of these talented floral artists create the right mood, and tea in season includes a tour of the gardens, where you can wander on your own afterwards. Perennial flowers, herbs, and vegetables decorate the pastoral landscape, changing with the seasons from tulips, daffodils, and other spring bulbs to the asters and colorful foliage that highlight the gardens in Sept and Oct. Every Fri and Sat from Thanksgiving until Christmas you can tour the twelve rooms of the nineteenth-century farmhouse, each decorated for the holidays. Refreshments are served, and the shop is filled with floral and herbal gifts and holiday decorations. From exit 22 on I-93 follow Route 127 south, turning right on Prescott Road; when it ends, go left onto Brook Road, where Owl's Rest Farm is the second driveway on the left; (603) 934-3221.

Ossipee

Unlike New Hampshire's western border, where the Connecticut River makes a clean separation with Vermont, the border with Maine, north of Wakefield, is merely a surveyor's line. Roads and villages that grew up prior to this line sprawl and meander from one side to the other. Route 153 is one of these, not only a lovely road to travel, but also a good alternative for shunpikers seeking to avoid the traffic on Route 16. On its way to Conway, this road weaves through valleys and around the shores of little lakes. Province Lake nudges it over the line into Maine for a few miles until it reenters New Hampshire at South Effingham.

The Effinghams, and there are four of them, were once a very prosperous community based on a group of mills built along the Ossipee River in the 1820s. **Center Effingham** overlooks the road from a hill, with an imposing town hall that doubled as a Masonic lodge. That accounts for the emblem on the clock face. A Grange hall, a Baptist church at the foot of the hill, and several eighteenth- and nineteenth-century farmstead homes complete the historic village. Learn more about this surprising town's architecture at the **Effingham Historical Society,** whose free museum is open Tues and Thurs afternoons, June through Oct. Effingham Historical Society, Route 153; (603) 539-6715.

To the north is **Effingham**, also known as Lord's Hill. This cluster of early-nineteenth-century buildings includes a church, a 1780s hip-roofed house, and several impressive homes of 1820s origin. Just down from the crest of the hill is a road with a historic marker describing the Effingham Union Academy. A short distance up that road, set among manicured lawns and huge shade trees, is **Squire Lord's Mansion.** For its size and the quality of its architecture, this would be an impressive building in Portsmouth or Exeter. Here, come upon suddenly in such a rural setting, it is astonishing. Its three stories rise in clean lines, the eye drawn upward to the tall, octagonal, domed cupola. A Palladian window in the second floor surmounts the wide Federal doorway. No longer open for public tours, the mansion is now a private home. Please respect this and continue down the road a few yards to the **Effingham Union Academy**, on the right, to turn around. This stark building was erected in 1819 as a school, but was reorganized in 1829 as New Hampshire's first "normal school," a teachers college, under the leadership of James W. Bradbury, a first in education.

For an unbeatable fall-foliage tour and a once-a-year chance to visit more than twenty such historic buildings, homes, and gardens that are not open to the public, reserve early for **Tour of the Towns,** usually held the first Saturday in October. A limited number of tickets are sold at slightly discounted rates in advance, with full price expected the day of the tour, provided there are any tickets left. The ticket includes admission to a Friday evening preview party, where a presentation about the sites helps you choose which to see. The tour sites vary from year to year but include the towns of Freedom, Effingham,

Ossipee, Chocorua, Tamworth, and Wolfeboro. Past tours have included the Squire Lord's Mansion, an Italianate Masonic temple with trompe l'oeil murals, and several early homes with antique interiors. For information on obtaining tickets, write to Tour of the Towns, PO Box 2559, Conway 03818.

The town of *Freedom* lies along a small river, its two streets lined by fine homes, many with interesting decorative trim. On Maple Street is the *Freedom Historical Society,* which operates *the Allard House and Works Museum* on Old Portland Road. The Allard house collections include furnished rooms and the attached barn has collections of farming tools, pre-motor vehicles, and equipment. The house's Victorian parlor is particularly illustrative of life in these prosperous mill towns during their heyday, with its ornate fainting couch and stereoscope viewer. Open Memorial Day to Labor Day, Sat 10 a.m. to noon or by appointment. Call John Shipman at (603) 539-5799 or Nadine Chapman at (603) 539-6594 or visit freedomhistoricalsociety.org for additional details and information, regarding your visit.

If you're staying at *Purity Spring Resort* (purityspring.com), you don't have to look for activities to keep your family busy, since each day at this casual family resort brings new activities, from a Monday morning breakfast cooked over a campfire, a Thursday lobster-and-steak cookout on a private island, to a Friday night steamship smorgasbord. The dining room in the old-fashioned, American-plan resort offers a choice of five entrees each evening, always including a meatless alternative. Non-guests are welcome at meals— some families come every week for the lobster cookout, and reservations are highly recommended.

Everything here is included: day care, tennis, canoes, rowboats, and all outdoor activities, except an all-day canoe trip on the nearby Saco River. Grandparents who first came here as children are still returning to this comfortable, homey resort. It is also wheelchair accessible. Write them at 1251 Eaton Rd., Route 153, East Madison 03849; (603) 367-8896 or (800) 373-3754; purityspring.com.

Purity Spring Resort is on *Purity Lake,* and you don't have to be a guest there in order to explore this beautiful spot. It's surprising to discover that, although the lake stretches along a road, there is very little settlement around its shores. The pond is long (about a mile and a half), narrow, and fairly shallow at the edges, making it a great place for flat-water paddling.

Start at the south end at the intersection of Toll Hill Road. There you will see a grassy area with a path to the Audubon sanctuary. You will usually be able to drive up the path about 75 feet to the south end of the pond, next to the dam. Put in and paddle past Purity Spring Resort's beach. This is in a small pond, and at the end you will find a narrow, river-like, stretch of water that leads to the next pond. Watch for the kingfishers that guard this narrows. Along here on the right is an esker, a long ridge of sand and gravel deposited during the last ice age.

At the end of the esker, you will see an opening to the east, leading to a totally natural place with lots of wildlife. Even this close to a resort, there is not a sign of mankind. In places you will see bog plants, where a base of thick peat and sphagnum moss grows over the water and supports a number of plants on its surface. Look for pitcher plants, cotton grass, bog laurels, and other species of grasses and sedges. Along one shore is a big beaver lodge. You will also find a number of different bird species in this deep cove; the Audubon Society has placed duck houses here to encourage black ducks.

Back on the lake, follow along the undeveloped east shore to a secluded cove at the far end. There are some nice marshy areas to explore here, too.

To reach Purity Lake from the south on Route 16, take Route 25 east in **Ossipee**, just south of Ossipee Lake. When you reach Effingham Falls, take Route 153 north to Purity Lake. From Conway, take Route 153 south.

King Pine Ski Area, just up the road, is small, but it has trails for those of all skill levels. Six trails and slopes are lighted for night skiing. Facilities are up to date, but prices are old-fashioned and made even better with joint ski-lodging packages with Purity Spring. A complete ski school and the relaxed atmosphere of King Pine make it a particular favorite of families. It's located on 1251 Eaton Rd., Route 153 in Madison; (603) 367-8896 or (800) 373-3754; kingpine.com.

The **Madison Boulder,** off Route 113 between **Conway** and **Madison,** is the largest known example of a glacial erratic in New England and one of the largest in the world. Enormous freestanding boulders are not uncommon in New Hampshire, but none even approaches the size of this 83-foot, 5,000-ton giant. This is not just another big rock. Such erratics were broken from large outcrops of granite by glaciers, then carried away and dropped in spots sometimes several miles distant. This one is thought to have come from cliffs about 4 miles away, but some geologists believe it came from Mount Willard, 25 miles north in Crawford Notch.

One beautiful way to see the White Mountains is from the saddle of a bike. Whether it is in spring, summer, or foliage season, this is one way to connect to the land. **Bike the Whites** has tours of the region throughout the summer and fall seasons. Beginning on Sunday, these three-day tours include lodging, breakfasts and dinners, maps with points of interest noted, luggage transfers, transportation to the starting point, and emergency assistance if needed en route. Other itineraries can be arranged. For information call (603) 356-9025 or (877) 854-6535; bikethewhites.com.

Overlooking the postcard-perfect **Crystal Lake** in "downtown" **Eaton**, the **Inn at Crystal Lake** looks exactly like what it is—a hostelry that has welcomed travelers to this tiny village since the 1880s. Its three layers of porches, rows of rockers, and columned facade mark it even before you see the sign. Inside this period piece, simply furnished rooms are comfortable and breakfasts delicious. The pub serves hearty dishes, such as shepherd's pie. Unique in New Hampshire is the live opera that accompanies the inn's monthly opera nights, held on the fourth Thursday of the month from September through May. These are so popular that advance reservations are essential to get a table. Discussions, illustrated by recordings and live singing by innkeeper Tim Ostendorf, cover operas that are announced in advance, so you can choose a favorite. The program is included with a four-course dinner and a glass of wine. Ostendorf trained as an opera singer and has sung professionally. The chef creates each dinner menu to fit the featured opera. The dining room and pub are open Tues through Sun, 5 to 8:30 p.m. The inn is on Route 153, 2356 Eaton Rd., Eaton Center; (603) 447-2120; innatcrystallake.com.

Around the corner from the inn, the **Eaton Village Store** faces the lake. Along with being the general store and community gathering spot, it also serves a good lunch. Eaton Village Store, Route 153, Eaton; call (603) 447-2403.

White Lake State Park packs three attractions into one compact park that surrounds a crystal-clear lake. The lake's swimming beach stretches along one end, with the rest of the shore bordered by trees. A walking trail encircles its perimeter; a campground offers well-spaced sites under tall pine trees, and a soft carpet of pine needles pads the forest floor. Across the lake is a stand of pitch pines that have been declared a National Natural Landmark. Close to the northern tip of their range, the pitch pines here are especially large, which indicates age, but they are hard to date because they don't grow even rings for each year's growth. Pitch pine trees have difficulty reproducing except after a forest fire, since their cones need the heat to spring them open and release the seeds. White Lake is in Tamworth; call (603) 323-7350 or visit nhstateparks.org for updated admission prices and additional information.

Another interesting pine-forest environment is located a short distance away along the road between Silver Lake and **West Ossipee.** The **West Branch Pine Barrens,** part of which is owned by The Nature Conservancy, is considered one of the world's finest examples of pine barrens. Its layer of birch and scrub oak grows under a canopy of pitch pine, with blueberry bushes closer to the ground. The barren is home to several rare moth varieties that feed on its trees.

Tamworth doctor Edwin C. Remick joined his father's practice, which had begun in 1894, and continued it until his own death in 1993, missing a round century by less than a year. When he died he left the family farm, dating from the late 1700s, to the town as the *Remick Country Doctor Museum and Farm.* Much of the interest of the museum, which includes two homes, barns, and outbuildings, is its emphasis on how the traditional country doctor grew vegetables and kept livestock just like his neighbors. The interplay between the two themes—medicine and farming—keeps the Remick property lively. Two doctors' offices show the two generations at work, and a fascinating set of photographs and artifacts discusses topics from World War II to how the doctors reached patients' homes in the winter. During special events, the farm is abuzz with activity: butter churning, cheese and sauerkraut making, sleigh rides behind a team of draft horses, barn tours, a chance to use a corn sheller, and blacksmithing demonstrations.

Tamworth is west of Route 16. *The Remick Country Doctor Museum and Farm* (58 Cleveland Hill Rd.) is open Mon through Fri 10 a.m. to 4 p.m. year-round; closed on Sun. July through Oct it is also open on Sat and occasionally on Sun of special-event weekends. Admission is $5 per person, with free admission for children 4 and under. For information call (603) 323-7591 or (800) 686-6117, or visit remickmuseum.org.

Founded on the adage "Enter as Strangers, Leave as Friends," *Rosie's* embodies approachability and affordability when it comes to dining. Using locally-sourced ingredients, visitors to the area should treat themselves to breakfast or lunch, served Mon through Sat from 5 a.m. to 2 p.m., and Sun from 6 a.m. to noon. Between the fresh-baked cinnamon rolls, fruit smoothies, and range of eggs, pancakes, and omelet offerings, you can even take home loaves of Rosie's homemade bread . . . assuming you're not too stuffed. Rosie's

Something Was Missing

On an October morning in 1915, as she was hanging out her daily laundry, a woman glanced up at the mountain that she had looked at every morning since she could remember. But something was different about the familiar view of Mount Chocorua. The white two-story house that stood just below the summit seemed to have disappeared overnight.

Peak House, built in 1884, was an inn for climbers, anchored firmly (or so its owner thought) by chains to the surrounding rock of Chocorua's barren summit. But an October gale ripped the chains loose and literally blew the house away, scattering it board by board all over the craggy slope. Only bits and pieces of either the house or its contents were found. It was never rebuilt, but the Jim Liberty shelter for hikers was later built near the site.

they're smaller now

Virgil White, longtime owner of White's Garage, a familiar landmark in West Ossipee, invented the snowmobile, where more than 20,000 of these were made between 1913 and 1929. They worked on two axles of rear wheels joined by caterpillar traction, fitted onto a Ford chassis with two runners on the front; he patented the name, along with the machine.

Restaurant is located at 1547 White Mountain Hwy., Tamworth; (603) 323-8611; rosiesnh.com.

Climb out of town on Cleveland Road, past the Remick Museum, to find a most unusual monument beside the stone enclosure of the 1801 **town pound.** There, atop a large glacial erratic boulder, is a memorial to Tamworth's first minister, who was ordained on top of the boulder. You'll have to climb the seventeen steps to the top to read about it.

The distinctive silhouette of **Mount Chocorua** is probably the state's most photographed view. Not only is it a perfectly shaped mountain, it rises alone, and at its feet is a lake placed like a looking-glass to reflect it. Behind the lake rises a hill, and as Route 16 drops over the crest, travelers are treated to a view, across an open field, of the mountain and lake. Below, just at the foot of the hill, a left turn takes you to the shore of the lake, where there are parking spaces and benches under a stand of giant red pines.

Chocorua offers more to travelers than its pretty face. Several trails ascend to its rocky peak, one of the most satisfying to reach, since it really is pointed on top. (So many mountains are really quite flat at the summit, even though they appear to form a point.) The easiest climb is via the Piper Trail, which begins on the left side of Route 16, not far north of Chocorua Lake. A tougher climb, but also very scenic, is the Champney Falls Trail, which begins from Route 112, the Kancamagus Highway, not far west of Rocky Gorge. A short distance up (straight up, it often seems) is Champney Falls, at their best in the spring or after a heavy rain.

After your climb, settle in for the night at a B&B that offers a unique blending of a bed-and-breakfast with a seasonal farm stand, and unique venue for special events. Located on 7 acres in **Chocorua**, **The Farmstand** features four guest bedrooms, two shared baths, and a full breakfast created from local ingredients every day. Accommodations range from twin, double, queen, or king rooms, with reservations easily made online or over the phone. The Farmstand is located at 1118 Paige Hill Rd. in Chocorua; (603) 323-6169; thefarmstand.net.

Don't be put off by the fear of looking like the two fat pink pigs on the sign of The **Yankee Smokehouse** at the intersection of Routes 16 and 25 in **West Ossipee**. This is an authentic open-pit barbecue, one of the few in New England. The service is so unremittingly cheerful and eager here that it reminds us of Disney World. Servers describe each specialty and suggest the best deal. "You'll get more of the same thing for less money by ordering the sampler for one and splitting it," our waiter once advised us after mentally totting up our order. Beef or pork ribs or slices, chicken, and delicious baby back pork ribs are their specialties, but you can have the sliced smoked beef or pork in a sandwich or the chicken made into a wonderful smoked salad. Don't miss the corn chowder (it's unlikely that your waiter will allow you to order a meal without it), which is rich with chunks of potato, bacon, and corn, seasoned with herbs and plenty of pepper. You can roll up your sleeves and eat until you can't hold another bite and still have trouble making the bill come out to $12 each. If you have a group of at least eight, order the Smokehouse Feast. It says on the menu that it feeds four to six, but it's enough for a regiment on the march. Open Sun through Thurs, 11:30 a.m. to 9 p.m., and Fri and Sat from 11:30 a.m. to 9:30 p.m.; (603) 539-RIBS (7427); yankeesmokehouse.com.

South of the Yankee Smokehouse on Route 16, a former state fish hatchery has been converted to **Sumner Brook Fish Farm**. Fly-fishing enthusiasts can practice their skills in the pond on a catch-and-release basis, or those who prefer can catch their supper for a per-fish-inch fee. The farm also sells trout or will stock your own pond. Open weekends spring and fall, daily Memorial Day through Labor Day; (603) 539-7232; jessherbs.com.

The Sandwiches

Some of New Hampshire's quirky private museums—collections gathered over the years by people with a particular hobby or interest—have signs by the roadside inviting people in, and some don't. Even when you're in the **Old Country Store** (603-476-5750; nhcountrystore.com), at the crossroads of Routes 25 and 109 in **Moultonborough**, you might not notice the sign by the stairs pointing to the museum. The whole upper floor is filled with local history—saws, axes, and other tools; a wooden snow shovel; blacksmithing tools; maple-sugaring equipment; advertising cards; cigar-store Indians; yarn winders—neatly labeled, often in some detail. Much of what is up there was probably sold downstairs when it was new. The building and the store are believed to date from the late eighteenth century. There is no curator and no charge; you just wander around at your leisure. You might want to show your appreciation by taking home some common crackers or some cheddar cheese from the wheel in the glass case downstairs or stopping for a Moxie or a cream soda from the big old ice chest, but everybody's very pleasant even if you don't buy anything. Outside in the barn, visible through a large window, is an original Concord coach that is thought to be the oldest Concord-built stagecoach in existence.

DDT and other pesticides of the last century, as well as increased pressure from the growing popularity of lakes as recreational assets, almost led to the extinction of the American loon. These beautiful birds with their black heads, red eyes, and gray-and-white-striped breasts are perhaps best known for their plaintive cry in the evening. The **Loon Center** and **Markus Wildlife Sanctuary** have the dual mission of creating a habitat for the protection and propagation of the species and teaching the public about the birds and the impact of human activity on their welfare. Displays and materials in the center teach about the birds. Outside is the sanctuary, covering 200 acres of rare wilderness land on the shores of Lake Winnipesaukee. The **Loon Nest Trail** travels through the forest to the shore of the lake. It then follows along the shore, passing among huge glacial erratics left here in the last ice age, and continuing into a marsh where the loons nest. The **Forest Walk Trail** is another pleasant option for a walk in the woods. A gift shop features loon material, of course, including framed photos, carved decoys, and books and pottery with a loon motif. From Route 25 in Moultonborough, take Blake Road at the Central School, following signs for The Loon Center. At the end of the road, turn right onto Lee's Mill Rd and look for the center on the left. It is an Audubon sanctuary and is free to the public. Open Mon through Sat 9 a.m. to 5 p.m. year-round and the same hours on Sun in July and Aug. Visit the center at loon.org/loon-center.php.

The village of **Center Sandwich** is largely made up of houses built in the first half of the nineteenth century. The houses are clustered into a handful of tree-lined streets, an open invitation to stroll through town. Along with the antiques and craft shops, be sure to stop at the **Sandwich Historical Society Museum.** Its furnishings include a kitchen, household implements, and a wide

Get Your Big Foot Out of My Sandwich

Hollis is not alone as a sighting spot for Sasquatch. In the area around Sandwich—Mount Israel and Sandwich Dome—there have been reports since the early 1940s, and they have even been backed up by 3-foot-long footprints, four-toed and clawless, similar to other Big Foot tracks recorded, after being found in the mud beside the road. Recent reports on file with the state police all describe a fur-covered creature about 8 feet tall. Everyone agrees that however startled and alarmed they were, Big Foot seemed just as frightened and ran into the woods immediately.

variety of artifacts from the town's eighteenth-century beginnings through the early twentieth century. Open late June to late Sept, Wed through Sat, 10 a.m. to 4 p.m. The museum, at 4 Maple St., has events throughout the summer and fall. Call (603) 284-6269 or visit sandwichhistorical.org.

Follow Grove Street and then bear left at road signs for **Sandwich Notch,** which is reached via a gravel road that is not maintained for winter use. The stone walls beside it once outlined the fields of farms now overgrown into forests. A cart track, the road was put through the notch in 1801 as a route for the North Country farmers to get their produce to the markets of Portsmouth and Portland and return with supplies and goods not made on their own farms. Later bypassed by other routes, the road through this notch has not changed very much for the past century and a half.

A parking area on the right marks the short trail to **Beede's Falls.** Where the trail meets the river, an island cuts the river into two small channels. To the right, the water slides over ledges and drops in a series of cascades into a moss-lined pool below. The wooded area at the bottom is surrounded by a tumble of boulders, some of which form caves and crevices. If you go upstream along the island, you will see the brook rushing through a foot-wide shoot. A short distance above that, the river flows down a ledge and then drops 40 feet into a sandy pool. More rocks lie in giant tumbles here, too. Some of these overhang enough to form a cave that, legend has it, sheltered a stray cow for an entire winter. Above the main falls there are two more cascades. Because there are no signs here, it would be easy to miss the main falls to the left and to assume the cascades downstream were Beede's Falls.

Not far up the road, between two bridges over the Bearcamp River, is a cliff shaped like the prow of a ship. Called **Pulpit Rock,** it was used as a pulpit by a long-ago Quaker pastor. The head of the notch, 7 miles from the center of Center Sandwich Village, is marked by a small sign high up on a tree and not easy to see. For a well-written history of the notch, read *The Road Through Sandwich Notch* by Elizabeth Yates.

There are more entrees on the daily specials blackboard at the **Corner House Inn** (603-284-6219) in Center Sandwich than most restaurants have on their printed menus. These dishes allow the chef to take advantage of ingredients with short seasons and the chance to serve his latest original dish. This might be a double lamb chop stuffed with a blend of ricotta, Parmesan, and spinach. The printed menu is not ho-hum either, with offerings like medallions of chicken breast stuffed with ham and artichoke hearts or veal smothered in chunks of lobster with broccoli and béarnaise sauce. A grinding of nutmeg on the cappuccino tops off a fine dinner here. Prices are moderate; lunch (try the crab cakes) and dinner daily and Sunday brunch are served year-round. Visit the restaurant's website at cornerhouseinn.com.

At the edge of the village on the road to **North Sandwich,** the **Quimby Barn** is the home of the town's Concord coach. **Sandwich Creamery,** in North Sandwich, isn't a place you will stumble upon, unless you are a really dedicated back road follower. But it's worth looking for this dairy farm of placid cows that produce the milk and cream for a cave-full of farmstead cheeses: aged or smoked cheddar, Caerphilly, Coulommier, Jersey jack, brie, and several fresh soft cheese spreads. It's the ice cream they're best known for, creamy and rich, made with fresh local peaches, berries, maple syrup, and even pumpkin in season. We like the black raspberry with chocolate chips and the black currant sorbet. The door is always open, so if you crave a pint of ginger ice cream at 7 a.m., you can get it from this honor-system dairy. Picnic tables in the yard invite you to sit right there and eat it from the box as you watch the butterflies play in the flower garden. To get there from Route 113A, turn onto Wing Road, going right onto Hannah Road. As you go down the hill, you will see the creamery on the left. Sandwich Creamery is at 130 Hannah Road, North Sandwich; (603) 284-6675.

Squam

The quiet of **Squam Lake** is almost legendary. Its irregular shape, with bays, inlets, and islands, makes it virtually impossible for powerboats to get up any speed, so there is very little to disturb the loons that nest here. Cottages along the shore are tucked behind the trees, giving it the feel of a wilderness lake.

Squam, along with Winnipesaukee, is one of the best landlocked salmon lakes in the state. Squam is a gem of a lake with nesting loons, and **Science Center Lake Cruises** has ninety-minute boat tours that showcase the high points. Explorer Cruises depart daily late May to mid-June at 1 p.m., and from mid-June to mid-Oct daily at 11 a.m., 1 p.m., and 3 p.m. from the docks on Route 3 in downtown **Holderness.** From July through mid-Oct there is also a Nature of the Lakes Tour led by a naturalist at 4 p.m. on Tues, Wed, and Thurs. A Loon Cruise is added on Fri from mid-June through mid-Sept at 3 p.m., led by a naturalist from the Loon Preservation Society; (603) 968-7194; nhnature.org.

A group of businesses in Holderness has prepared maps of summer and winter recreational routes showing mountain bike and hiking trails, and snowmobile and cross-country trails, respectively. You can get a copy from most businesses in town or from **Squam Lakes Association** (Box 204, Route 3, Holderness 03245; 603-968-7336; squamlakes.org), or **Riverside Cycles** (Route

3, Ashland 03217; 603-968-9676). The association also has boat rentals at its headquarters on Route 3 and manages twelve remote non-serviced campsites on islands in the lake and in a forest preserve. Camping is also available at the **Mead Conservation Center** in **Sandwich Notch.** Check the website for details on the campsites.

The **Manor on Golden Pond** is a romantic lodging choice with its broad lake and mountain views. It started life as the country retreat of Florida real-estate magnate Isaac Van Horn in 1907 but has spent much of its existence as a manor-house inn. The rooms are beautifully decorated in a style that matches the elegance of the home, but with easy comfort in mind. The inn has its own dining room, and six times a year the inn's chef has specially themed cooking lessons. Packages are available. The manor is on Route 3, Holderness; (603) 968-3348 or (800) 545-2141; manorongoldenpond.com.

In 1897, two summer encampments were started on the shores of Squam Lake, one Rockywold, and the other, Deephaven. Over the years, the tent platforms became cabins and the two camps one, now **Rockywold-Deephaven Camps,** but the magic remains. They don't advertise, and families have returned here for generations. Rustic wooden cabins, many with fireplaces, sit spaced among tall pines and granite outcrops on trails over a peninsula jutting into the lake. Meals are family style in one of two large, open wooden dining halls. Ice cut on the pond over the winter and stored in an old-fashioned icehouse is delivered to each cabin daily, along with firewood. Check their website to watch a video of the ice harvest from Squam Lake. Two libraries

Riding Rails in the Lakes Region

Wide-open lake vistas mark the route of the **Winnipesaukee Scenic Railroad.** On its regular one- and two-hour trips between Meredith and Weirs Beach, the train is rarely out of sight of the lake as it travels along the tree-lined shore, making it especially appealing in the autumn foliage. Along with these daily runs, longer trips during foliage season cover sections of rail that are rarely seen. On weekends in October a train makes the four-hour round-trip from Meredith to Livermore Falls in Campton, north of Plymouth. This route climbs over a hill to Ashland, where the old rail station has been restored. It then follows the Pemigewasset Valley northward, crossing the river on a three-span bridge and providing views of waterfalls and rapids, as well as long vistas of the valley framed by red maple hillsides. At Livermore, the river flows through a deep canyon, where an old bridge framed in foliage begs for photos. A buffet lunch is served in the historic Plymouth railway station and is included in the ticket price. Contact the Winnipesaukee Scenic Railroad at (603) 745-2135 or foliage trains.com.

and lodges also serve the campers. This is an authentic, old-fashioned family camping experience, a treasure that we thought had left with the fifties. If you want modern conveniences, creature comforts, and speedboats, don't even think about this place. If you want peace, camaraderie, connection with nature, and space for thought, you'll find it here. Call or write them for rates and family packages; it's all by reservation. The address is Rockywold-Deephaven Camps, PO Box B, Holderness 03245; (603) 968-3313; rdcsquam.com.

One of the nicest views in the lakes region is reached by a gentle climb up **West Rattlesnake Mountain,** just east of Rockywold-Deephaven. All you snake lovers out there will want to know that it overlooks **Rattlesnake Cove** on Squam Lake, but there's no recorded history of rattlesnakes at either of them. A bit over 5 miles east of Holderness on Route 113, look for a parking area on the north (left) side of the road. You have to park here, even though the trailhead is a five-minute walk back along Route 113. The Old Bridle Path leaves from the opposite (south) side of the road, easy to follow as it climbs at a gentle grade. The only fork is well marked to the left. Although this is an easy climb for children, be aware that the view is from the top of steep ledges, not a place for an untethered small fry.

The **Squam Lakes Natural Science Center** on Route 113 in Holderness encourages visitors to explore six different natural communities along its exhibit trail. Signs and staff members explain the ecosystems of the marsh, field, pond, stream, forest, and lake, showing how plants and animals live together in each setting. Signboards explore such questions as, "If the marsh were drained, who would suffer?" The marsh community can be reached by boardwalk, often covered with little bodies lying on their stomachs watching painted turtles, leopard frogs, and trout below. Birds are everywhere, perched on fences or signposts or darting among trees. The setting is attractive and well maintained, a good way to understand the woods, fields, and waters as you travel around the state. Young travelers will enjoy the Children's Activity Center, where they can descend into a groundhog hole, climb a giant spider web, or invent an insect of their own design. The Science Center is open May through Oct 9:30 a.m. to 4:30 p.m.; last admission at 3:30 p.m. For a calendar of the science center's many special events, write PO Box 173, Holderness 03245; call (603) 968-7194 or visit nhnature.org.

Kirkwood Gardens is a one-acre garden at the western side of the historic **Holderness Inn,** a building listed on the National Register of Historic Places but currently in use as **Squam Lake Artisans Gallery,** filled with high-quality local crafts. A bluestone terrace overlooks a garden of ferns, one to attract butterflies and another with a fountain and native shrubs chosen to attract birds. You can also reach the gardens on trails from the Squam Lakes

Natural Science Center. Admission to the garden is free, and it is located on Route 3 in Holderness; (603) 968-7194; nhnature.org.

Anyone interested in art will want to stop in **Meredith** to see **The Old Print Barn,** one of the largest galleries in New England dedicated primarily to prints. Their collection includes more than 2,000 graphics from the United States and Europe, covering the period from the eighteenth century to the present. Media include all techniques: lithograph, metal plate, woodblock, linoleum, and photography.

The gallery started life as a nineteenth-century barn but has been artfully remade into a series of mini-galleries to better showcase the prints. Their New Hampshire pieces include works of the nineteenth-century artists W. H. Bartlett and William Oakes. The Old Print Barn has put together an illustrated paperback book entitled *New Hampshire's First Tourists in the Lakes and Mountains,* which uses reprints of antique materials to tell the story of the birth of the tourism industry in the state. More contemporary works of New Hampshire artists include those of wood engraver Herbert Waters, considered to be one of the top ten in the country. Their European collection includes older works of Manet, Piranessi, Delacroix, Lalanne, Legros, and Daumier, as well as works by newer artists such as Joop Vegter, Pino Finocciaro, and Fulvio Ara and contemporary Egyptian and Chinese prints.

In addition to their prints, the print barn has a collection of nineteenth- and twentieth-century oil paintings that can be seen upon request. These works include some by **Benjamin Champney,** one of the earliest New Hampshire painters of the White Mountains.

ALSO WORTH SEEING IN THE LAKES REGION

MS *Mount Washington,*
(603) 366-5531
cruisenh.com
Cruises depart Weirs Beach two or three times daily, May through Oct, calling at Wolfeboro, Center Harbor, and Alton Bay. Evening cruises offer dinner and dancing to live music.

Hobo Railroad
Winnipesaukee Scenic Railroad
(603) 279-5253
hoborr.com
Carries passengers along the scenic shore between the stations in Meredith and Weirs Beach for two-hour rides, leaving at 10:30 a.m., 12:30 p.m., and 2:30 p.m., with a one-hour tour leaving at 4:30 p.m., May through Oct.

The gallery is also engaged in the sale of estate art and as such often has private collections on view and for sale. As one would expect, these change frequently. The Old Print Barn also provides authentication, evaluation, restoration, and framing services. From Route 104 in Meredith, take Winona Road north at the traffic light (look for White Mountain Orthopedic) about 2 miles, following signs. It is open daily 10 a.m. to 5 p.m. all year, closing only on Thanksgiving and Christmas; (603) 286-8008. You will need to make an appointment for appraisal or other services.

Ashland has a trio of small museums—quite an accomplishment for a town of its size. The ***Whipple House Museum*** is a home built in 1837 and occupied by the same family until the 1970s, at 14 Pleasant St., just off Main Street (Route 3). It is open July through Labor Day, Wed through Sat 1 to 4 p.m. The ***Pauline Glidden Toy Museum*** is an 1810 cape displaying a collection of more than 2,000 antique toys, including dolls, miniatures, games, trains, and books. It is entered from the Whipple House and open during the same hours (and sometimes even more frequently). The third is the ***Ashland Railroad Station Museum,*** an 1869 station, one of the state's best preserved. In it are collections relating to rail history, and it is open July and Aug, Sat 1 to 4 p.m. The Glidden Museum charges a $1 admission, but the other two are free. All are run by the Ashland Historical Society, PO Box 175, Ashland 03217; oldashlandnh.org.

More Places to Stay in the Lakes and Foothills

ALTON BAY

Lakehurst Cottages
4 McKone Lane
(603) 387-0996
lakehurstcottages.com
Available May and June by the night; July, Aug, and Sept by the week only.

Nice, well-kept cottages on the water. Reservations suggested, heavily booked. Call for seasonal rates.

HOLDERNESS

The Inn on Golden Pond
1080 US 3
(603) 968-7269
innongoldenpond.com
Beautiful inn/B&B accommodations overlooking the lake in an 1879 farmhouse. Expensive, lower

off-season; including full breakfast.

Squam Lake Inn
28 Shepard Hill Rd.
(603) 968-4417
squamlakeinn.com
Elegant, Victorian-style country inn. Expensive; includes full breakfast and afternoon tea.

TO LEARN MORE ABOUT THE LAKES AND FOOTHILLS REGION

Greater Ossipee Chamber of Commerce
PO Box 121, West Ossipee 03890
(603) 651-1600
ossipeevalley.org

Squam Lakes Association
Route 3, Holderness 03245
(603) 968-7336
squamlakes.org

Wolfeboro Chamber of Commerce
32 Central Ave., Wolfeboro 03894
(603) 569-2200
wolfeborochamber.com

LACONIA

Lake Opechee Inn
62 Doris Ray Court
(603) 524-0111
opecheeinn.com
The newly renovated mill building overlooks Lake Opechee. Along with a spa, the inn has thirty-four individually decorated guest rooms with fireplaces. Many rooms have balconies with lake views and double whirlpool tubs. Expensive, with both packages and spa packages available.

MOULTONBOROUGH

Olde Orchard Farm
108 Lee Rd.
(603) 476-5004
oldeorchardinn.com
A 1700s Federal home with attractive rooms. Moderate to expensive.

WOLFEBORO

The Inn on Main
200 N. Main St.
(603) 569-1335
innnewhampshire.com
Known as "The Oldest Summer Resort in America"; now features a brand new restaurant onsite, the O Bistro.

Windrifter Resort
337 S. Main St.
(603) 569-1323
windrifterresort.com
No matter the season, the Windrifter Resort offers fun for families. Close proximity to Wolfeboro's other lake options, along with golfing, nearby shopping, and opportunities to lounge pool-side.

Wolfeboro Inn
90 N. Main St.
(603) 569-3016
wolfeboroinn.com
Situated on Lake Winnipesaukee with its own private beach; short walk from shopping and dining in downtown Wolfeboro.

More Places to Eat in the Lakes and Foothills

ASHLAND

The Common Man
60 Main St.
(603) 968-7030
thecman.com
Right in the center of town, with a dependable and varied lunch and dinner menu; moderate prices.

For other dining options, see Plymouth, in The Dartmouth-Sunapee Region chapter.

MOULTONBOROUGH

The Woodshed
128 Lee Rd.
(603) 476-2700
newwoodshed.com
Best known for its prime rib, lamb, and breads; moderate to expensive prices.

WEST OSSIPEE

Purity Spring Resort
1251 NH 153
(603) 367-8896
purityspring.com
This resort features a lovely dining room open to the public.

WOLFEBORO

El Centenario
14 Union St.
(603) 569-3445
elcentenarionh.com
Serves authentic Mexican dishes.

Dockside Grille
11 Dockside St.
(603) 569-3456
wolfeborodockside.com
Seafood platters, burgers, and more. Open all year.

Morrissey's Front Porch
286 South Main St.
(603) 569-3662
morrisseysfrontporch.com
A family restaurant and ice-cream bar, serving three meals daily Apr through Dec.

The Eastern White Mountains

The **White Mountains** are the stuff of native legend and settlers' folktales, of larger-than-life explorers and pioneers. Until the discovery of Crawford Notch, these mountains presented a barrier that kept the lands to the north in isolation.

In the nineteenth century they were "discovered" again, this time by wealthy families from the cities escaping the heat and dust. With maids, nannies, and enormous trunks, entire families boarded trains in New York, New Haven, Boston, Hartford, and other cities bound for Jackson, Glen, Twin Mountain, and Bretton Woods. Hotels sent elegant Concord coaches, resplendent in canary yellow or cherry red with gold-leaf scrollwork, to welcome guests. They stayed all summer, hiking, riding, swimming (called bathing), playing lawn sports, and dancing to a full orchestra every evening. This annual social season lasted until World War II and the invention of air-conditioning. Now most of the grand hotels are gone, but the few that remain have retained the fine traditions that made them famous in their golden age.

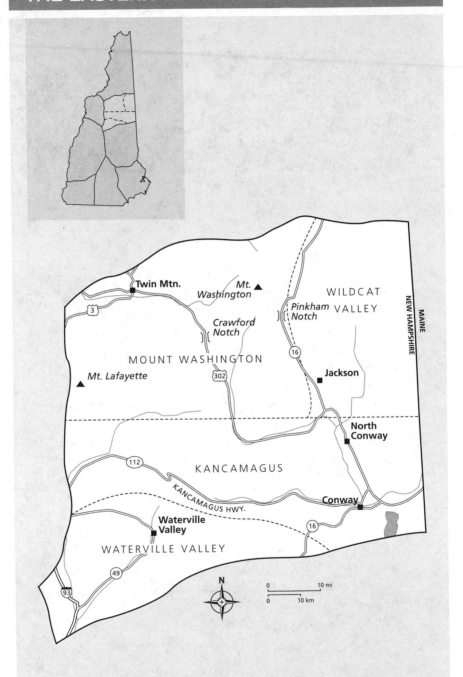

Waterville Valley

Waterville Valley is a cul-de-sac cut deep into the White Mountain National Forest. Route 49 follows the Mad River, which is really quite benign except in the spring, when it carries the runoff from a vast watershed and pours it into the Pemigewasset River. After 12 miles of narrow wooded passage, the valley opens suddenly into a broad floor of fields and a resort village reminiscent of an Alpine ski town.

During the 1960s, the little town of Waterville Valley became known as a purpose-built resort with all-season facilities, and as the occasional playground of the Kennedy family and other well-known celebrities. Since then the resort has continued to grow into a mature and well-designed operation, offering year-round sports, from skiing and skating to mountain biking and hiking.

The *Waterville Valley Resort* ski area covers one of the largest areas in New Hampshire, with more than 255 skiable acres on fifty-two trails. The vertical on this big hill is more than 2,000 feet, making it one of the highest in the state, and one of the trails is almost 3 miles long, perfect for cruising. As with most of the true resorts, lodging is available close to the slopes and a regular free shuttle service takes skiers to and from the slopes all day, as long as the trails are open. Waterville is especially popular for its attention to families. Ski lessons are given in a separate area to free learners from interference. Lift capacity is good and long lines are rare, meaning increased time on the full range of slopes. While many of the skiers here are staying at the resort, it is a very popular area for day skiers as well. In addition to alpine skiing, Waterville also has about 75 kilometers of Nordic skiing trails and a full Nordic center with lessons available. The resort also offers indoor skating and sleigh rides. Waterville is off I-93 at exit 28; follow Route 49 northeast. Contact Waterville Valley Resort, 1 Ski Area Rd., PO Box 540, Waterville 03215; call (800) GO–VALLEY or (603) 468-2553; visitwatervillevalley.com/lodging.

Waterville also includes 22 miles of hiking trails and several mountain summits whose trails begin in the valley. One of the shorter trails for more casual hiking begins at the bottom of the Snow's Mountain ski lift and leads to *The Cascades.* Follow the signs, climbing up the ski slope and then to the left. Be sure that you are following the sign for the Cascades trail and not the Snow's Mountain cross-country ski trail. Once you are in the woods, look for yellow trail blazes. There are very few steep places on this easy trail. Once you get to the cascades, cross the brook and continue up the other side for the best views of the continuous series of waterfalls and pools.

A pleasant, if moderately difficult hike, the *Welch-Dickey Mountain Trail* combines views and natural history with a touch of mystery. To reach the

Walking Lightly

Many casual—or even serious—hikers don't think about the effect their shoes or boots can have on the landscape and flora along the way. Each trail disrupts the landscape to some degree, packing the surface so water flows over, rather than into, the soil. During the spring melt, trails often create miniature streams that wash out steep places, form mud holes, or make the going rough. To avoid these, hikers take detours, trampling plants to create a new trail, which only increases the damage in following years.

Hikers also take shortcuts, bypassing a curve in the trail by making a beeline through the woods. Not only does this practice kill a new set of plants and damage more tree roots, but these straight lines make more direct paths for water runoff, increasing the danger of erosion.

Staying on the trail and avoiding trails altogether in the early spring or after prolonged heavy rains, when the trails are muddy, protects both them and the plants around them that would be damaged by detours when wet.

Staying on the trail and boardwalk while hiking through a bog is even more important, since bog plants are especially vulnerable to crushing. Also, in a floating bog you always run the risk of stepping right through the delicate mat.

When hiking above the timberline, stay on the trail—if there is one—or step from rock to rock, carefully avoiding tiny plants and trees that grow between them. These alpine plants are fragile and often rare, and they have enough trouble surviving the extreme weather and winds without being kicked or stepped on by hiking boots. The little stunted tree beside the trail may have been clinging to that crack between the rocks for one hundred years.

trailhead parking area, take Upper Mad River Road, near the **Thornton** town line, and then follow signs at the third junction to the right. Two trails begin here, joined into a loop that connects the two small mountains; the easier route begins with the right-hand trail toward Welch Mountain. Much of the trail is in the open, across ledges that give good views to the south and east. Before reaching the summit of Welch Mountain, the trail passes several stands of jack pine, exceedingly rare in New Hampshire. On Dickey Mountain, look for a cairn marking a stone circle carved into the bedrock. The origin of the circle is unknown, but if you stand inside it and look back toward the large triangular rock, you are looking at the exact point of the sunrise at the summer solstice. The 4.5-mile climb takes about three and a half hours.

Okay, we admit it: We like the trappings of luxury, and our favorite place to stay in the valley is the **Snowy Owl Inn.** Summer or winter, its three-story-tall fieldstone fireplace identifies it as a ski lodge. In the big downstairs lounge area, a sunken pit provides guests a place to gather by the fire in the evening. In the afternoon, wine and cheese await returning hikers and skiers. Rooms are spacious; especially nice are the upper-level rooms with loft bunks for the kids. En-suite whirlpool baths, an indoor swimming pool, and a kids-stay-free policy make this contemporary inn an old-fashioned value. Rates drop in spring, fall, and summer. Call (800) 766-9969 or visit snowyowlinn.com, for seasonal rates and reservations.

Several lodging options cluster around *Corcoran Pond,* including *Town Square Condominiums.* These are geared to families, with multiple bedrooms and big kitchens. In the same complex are a coffee shop, restaurant, and convenience store, and the condos all have Wi-Fi. Kids love the third-floor bedroom space all to themselves in the three-bedroom condos, with bunk beds and their own TV. Reserve Town Square Condominiums at (888) 462-9887; townsquarecondos.com.

Except in winter, when the road is closed, a nice alternative route out of the valley is over *Thornton Gap,* a small notch reached from a road to the left at the village library. Follow signs to Tripoli (pronounced "triple-eye") Road, following a mountain brook through the forest.

After you crest the gap, you drop down into the Pemigewasset Valley near *Russell Pond Campground.* For those who enjoy camping as a sport, not simply as a way to reduce lodging costs, this national forest campground offers well-separated sites, deep in a hardwood forest that drops into a lovely small pond. No buildings mar its shore; there are a canoe launch, a fisherman or two, and the deep quiet that only lakes that ban motorboats can offer. There are no electric outlets at the campground and no RV hookups. It's hard to believe that

EVENTS IN THE EASTERN WHITE MOUNTAINS

July Fourth Family Day
North Conway
(800) 367-3364
attitash.com/4th-july/

Highland Games
mid-Sept, Loon Mountain Resort, Lincoln
(603) 229-1975 and
(800) 358-7268 (tickets)
nhscot.org

Fall Railfan's Day
mid-Sept, North Conway
(603) 356-5251 or (800) 232-5251
railserve.com/events/

Polar Express
Dec, North Conway
Tickets available for purchase online by
visiting polarexpress.org
(603) 356-9980
conwayscenic.com

such quiet wilderness can be so close to an interstate highway. On Saturday afternoons, rangers present nature programs. Call the Pemigewasset Ranger Station at (603) 536-6100 for open dates.

Leaving or entering Waterville Valley on Route 43, it's a 4-mile side trip north on Route 175 to have breakfast at ***Benton's Sugar Shack.*** From mid-February through mid-April, they are likely to be boiling maple sap into syrup in the back room, but they serve weekend breakfasts year-round. They are best known for stacks of pancakes swimming in their own maple syrup, but they serve a full menu that includes French toast, omelets, even biscuits and gravy. Buy their syrup, maple candy, and jams at the shop. Serving from 8 a.m. until 2 p.m. on weekends and during holiday weeks. Benton's Sugar Shack, 2010 Route 175, Thornton; (603) 726-3867; bentonssugarshack.com.

The Kancamagus

Only one road cuts directly east and west through the center section of the White Mountain National Forest—the Kancamagus Highway. Not really a high-way but a paved two-lane road, it climbs from Lincoln to Conway over the 2,860-foot ***Kancamagus Pass*** via a long switchback. Be sure to stop at the pull-out areas to enjoy the view back across the mountains. No commercial development mars this route; you'll just find the woods, the views, small trail-head parking areas, and a handful of national forest campgrounds.

At its beginning on the west end is ***Loon Mountain,*** well known for its ski area. Less known is the geological site at its summit, reached by a trail from the top of its chairlift (which runs in the summer). A well-built stairway allows you to climb down among a tumble of giant boulders tossed there by a glacier to form caves and passageways that will fascinate kids (and adults). On Sunday mornings there is a nondenominational service in an outdoor chapel at the summit, provided by Loon Mountain Ministries (loonmtnministry.com), and a pancake breakfast is served at the Summit Café.

With the addition of South Peak and Loon's first double–black diamond trail, Rip Saw, in 2008, there are now even more trails to enjoy. Ski it if you dare, but don't say you weren't warned. The resort's Adventure Center, located opposite the main parking areas, has a cross-country center and skating rink, with rentals of skates, skis, and snowshoes.

Loon Mountain and the town of ***Lincoln*** combine to make this a major center for outdoor activities year-round. Near the ski area, rent snowmobiles and join guided tours of the snow-covered mountains with ***SledVentures*** (603-238-2571; sledventures.net), and in Lincoln, ***Art's Outdoor Outfitters*** offers canoe and kayak rentals, complete with pick up and drop off for paddles down the Pemigewasset River. Bicycle rentals are also available (603-745-4806).

At the eastern end of the Kancamagus, watch the south side of the road for the sign for *Sabbaday Falls.* From the picnic area, the path is broad, smooth, and quite well marked to the foot of a flume, where the river flows through a 10-foot gap between straight rock walls more than 40 feet high. At the base there is a water-worn pothole about 4 feet in diameter, and nearby a 2-foot-wide stripe of dark basalt runs through the granite shelf that forms the viewing platform.

The trail along the rim is secured by a log railing, so you can safely look straight down into the flume. Full-grown trees cling to the opposite wall, their roots like giant fingers gripping the rock. You can see here very clearly the dramatic upstream march of the vertical wall of a waterfall. As potholes are formed by whirlpools, their walls are washed or worn away, and the ledges are undercut.

About 3 miles east of the Sabbaday Falls trailhead is the *Russell-Colbath House.* This 1805 farmhouse has been restored to the mid-nineteenth century, providing an interesting look at the isolated lives of the families who settled the Passaconaway Valley. Ruth and Thomas Colbath lived here in the late nineteenth century in the house built by her father. One day in 1891, Thomas told Ruth that he was going out for a spell but didn't return. For the next thirty-nine years Ruth kept a lighted candle in the window every night waiting for his return. She died without ever seeing him again, but he finally did show up three years later. The house is in Passaconaway, on the Kancamagus Highway, and is open daily 9 a.m. to 4:30 p.m. between mid-June and Labor Day and on weekends after Memorial Day and until Columbus Day. Call (603) 447-5448 or visit the website, fs.usda.gov/detail/whitemountain/learning/history-culture, for information.

Behind the house, *Rail 'n River Forest Trail* is a 0.5-mile level loop that offers a unique view of the logging that once took place here and of the regrowth of the forest. Signs and a free leaflet explain different kinds of forest environments, how timber was carried out of the valley by rail, and methods used to fight forest fires. The tale of the timbering that once stripped this entire area of its forests is now told only by ghosts, such as the pilings of a railroad bridge in the bed of the Swift River, visible from this trail. For a closer look at these rough-and-tumble days read *Tall Trees, Tough Men* by Robert E. Pike. The trail is wheelchair accessible.

On Route 16, after it becomes the main street of *Conway,* you'll see the *Eastman Lord House,* a museum run by the local historical society at 100 Main St. It's no ordinary period house but an 1818 home with each of its twelve

Forest Service Parking Fees

Be aware that the White Mountain National Forest charges a use fee. A $20 charge ($5 for a one-week pass) is levied not on the person but on the car, whether you take a five-minute walk to a waterfall or spend the whole summer hiking. You can use the trails all you want, as long as somebody drops you off or you park outside the national forest. It is hard to find a place to get a pass. You can buy a site-specific pass for $3 per day at some national forest parking lots (look for a box on a post near the trailhead), but don't count on it. There is a fine for not having a pass. For locations of sales points visit fs.fed.us/r9/white, ask at information booths, or call (603) 528-8721 for the current list of places to buy passes. Canada has done this with its national parks for years, and it's happening in other states as well. Don't blame New Hampshire, as many people have done quite loudly: It was a decision made in Washington, NOT, we can assure you, something the state volunteered for.

On the plus side, the Forest Service and the White Mountain Interpretive Association provide free nature programs all summer long at the campgrounds throughout the national forest. You may learn about medicinal plants, weather, lumbering, raptors, canoeing, animals, llama trekking, salmon, geology, or any other facet of the White Mountains. Programs begin at 7:30 p.m. on Friday and Saturday evenings at Dolly Copp Campground, Saturday nights in others. For a schedule, stop at any ranger station or call (603) 466-2713.

rooms restored to a different period, from the year of its building to 1945. The last is the kitchen. Instead of showcases of artifacts with placards, each item is displayed in its place of use, so it's like walking from era to era through someone's home. Their enlightened view of history as a continuing story has created a museum well worth seeing. It's open Memorial Day through Labor Day, Wed 2 to 4 p.m., Thurs 6 to 8 p.m., and by appointment other days in the summer and in May, Sept, and Oct; (603) 447-5551; conwayhistory.org.

Route 16 from the northern end of Conway to above **North Conway** is so beaten a path that on summer and fall weekends the traffic may be backed up for hours. But there is a way around it, and it takes you past two delightful corners that people honking their horns on Route 16 never hear about. But first, you have to find West Side Road. Just opposite the intersection where Route 153 heads south to Eaton Center is a street going north. Take it and then the left at the fork (straight ahead is one of Conway's covered bridges, and to the left you will pass another one just a few yards up the road). Follow this road through lovely farmlands that open out to some of the valley's finest views of the Presidential Range. When the road comes to a T, you should go left to bypass North Conway or right to reach the ski area or the northern edge, above the outlets.

Taking full advantage of those views with a beautiful 70-acre setting along the Saco River, *Stables at Farm By the River* is a year-round center for horseback riding, as well as sleigh, wagon, and carriage rides. Pony rides for children and riding lessons for all ages are also available. Stables at Farm By the River, 2555 West Side Rd.; (603) 356-2694 or (603) 356-6640; farmbytheriver .com/stables for reservations.

Less than a mile north of the North Conway intersection, on West Side Road, is the trailhead to *Diana's Baths.* Look for a sign on the west side of the road after two fenced fields. A parking lot is cut into the woods. The falls, only a short distance along a fairly level trail, were once the site of a gristmill. You can still see the foundations and the chute that fed it water. Above, falls and pools are interspersed with cascades over sloping granite. Each of these succeeding shelves is marked by potholes cut into its surface, like a series of children's marble holes on a playground. As you continue to climb, you will find the ledges flatten and the falls shorten. But the swirls and scoops in the granite become even more dramatic.

Another way of getting to North Conway without encountering the outlet traffic is to ride the *Conway Scenic Railroad* from the quieter town of Conway. The tracks cut through the peaceful, historic heart of the valley, passing fields, meadows, woodlands, the Saco River, and an abandoned lumber mill. The Presidential Range fills the north end of the valley, and dramatic ledges line the west. Or, if you begin the trip in North Conway, you can enjoy a good lunch en route in the dining car, a period piece in honey-colored wood and etched glass. Trains run daily from mid-May through foliage season and on

Green B&Bs

Bed & Breakfasts INN Mount Washington Valley is a group of ten B&Bs between North Conway and Shelburne that have joined not only to promote their inns but to promote green initiatives for themselves and their guests. Throughout the year, the inns find ways to make getaway weekends more fun for their guests with programs such as March Maple Madness, Ghost and Goblin Trail in October, and a June weekend celebrating green living. At March Maple Madness, guests receive a booklet mapping out the locations of local sugarhouses and the participating inns. Part of the fun is the "Sap-enger Hunt" and a puzzle to assemble of pieces gathered from each inn. Questions involve the inn or the local attractions. Clues and hints are liberally provided by the innkeepers, as are the items needed for the scavenger hunt. The prizes are well worth competing for, but the other reward is sampling each inn's favorite maple recipe, along with sweets from the maple sugar houses on the trail. To learn of upcoming events, visit bbinnsmwv.com.

weekends as early as April and as late as November, but to ride from Conway and have any time in North Conway, you have to ride between May and October, when there are multiple trains each day. The train also travels north to **Bartlett** and, once a day, beyond and all the way through **Crawford Notch** to the tiny Victorian railway station that once served Crawford House. It's five hours of mountain scenery and a don't-look-down crossing of the Frankenstein Trestle. The trains begin at the depot in downtown North Conway; (603) 356-5251 or (800) 232-5251; conwayscenic.com.

You don't have to ride the train to enjoy the museum at the **North Conway Depot,** a beautifully restored **Victorian railway station** in the center of town at the northern terminus of the trip. Displayed in the old waiting room are brochures, lanterns, uniforms, photos, and other historical items. Be sure to ask for the flyer identifying the buildings, railway cars, and engines in the rail yard. Many of the cabooses are private homes; other cars and engines are in the process of restoration. For information call (603) 356-5251.

Before the return ride to Conway, walk across the wide town green to **Zeb's General Store,** which carries only products made in New England. Look for fine foods from small farms and bakeries, unique handmade items, books, soaps, and an array of other items you won't find elsewhere. Call (800) 676-9294 or visit zebs.com.

Under the towering rock cliffs of **Cathedral Ledge,** in the White Mountain Hotel, **The Ledges** dining room is defined by a large semicircular glass wall, with views over the forest to Mount Cranmore. Inside, a split-level floor affords patrons in the back of the room the same views. But the food beats even the views. Specials may include smoked duck, mako shark, or ribs of Angus beef, but the menu's fifteen entrees give a wide range of choices, such as orange-scented scallops in Grand Marnier and crème fraiche. Dinner is served nightly all year, and lunch is served from late spring until mid-fall. The Ledges is at the **White Mountain Hotel** resort, West Side Rd, North Conway; (603) 356-7100; whitemountainhotel.com.

Dog-owners will be happy to hear that North Conway has a B&B where the dogs are welcomed with the same warm hospitality as their owners. In fact, Whitman and Lilly will be right at the door of **Spruce Moose Lodge and Cottages** to join the innkeepers in the first hello. Cheery sunlit rooms are decorated in a comfortable cottage style in the lodge, and the cottages and bungalows sleep as many as twelve, making them ideal for family groups. Visiting dogs get a discount on anything they (or their traveling companions) buy at **Four Your Paws Only,** North Conway's center for all things canine. Spruce Moose Lodge and Cottages, 207 Seavey St.; (603) 356-6239; Spruce MooseLodge.com.

Very few people know about the ***Pudding Pond Trail*** in North Conway, which we found while looking for something else. It's a nice walk in the woods, good for a family, and not too strenuous, but don't expect to swim there. Pudding Pond is actually a string of small ponds connected by marshlands and a stream. The trail is a joint effort of The Nature Conservancy and the town of Conway.

You will notice signs of beaver activity as soon as you reach the water. Several beaver lodges are visible, as well as the telltale gnawed stumps of small trees that were used as building material. Especially in the morning and evening, keep a sharp lookout for the typical V-shaped wave that beavers make in the water as they swim. You will also notice, especially in the spring, the large variety of wildflowers that abound here, which seem to be guarded by their own air force of voracious mosquitoes—the price you must pay to see spring wildflowers in such moist places.

The trail starts along a wide old road and parallels a power line easement and then forms a T intersection with other trails. At the intersection, take the trail to the right. A wide and easy dirt trail leads uphill before descending a gentle slope. Ignore the first trail that goes off to the right. At the base of the hill look for a sign that shows the Pudding Pond Loop Trail to the left. This is the other end of the loop trail, and we suggest that you follow the path to the right. It leads to a small stream that is the exit of the pond. Take the path left as it changes direction and follows along the marsh. The trail can become rough in this area, with lots of roots protruding to catch your feet, so be careful. Another part of the trail is over planks that span the low spots. To find Pudding Pond, take Artists Falls Road, which leaves the north side of Main Street (Route 16) in North Conway, beside the Eastman Inn. Go right onto Thompson Road and look for the Pudding Pond sign on the right, with parking at the trailhead.

Green Hills Preserve is a 4,222-plus-acre tract of Nature Conservancy land in North Conway, with 1- and 2-mile trails. One leads up 1,734-foot Peaked Mountain, where rare plants grow. Also on the property is a red pine forest, an unusual phenomenon for its altitude. Take Artist Falls Road to the east (left as you head south) off Route 16/302, at the southern end of North Conway. Just short of its end is a public parking space, with a trail board at one side. Pick up maps here before hiking the trails. For information call (603) 356-8833 or visit nature.org.

Just south of North Conway, US 302 diverges east from Route 16 through a dot on the map marked ***Redstone.*** This was once a very active village because of the Redstone Ledge, where richly colored red granite was quarried, and because of a spring known for its restorative properties. During the Victorian era, "taking the cure" became high fashion, and grand hotels were built around

The Case of the Missing Tourist Attraction

In the heyday of the grand hotels—from the Civil War to the end of the century—guests arrived by train and stayed for weeks, so it was up to the hotels to amuse them. Each day they offered excursions, and one of the favorites near Conway was a circuit that stopped first at Echo Lake, then at the gigantic Washington Boulder, and then at White Mountain Mineral Springs in Redstone. The wooden springhouse, as you know, is still there, but not a trace remains of the presumably more durable Washington Boulder. Despite its having been named for the "Father of his Country," it was quarried in 1900, and you can see it now in neat blocks as the foundation to the public library in Conway, at the intersection of Routes 113 and 16.

springs whose water tasted even faintly odd. These mineral springs were fairly common in Vermont and the Hudson Valley, but quite uncommon in New Hampshire, where we've been able to track only three. All that's left of the fashionable **White Mountain Mineral Springs** are some foundation stones and one of the most surprising sights you'll come upon in a walk through the New Hampshire woods.

Only a short distance from the Route 16 intersection, look for a pull-out area in a pine forest, where you'll see a gate barring an old road. You'll also see a sign and a trail map, but you won't need a map. Park and follow the old road on foot through woods and across a power line cut to a large, round field. As you enter the field, look to the woods on your right. You'll see what, at first, appears to be the fanciful cupola of some long-collapsed grand hotel, but if you walk to it, you'll find a pavilion under a spreading curved dome, sort of an offshoot of the Karelian/Victorian architectural style of the North Conway railway station. The spring still fills the pool in its center, and the place stands dilapidated and overgrown; near where the road enters the field, you'll find some foundations of a guesthouse, really a large farmhouse, and a building where the water was bottled.

It's the terrible weather—world-record winds, driving rain, dense fog, sleet, snow—that makes conditions at the top of **Mount Washington** so formidable, and so interesting. And you can learn all about it, without going to the top, at the **Weather Discovery Center** in North Conway. Small, but very well done, it's filled with hands-on exhibits that demonstrate the forces of wind and show how (and why) we study weather patterns. The center is in direct contact, by photo and weather instruments, with the **Mount Washington Observatory,** so you can see the wind, barometric pressure, and other readings as they happen. Exhibits are designed for all ages, with plenty of interactive displays for kids and the scientifically challenged. The Weather Discovery Center is at 2779 North Main St. (Route 16) in North Conway; (603) 356-2137, ext. 211; mountwashington.org.

Mount Washington Valley Children's Museum is a low-tech museum designed for children 8 years and younger, offering a puppet theater, costumes for impromptu plays and make believe, a construction area with a kid-size log skidder, a carpeted wall where children can arrange their own village of movable buildings, and an area designed just for toddlers. The museum is open 10 a.m. to 3 p.m. daily. The cost is $8 per person for a day's multiple admission (good for short toddler attention spans or a lunch break). The museum is located at 2936 White Mountain Hwy, (Route 16), north of the village center; (603) 356-2992; mwvchildrensmuseum.org.

In the same little shopping center is the (literally) world-famous *Stan and Dan's Sports,* where you can get custom-fitted ski boots at prices real people can afford. *Snow Country* called Stan and Dan's the top ski shop in the country and *Ski Magazine* has twice awarded them gold medals for their custom boot fitting. Not surprisingly, the owners are named Stan (Millen) and Dan

For Cookie Lovers

Every winter season, the annual *Inn-to-Inn Cookie Tour* features participating inns that offer lodging packages, including two-night accommodations with breakfast each morning, two tour tickets, recipes exclusive to each inn, a souvenir ornament, and the opportunity to enter a drawing for a $250 gift certificate. At least eighteen inns and B&Bs dress up in their holiday finest and bake up their favorite cookies. Popular participants include the Darby Field Inn in Albany; Inn at Crystal Lake and Pub in Eaton; Inn at Ellis River in Jackson; 1785 Inn, Cranmore Inn Bed and Breakfast, Eastman Inn, Samuel O'Reilly House, Old Red Inn & Cottages, and White Birch Inn in North Conway Village; Snowvillage Inn in Snowville; and Admiral Peary Inn Bed & Breakfast in nearby Fryeburg, Maine.

It's a good idea to get tickets in advance for this popular, tasty event. To do so, call (603) 356-9460 or visit countryinnsinthewhitemountains.com.

Though it's tough to choose a favorite among the dozens of beautiful B&Bs in Mount Washington Valley, the *White Birch Inn* (54 Kearsarge Rd., North Conway; 603-730-5267; whitebirchinnnh.com) is certainly one of our top choices. Built in 1873, this rustic farmhouse provides the romantic setting with thoroughly modern accommodations. Of course, given its location in the heart of the Village of North Conway, there is no shortage of things to do, including skiing, snowmobiling, and sampling those sweet recipes at the annual Inn-to-Inn Cookie Tour.

(Lewis), both of whom acquired their expertise at Carroll Reed's, a gone-but-not-forgotten North Conway landmark. Their shop fits about 1,100 pairs of ski boots in an average season. At two to three hours a pair, that's a lot of hours spent heating boots and snapping buckles. The best time of year to shop is September through Thanksgiving, when they have the largest stock. If you go in ski season, the best time of day is between 10:30 a.m. and 3 p.m., although they are open 8 a.m. to 6 p.m. Stan and Dan's is in North Village Common on Route 16, just north of the village; (603) 356-6997; stananddansports.com.

Bernerhof Inn is surrounded by beautifully kept gardens, and its rooms are just as well maintained. We like the quirky arrangement and shapes of rooms tucked into the turrets and gables of this Victorian mansion. Prices are moderate and include a full breakfast. You can't miss it beside Route 302 in Glen; (603) 383-4200 or (800) 548-8007; bernerhofinn.com.

Wildcat Valley

Tucked into a corner, away from the bustle to the south, is the village of *Jackson,* with its red covered bridge and white church. Artists discovered its scenic beauty in the mid-1800s, and by the turn of the twentieth century, Jackson had twenty-four lodging places, including several grand hotels. By the late 1970s, only *Eagle Mountain House* and a few smaller guesthouses were still operating.

But this story has a happier ending than most. Today, a number of these have reopened, including the Victorian treasure Wentworth Hall. Not all of its original thirty-nine buildings could be saved from years of neglect and abandonment, but the three central ones and several other cottages, with their curved porches, round towers, wide gables, and quirky architectural detail, are once again the showpiece of the village center.

The *Wentworth Resort* is just as nice inside as it is outside, with real feather pillows, giant bathtubs, and an air of grandeur that is comfortable, not intimidating. Rooms in the Arden, Wildwood, and Amster cottages are unique, taking advantage of the architecture of each. In the main building, the Thornycroft suite is our favorite, with its carefully restored antiques, custom-built bed, window seat, sleigh settee, marble fireplace, and even a fireplace in the ample Jacuzzi room.

The dining room is just as memorable; the menu is innovative, and each season brings new dishes as the chef takes advantage of the freshest ingredients. A meal could begin with smoked trout or a monkfish medallion with a coriander crust and shiitake mushrooms. Entrees may include lemon-thyme chicken breast with stone-ground polenta or lamb shanks in a white bean cassoulet. The public is invited to dine here but should call to make reservations. The hotel is open year-round. Expensive. Write the Wentworth Resort Hotel, Box M, Jackson 03846; (603) 383-9700 or (800) 637-0013; thewentworth .com.

A short walk up the road is *Jackson Falls,* a series of cascades with potholes that invite jumping into, if the weather is only halfway nice. The hotel has a pool, of course, but these falls must have been the original inspiration for water slides. There is a circular route of 6 miles (called, for some reason, the Five Mile Drive) that begins at the Wentworth and goes up the Carter Notch Road past the falls. Instead of continuing to the top of the notch (where the road turns into a trail), turn right and cross the river for views across highland meadows to the mountains.

Eagle Mountain House itself was one of the smaller of the grand old White Mountain hotels, with a mere ninety-three guest rooms, and one of very few to survive. Lodging is expensive. The menu is classic New England with nice seafood options, and they have kept some old favorites from the hotel's previous life, including the roast turkey dinner—slow-roasted turkey breast with stuffing, gravy, and cranberry sauce. Moderate. Eagle Mountain House is in Jackson; (603) 383-9111; eaglemt.com.

On the way to *Carter Notch,* tucked under the wing of the Eagle Mountain House, is the bright and appealing *Carter Notch Inn.* Engaging hosts have created a haven filled with character, including a room with a loft that kids love. Rooms range widely in price, higher in summer and fall, including breakfast—but all are nicely furnished and very pleasant. Moderate. Eagle Mountain's golf course, with fine views, is in sight. 163 Carter Notch Rd., Jackson; (603) 383-9630 or (800) 794-9434; carternotchinn.com.

Black Mountain Ski Area (800-475-4669; blackmt.com) is usually forgotten in the razzmatazz of its bigger neighbors, but this end-of-the-road place is a

Golf Clubs

At least a dozen golf clubs in New Hampshire are over a century old, built in the 1890s when golfing was the latest rage. By the 1920s, dozens of golf clubs, most attached to grand hotels, flourished in the White Mountains alone. Several of these have outlived the hotels—the Maplewood in Bethlehem and the Waumbec in Jefferson among them—and others are long gone. But at the *Wentworth Resort Golf Club* you can still play the two oldest holes in the state. Holes Twelve and Thirteen were in use when Grover Cleveland was president. Of the original six holes, two have been altered and two taken out of play entirely.

favorite of anyone who has ever skied there. This is a real gem of a mountain, with over 1,100 feet of vertical drop and more than 98 percent of the trails covered by snowmaking. Black Mountain is popular with families for more than one reason. First is cost, since it has some of the least expensive rates in the state, with correspondingly less expensive rates for kids and seniors. Special packages, including room and lift tickets (some with meals), are available from Whitney's and other local inns and B&Bs. Another reason is its genuine North Country hospitality and friendliness. Kids are safe here, and they are treated like family. Black Mountain has an exceptional ski school for all ages, with an atmosphere that provides just the right setting to make novices into confident skiers. And the mountain itself, served by four lifts, is another reason for Black's popularity. Beginners can ski with confidence, and advanced skiers will find some nice challenges.

Skiing on Black Mountain has been synonymous with Whitney's since "Ma" Whitney bought the old Moody Farm in 1936 and welcomed skiers to the first overhead ski lift in the East on Black Mountain, literally out her back door. The lift was made from Sears Roebuck shovel handles. Generations of skiers later, **Whitney's Inn, Jackson,** still welcomes skiers, Black Mountain has grown into a full-service ski area whose lift rates are one of the best ski values in the White Mountains, and "Ma" Whitney has retired to a house on the edge of the slopes above the inn. There has been a complete renovation of the old inn recently, bringing the inn to the next level. Comfortable rooms, a hearty breakfast, and special facilities and programs for children make Whitney's popular with families. It's a year-round resort as well, with special summer packages that include a Wednesday night lobster cookout. Starting rooms rates are on the low end of moderate. Whitney's address is PO Box 822, 357 Black Mountain Rd. (Route 16B), Jackson 03846; (603) 383-8916 or (800) 677-5737; whitneysinn.com.

Christmas in the Mountains

In early December, the Jackson area is abuzz with its annual *Traditionally Yours* holiday celebrations. Santa arrives and the Christmas tree is lighted the weekend after Thanksgiving, but the following weekend brings the Jingle Bell Chocolate Tour, when horse-drawn sleds stop at inns and restaurants for chocolate goodies. The Women's Sewing Club Silver Tea and Christmas sale is at the Community Parish House. On Sunday, Eagle Mountain House hosts a gingerbread workshop for children, and in the afternoon, Nestlenook Farm hosts a Winter Wonderland, with free ice-skating on their big pond. Contact the Jackson Area Chamber of Commerce at (603) 383-9356 or jacksonnh.com.

In summer, **Black Mountain Stables,** located at the ski area, offers horseback riding. The hour-long guided ride is $45. Trail rides start at 10 a.m., 11:30 a.m., 1 p.m., 2:30 p.m., and 4 p.m. For kids there are pony rides on gentle Tinkerbell at 10:30 a.m. and 3:30 p.m. They also have two five-day riding camps (9 a.m. to 4 p.m.) in July, and Stay and Ride packages are available using local inns and B&Bs. Reservations are suggested. Black Mountain Stables, 373 Black Mountain Rd., Jackson; (603) 383-4490; blackmt.com/summer.

Cross-country skiing is an art form in Jackson. This is the home of the **Jackson Ski Touring Foundation,** which maintains 150 kilometers of exceptionally well-groomed trails throughout the village and all over the surrounding hillsides. In winter, with no leaves to obscure the view, the neighboring mountains, including the southern slopes of Mount Washington, are visible from every hillside. It's so beautiful on a crisp winter day that it's hard to concentrate on skiing. Grooming here is state of the art, and they offer quality rental equipment and lessons. Jackson XC, as they call themselves, hosts an amazing array of programs from the beautiful new lodge, often several per week. These range from wax demos to snowshoe nature tours, "ski with a ranger," group skiing, and ski demo days, when you can try out the new stuff. If you have never tried Nordic (cross-country) skiing, we urge you to start here. Look at the page for beginners on the website, then sign up for lessons. The scenery around Jackson is one of the world's best stress relievers. For the latest conditions and the calendar of events, contact them at 153 Main St., Jackson 03846; (603) 383-9355 or (800) 927-6697; jacksonxc.org.

High above Jackson, with a full view of Mount Washington, **The Inn at Thorn Hill** sets a standard for relaxed, but luxurious, country lodging. The original inn, designed in 1895 by Stanford White, burned in 2002. The new inn follows White's style and perhaps trumps it. The rooms are decorated in Victorian style, with elegant, comfortable furnishings and stunning views from the windows. Each room has a gas fireplace and a two-person Jacuzzi tub. Accommodations are available at the Main Inn, the Carriage House, or cottages, and rates vary. Rates in the Carriage House are lower. The Main Inn is expensive; however, frequent specials are offered.

There are several outstanding restaurants in Jackson, and the dining room at the inn is among them. Guests can dress casually, but the settings and surroundings are undeniably elegant and the service far from casual. The menu adds a Mediterranean accent to New England traditions and is based on fresh local ingredients when possible. Pignoli nuts add sparkle to a crisp-skinned salmon served with braised baby beets, and roasted halibut is served with a roasted red pepper coulis and truffle vinaigrette. And the Thorn Hill wine cellar, with more than 3,000 bottles of the world's finest wines, remains as outstanding as before. Along with direct access to the network of cross-country trails and proximity to four ski areas, the inn offers tobogganing on the property, even at night. Art and photography workshops with artists from Cape Ann are a long-standing tradition at the inn, which is on Thorn Hill Road (PO Box A), Jackson Village; (603) 383-4242 or (800) 289-8990; innatthornhill.com.

If you ever long to slip into an idealized, Currier and Ives world that never was, spend some time at **Nestlenook Farm** in Jackson. No one at Nestlenook pretends that this is what life was really like in the good old days, although the gingerbread trim, patterned shingles, splendid woodwork, stained glass, and furnishings are all quite authentic.

The inn faces a pond that meanders into coves and past islands and under arched wooden bridges. Bonfires at its shore on winter evenings welcome skaters to warm their hands. On special winter weekends, people dress up in Victorian costumes to skate, a visual treat that adds to the fairyland ambience. At the inn's front porch, a team of Belgians and a large Austrian sleigh stop for passengers, then set off past the pavilion and into the snow-covered woods to circle the lake, with sleigh bells jingling along the way.

The inn has a fully equipped kitchen for guests' use. Fresh-baked muffins and cookies are always available. Multicourse breakfasts are sumptuous, and in guest rooms original oil paintings by Benjamin Champney and other White Mountain artists, whose works are usually seen only in museums, are proudly displayed. Call (603)383-7101 or visit nestlenookfarmsleighrides.com for more information.

If all this is too much and you long for a more modern take on easy living, head up the hill to **Nordic Village Resort**'s smart new condos, under the same management. Spacious rooms sport all the modern amenities and are within easy reach of swimming pools and a new state-of-the-art fitness center with views across the valley. Both properties are on Route 16A in Jackson. Call (603) 383-9101 or visit nordicvillage.com to make a reservation.

Near the top of **Pinkham Notch** on Route 16 is a trio of short, rewarding hikes. Look for the parking area for **Glen Ellis Falls** on the west side of the road. This short walk, beginning at the tunnel under the highway, leads to the cliff-lined Ellis River, which plunges over cascades and then through a narrow cleft in the granite, falling 65 feet into a basin before continuing through its boulder-strewn bed.

The **Appalachian Mountain Club Visitor Center**, just up the road, is the starting point for the 0.5-mile walk to **Lost Pond**. Cross Route 16 to the east side. The trail crosses a bridge, and then runs south for 0.5 mile to the pond. While the falls show the wild side of nature, this shallow pond shows a gentler, more tranquil wilderness. At the southern end is a beaver dam and a jumble of boulders dropped here from the slopes above. In dry weather the path continues on to *Glen Ellis Falls.* You can get your national forest permit here, but note that if you park here for Glen Ellis Falls, you don't need a pass. If you park in the area at the falls, you do.

Crystal Cascade is an easy fifteen-minute walk up the trail behind the visitor center, following the Cutler River upstream. Although called a cascade, this is really a waterfall, the water dropping almost vertically 60 feet into a deep chasm and then falling another 20 feet. We have always felt that the best place to view a waterfall is facing its midpoint, a vantage usually reserved for winged creatures. But the unique bend in the river provides an overlook at exactly the right point for viewing this one.

A wide variety of programs and classes are held by the *Appalachian Mountain Club* (AMC) at their Pinkham Notch Visitor Center. These go on year-round and include nature, mountaineering, hiking, botany, photography, igloo and snow-shelter building, animal tracking, and other subjects of interest to those who revel in nature and the outdoors. Some are day or half-day programs, others are weekend classes that include lodging and require advance reservations. Free evening programs with illustrated travelogues are often combined with inexpensive dinners, featuring dishes from the destination. The AMC operates a hikers' hostel inn here, with comfortable rooms and nightly dinners that are among the best values in the White Mountains. Served family-style at long tables and priced under $20, the multicourse dinners may feature hearty entrees, such as pork loin roasted with rosemary and garlic. There is always a vegetarian option, which might include risotto primavera or couscous with sautéed cannellini beans and a vegetable medley. It's a good idea to have reservations on weekends. For a complete schedule, contact them at PO Box 298, Gorham 03581; (603) 466-2727; outdoors.org/lodging/pnvc.

The 4,000-foot summit of *Wildcat Mountain* brings visitors face to face with Mount Washington's eastern slopes, carved and shaped by the deep glacial scours of *Tuckerman's Ravine* and *Huntington's Ravine.* The upper slopes of the mountain are so close across the narrow valley that without even using the telescopes at the summit, you can follow the progress of climbers making their way up the trails. Ascend to this view via New Hampshire's highest gondola ride, the four-passenger *Wildcat Express,* in a vertiginous twelve minutes; on a really clear day, from the top you can also see to the Atlantic Ocean and into Canada. Wildcat Express Gondola serves skiers in the winter, but it operates daily through the summer and until mid-Oct, 10 a.m. to 5 p.m.; (603) 466-3326; skiwildcat.com.

A bit farther up Route 16, at the head of Pinkham Notch, you'll find the entrance to the *Mount Washington Auto Road,* opposite the site of the long-gone Glen House, one of the grand hotels. Its carriage houses remain, and in them you can see some of the vehicles that have carried passengers up the scenic road since its initial construction: the first coach, two wagons, a Pierce Arrow, and a wood-paneled Beach Wagon. In the wagon days, they had to replace all the brakes entirely after each trip down the mountain. You can drive along the road in your own car or ride up in one of the fleet of new vans with a guide who'll point out everything from historic sites to the unusual geologic formations beside the road. Check auto and passenger fees by calling (206) 466-3988 or visiting mountwashingtonautoroad.com. Mount Washington Auto Road can be accessed on Route 16, Pinkham Notch, Gorham.

For a shorter climb on Mount Washington, rather than tackling the entire mountain, you can take the auto road to reach the ***Alpine Garden.*** Begin at the Huntington Ravine Trail crossing, where there is ample parking space. Follow that trail down (trying not to think about the reverse of the old axiom: "What goes down must go up") until it meets the Alpine Garden Trail in less than half a mile. The trail through the gardens is fairly flat and continues for more than a mile to the spectacular view down into Tuckerman's Ravine. Along the way are other fine views of the mountains to the east. Because the plants here are unique to the alpine environment, you should bring a guide to alpine wildflowers, available at the Pinkham Notch Visitor Center. The plants are interesting all summer, but bloom the best in June. Please be careful to stay on the trail; these plants are not only rare but fragile, despite their ability to survive their harsh environment.

Road Records

In 1853, a man descended the auto road on a tricycle in fifty-five minutes.

In 1887, a record ascent by a horse-drawn vehicle clocked in at one hour and nine minutes.

In 1899, Mr. and Mrs. Freeland Stanley made the first engine-powered vehicle ascent on the auto road in a Stanley Locomobile, taking two hours and ten minutes.

In 1907, two men made the first road ascent on skis, as far as Halfway House, and skied back to the base in twenty minutes. Members of the Dartmouth Outing Club made the first round-trip to the summit on skis in 1913.

In 1926, Arthur Walden (musher for several Arctic expeditions) and several friends drove the first team to the summit and back, which took fifteen hours. In 1932, Florence Clark was the first woman to make the trip with a dog team.

The Mount Washington Auto Road and ***Great Glen Trails*** share the same headquarters building. Great Glen has more than 40 kilometers of trails on Mount Washington that are available free to hikers. Mountain bikers are also welcomed but must pay a fee. Great Glen also has nature walks, archery, a concert series, barbecues, kite flying, and a climbing wall that's available all year. They also have full- and half-day paddling excursions on the Androscoggin River and rafting trips. In winter, the trails become cross-country trails, covered in natural snow. Several trails have snowmaking, so there is almost always skiing available. The lodge has skis for rent, as well as skates and kick sleds, popular in Finland, but relatively unknown here.

Great Glen also offers a snowcoach service, operating between December and March, which takes passengers 4.5 miles up the auto road to a point above the tree line where they can get out and experience the mountain in winter. Cross-country and telemark skiers and snowshoers then have the option of going back on foot. It's first-come, first-served and no reservations. Open daily 8:30 a.m. to 4:30 p.m. Located on Route 16, Pinkham Notch, Gorham. Call (603) 466-2333 or consult the website at greatglentrails.com to verify seasonal rates and hours.

Mount Washington

At just over a mile high, Mount Washington is the highest mountain in the Northeast, but its weather conditions are among the most severe in the world. Arctic equipment is tested at its summit. Only slightly below it stand other mountains named for presidents—thus the name ***Presidential Range.***

Crawford Notch, a break in the almost solid chain of the White Mountains, lies due south of Mount Washington. Geologically, the notch is a classic glacial scour. During the last ice age, boulders frozen into the ice caught onto chunks of loose bedrock as the glacier moved down mountain slopes. In valleys, where the action of the glacier became more concentrated, the scouring was at its greatest, carrying off boulders and pieces of broken cliffs, which in turn scraped even deeper as they moved, giving a characteristic U-shaped curve to the valley walls.

In the early days of settlement, vast forests of very tall trees covered all but the tops of the mountains, so the settlers couldn't tell where the notches and the passes were. About all they could do was to follow the riverbeds, hoping to find the easiest and lowest route.

Usually, these routes were discovered more or less by accident. So it was with Timothy Nash the day he climbed a tree on Cherry Mountain while moose hunting and saw the gap in the line of mountains. He went to Portsmouth to ask the royal governor (the same Benning Wentworth we met earlier) for a piece of land and a road through the notch. The governor told him to bring a horse through the notch, which Timothy and a friend did by lowering it over the cliff on a rope. Nash got his land, and eventually the road was built, opening a much shorter route to the North Country.

The trees that filled the notch, like those of the Passaconaway Valley, fell to the lumber market. Entire towns sprang up around the lumber camps, and some of them died with the industry. *Livermore,* a ghost town today, lies along Sawyer River Road, which meets Route 302 just north of the bridge over the Sawyer River about 5 miles north of Bartlett. A 1.5-mile walk up Sawyer River Road, you'll see a barred gate and some foundations, which are all that is left of Livermore. It was once a thriving community of 200, built in the late 1800s, and reached by both road and railroad. Of its homes, stores, boardinghouses, offices, and two sawmills, you'll find only ruins. Walk to the river and into the woods upstream to find cellar holes and the ruins of a beautifully constructed concrete-and-brick sawmill. All of these have full-size trees growing out of them now. It's easier to find the cellar holes in the fall, when the leaves are missing. Look for the one with the company safe clearly visible.

Just north of the Sawyer River Road is the *Notchland Inn,* a granite mansion that has been a Crawford Notch landmark since its construction in 1862. The front parlor of this Victorian home was designed by Gustav Stickley; an adjoining country schoolhouse has been transformed into two suites. Guests can join a guided walk to a dramatic gorge and swimming hole located on the property. Non-guests are welcome to dine here but must reserve for the fixed-price dinner. The Notchland Inn is on Route 302, Harts Location; (603) 374-6131 or (800) 866-6131; notchland.com.

bitofablow, itwas

On April 12, 1934, the highest velocity wind gust ever recorded rocked the observatory on top of Mount Washington with a force of 231 miles per hour. On the same day, the one-hour average velocity was as high as 173 miles per hour, also a record.

The head of the notch was once home to the historic Crawford House Hotel, unfortunately a victim of fire in the late twentieth century. Today the hotel site is home to the new *Appalachian Mountain Club Highland Center,* offering lodging, dining, outdoor activities, and learning. Simple but attractive rooms allow families to stay together, and a separate bunkhouse in the historic Shapleigh studio accommodates hikers. The center hosts a constant series of seasonal education programs throughout the entire year and serves as a center for hiking, bicycling, and other outdoor activities in the vast woodlands around it. While there, be sure to look into the environmentally friendly techniques used to build and operate it. Free environmental tours are offered daily, and all the evening nature programs are free and open to the public, not just to overnight guests. An added plus to all their programs, which include year-round hikes, climbs, and other sports, is free use of the abundant clothing and equipment provided by L.L. Bean. These range from winter boots, insulated gloves, and snowshoes to hiking boots, sleeping bags, and backpacks. Sophisticated, healthy, family-style dinners, which are worlds away from the pass-the-meatballs style of most hiker meals, are served nightly and reasonably priced. A vegetarian option is always offered, such as a hearty lentil and vegetable stew. The AMC Highland Center is on Route 302, Crawford Notch; call (603) 466-2727, or contact the Appalachian Mountain Club, 5 Joy St., Boston, MA 02108 (617-523-0655; outdoors.org/lodging/lodges).

The happy news is that with the reopening of the railroad through the notch, trains arrive once more, and if you check the schedule of the Conway Scenic Railway, you can be there to see one come through the "Gateway to the Notch" and pull up to the station. Better yet, you can be on one (see the Kancamagus section in this chapter).

Less than half a mile behind the railway station is a waterfall where the abolitionist Henry Ward Beecher liked to swim, so it was named ***Beecher's Falls*** after him. Follow the Avalon Trail across the tracks and over Crawford Brook. Shortly beyond, a side trail to the left climbs a very short way to the falls. The brook channels through a narrow chute and drops about 25 feet into a pool below. Follow the brook upstream to a second falls and then to a third.

The best view of Crawford Notch is down into it from ***Mount Willard,*** an easy climb (more accurately, an uphill walk) along an old bridle path to the summit. From there you can see the great scoop of the notch below you, as well as the shimmering cascades that fall off the mountains through rocky ravines. Watch overhead for peregrine falcons, which have nesting sites near the summit of Mount Willard.

Past Saco Lake, which is the source of the Saco River, is Mount Clinton Road, which leads to ***Jefferson Notch.*** Possibly the least known of the White Mountain notches, its 3,009-foot elevation is the highest point in the state reached by a public road. Gravel all the way, the road passes through deep woods along Monroe Brook, which cascades over rocks between moss-covered banks. At the top, the forest is still too tall to allow any panoramic views, but drive into the parking lot for a good, close view of Mount Washington's summit, 3,000 feet above you. The road descends into the town of Jefferson; the entire trip is 9 miles.

The First Trail

The Crawford Path, which begins at the top of Crawford Notch, is the oldest continuously used mountain trail in America, a fact confirmed by a sign erected on the path by the National Forest Service. Cleared in 1819 by Abel Crawford and his son, Ethan Allen Crawford, the trail reached the tree line near the summit of Mount Clinton. In 1840, it was widened to bridle-path width. Ethan Allen Crawford, by this time 75 years old, used it to make the first ascent of Mount Washington on horseback.

While the **Cog Railway** to the summit of Mount Washington is one of the state's best-known attractions, the **Cog Railway Museum** at the base station enjoys less celebrity. Located opposite the ticket window on the ground floor, its displays include cutaway versions of an early coach and boiler, showing how these were originally built and how they worked. There are also exhibits on the mountain's unusual weather, the history of the railway, and other related subjects such as the fall of the Old Man of the Mountain. There is no admission charge. The museum is open daily May through Oct. Call (603) 846-5404 or (800) 922-8825; thecog.com.

Our favorite trail up the mountain leaves from just below Base Station. The scenic **Ammonoosuc Ravine Trail** passes a waterfall before it begins any serious climbing, a pleasant short walk for those who do not wish to tackle the peak—or for days when climbing is unadvisable. High up on the mountainside, the trail breaks through the tree line and skirts **Lake of the Clouds,** passing **Lake of the Clouds AMC Hut** before the final climb to the summit via the Crawford Path. The round-trip will take about nine hours for someone in reasonably good shape, assuming the weather is good.

It's a beautiful climb on one of the easiest trails, but for many the summit is a great disappointment. Tourists arriving by train, van, and private car crowd the summit, which on a nice summer day seems more like Hampton Beach than a mountaintop. But the views are spectacular, and you can have lunch at the top and visit the observatory at which the world's highest wind velocity was recorded. A little museum in the lower level tells about the arctic flora and fauna. An older summit house is also a museum, restored to its original interior and furnishings. The museum is open whenever the road is open.

Although the busy tourist bustle at the top may diminish the sense of conquest afforded by lesser peaks with foot trail access only, the fact remains that climbing Mount Washington is an accomplishment in itself. We've been doing it since we were kids, and it's still a thrill to stand at the top and look out at 360 degrees of mountaintops below. Sometimes there are no mountaintops except the one you stand on, with only a sea of clouds bathed in sunlight.

With the world's worst winter weather, the top of the Presidential Range is not where you'd want to spend much time outdoors at that time of year, but it's cozy inside the ***Mount Washington Observatory.*** From December through March, a limited number of guests can spend the night, arriving after a two-hour ride up the mountain by snow tractor. It's an adventure suited only for those in good physical condition, because should the tractor break down halfway through the 4-mile trip, it means hiking back to the base or to the top of the mountain. Guests join the staff for dinner and a tour to learn about their work, and most trips include special programs and workshops with experts in related subjects, from winter photography and mountain safety to meteorology, global warming, and geology; mountwashington.org.

While the ***Mount Washington Hotel*** (now the ***Omni Mount Washington Resort***) is a White Mountain landmark, few know the ***Bretton Arms,*** a former chauffeur's quarters that served as home to the secretariat during the Bretton Woods Monetary Conference in 1944. Now an inn and a National Historic Landmark, the Bretton Arms offers newly renovated guest rooms and a more intimate atmosphere than the grand hotel up the hill. Be sure to see the magnificent Victorian stable building just past the inn, where horses, sleighs, and carriages are still housed. The Bretton Arms is located on Route 302, next to the cross-country ski center at ***Bretton Woods;*** (603) 278-1000 or (800) 314-1752.

The dining room at the Bretton Arms is small and intimate. The menu, too, is different, making the most of opportunities the grand hotel's large dining room doesn't have. Try as we might to sample different starters, we can't resist the smoked duck with cheddar-walnut ravioli. If wild boar in mountain berry plum sauce is on the menu, don't miss it.

If You Climb Mount Washington

Because of its infamous weather, this is not a trip to be undertaken on the spur of the moment. Wait for a day that promises good weather, begin early, and take layers of warm clothing. Even if you plan to lunch at the summit, take plenty of high-protein food and at least two quarts of water. Wear hiking boots (the top is rocky and, if wet, quite treacherous) and be sure you have a sturdy, waterproof windbreaker, even if it's hot and still, without a cloud in sight, when you leave the bottom. The weather above timberline can change from crystal-blue sky to a pea-soup fog in less than fifteen minutes. Never begin a climb here without being prepared to spend the night unsheltered on the mountain. The chances of that are very slight, but always there.

The Mount Washington Hotel exudes the opulence of its era, as it should, and it's been restored by owners who really care about the details. (They studied old photos and sent to England for replicas of the original Axminster lobby carpets.) It also exudes history. Nearly every nook and cranny has its story, many of which involve the princess. The hotel's first owner died only a few years after it opened, and his widow remarried a European prince. They continued to return to the hotel for summers, living in Paris in the winter, and she had her magnificent bed crated and shipped with her twice each year. The princess's bed, now retrofitted to queen (Why does this strike us funny?), is in an executive room at the hotel, with a Jacuzzi the princess would have had crated up and shipped to France each winter, too, had it been here then. Speaking of Jacuzzis, Room 114 has one in its bay window nook, overlooking the mountains.

For the first time in its history, and just short of its centennial anniversary in 2003, the Mount Washington Hotel remained open in the winter of 1999–2000, launching it into the spotlight as a winter resort. Renovations with complete insulation and winterizing have prepared it to do so for at least the next century. Along with the skiing and other winter sports, winter hotel guests enjoy a gala round of special theme events centering on food, holiday celebrations, and music. The Omni Mount Washington Resort is in Bretton Woods; (603) 278-1000 or (800) 314-1752; omnihotels.com/hotels/bretton-woods-mount-washington.

While you can argue that the hotel is not off the beaten path, the three free tours they give certainly are. You don't have to be a hotel guest to join; just ask at the activities desk. Each of the staff members who leads them has different stories to tell—perhaps of the princess sitting behind a curtain in a little balcony watching the ladies descend to the dining room each evening before choosing

ALSO WORTH SEEING IN THE EASTERN WHITE MOUNTAINS

Mount Washington Cog Railway
Off Route 302, Bretton Woods
(603) 846-5404 or (800) 922-8825
Operates Sat and Sun in May, daily June through late Oct. Departures hourly from 8 a.m. to 5 p.m. Reservations suggested for this memorable train that has been chugging to the summit of Mount Washington since the 1860s.

Attitash Bear Peak
Route 302, Bartlett
(603) 374-2368
Open daily mid-June to mid-Sept, weekends through mid-Oct with alpine and water slides, horseback riding, and a chairlift to the top for 360-degree views. In winter it is a ski resort.

which gown to wear to dinner—but you'll certainly see the Tiffany windows and the table where the Bretton Woods Monetary Agreement was signed, and you'll find out why the dining room is round.

The other tours take you to the print shop, where the menus are still hand set in type each day and printed on a press the Smithsonian wants, and to the *Stickney Chapel,* where Louis Comfort Tiffany signed one of the windows and the others were made by his students. If you can, go on a sunny afternoon when the sun is backlighting the chapel's front window. *Bretton Woods Mountain Resort* combines top-quality family skiing with eye-boggling views across the valley to the Mount Washington Hotel, with its distinctive red roof, and behind it in their full majesty Mount Washington, Mount Clay (now Mount Reagan by federal fiat), and Mount Jefferson. Once known as a small ski area, this is now the largest ski resort in New Hampshire, with more than 101 trails and glades spread over 434 acres of mountainside. Encompassing two (and soon to be three) peaks, the area has a vertical drop of 1,500 feet, access to which is provided by nine lifts. More than 92 percent of the trail area is covered by snowmaking. That, plus its North Country location and attention to grooming, assures good skiing all season. The trails here are well balanced in their challenge, with 29 percent beginner slopes, 39 percent intermediate slopes, and 32 percent advanced slopes. On a clear day it's very hard to concentrate on skiing with those views in front of you. Alpine and Nordic skiing are both available, as are equipment rentals and instruction in both styles of skiing. Skiers over age 65 take note: You get the astounding daily rate of $16. Located on Route 302, Bretton Woods; (603) 278-3320, snow phone (603) 278-3333, (800) 258-0330; brettonwoods.com.

Instead of leaving the area via *Jefferson Notch,* you can continue along Route 302 to the *Zealand Campground,* where there is a nice picnic area along the Ammonoosuc River. If you continue up the Zealand Road, about 3.5 miles to its end, you can take the Zealand Trail to *Zealand Falls,* a 2.5-mile easy hike. Getting to the top of the falls is the only climbing involved—there is only about a 350-foot difference in altitude from the parking lot to the top of the falls. The falls is really a cascade, and at its top, from the AMC hut, is a view of New Hampshire's hidden notch. Only hikers can see the dramatic shape of Zealand Notch, for no road penetrates it at any point. Take a lunch to eat by the falls as you enjoy the view. Along the trail you will follow the bed of a nineteenth-century logging railroad and pass through hardwood forests. It's hard to picture this entire valley laid waste by uncontrolled lumbering and the resulting fire and erosion damage, so great was the ability of the forest to rejuvenate itself here.

About halfway up the Zealand Road is the ***Sugarloaf Campground,*** one of the loveliest and most secluded in the mountains. Roomy sites are carved out of young forest, some with direct paths to the rocky Zealand River below. For information, write to the district ranger, White Mountain National Forest, Bethlehem 03574. Call (877) 444-6777 for reservations or (603) 536-1315 for information; https://www.fs.usda.gov/recarea/whitemountain/recreation/camping-cabins/recarea/?recid=74731&actid=29.

The ***Twin Mountain Fish and Wildlife Center,*** on Route 3 north of Twin Mountain, has a museum featuring local wildlife and an excellent exhibit on Water on the Move. It shows water in all its habitats, in a flowing stream, riffle area, cold-water pool, beaver pond, and wetland, each with its fish life. Although we think it was intended for kids, we found it fascinating, and we learned a lot about our finny neighbors. You can also tour the hatchery and hike a nature trail. It's free and open May through Oct daily 8 a.m. to 4 p.m.; the center is open 9 a.m. to 4:30 p.m. For information call (603) 846-5429 or visit twinmountain.com/hatchery.php.

More Places to Stay in the Eastern White Mountains

CAMPTON

Mountain-Fare Inn
5 Old Waterville Rd.
(603) 726-4283
mountainfareinn.com
An 1840s village house with antiques and flower gardens; rates low end of moderate.

CONWAY AND NORTH CONWAY

The Buttonwood Inn
64 Mt. Surprise Rd.
(603) 356-2625
buttonwoodinn.com
Spacious rooms with sitting areas, some with fireplaces and whirlpool tubs, are in a secluded setting with walking trails right out the back door. Families are welcome, and one of the owners is a chef, so breakfasts are a treat. Rates begin in the lower moderate range.

The Cabernet Inn
3552 White Mountain Hwy.
(603) 356-4704
cabernetinn.com
Elegantly furnished throughout, Cabernet is a pampering refuge for adults, with large, bright guest rooms and a common area that opens onto a garden terrace.

Farm By the River Bed & Breakfast
2555 West Side Rd.
(603) 356-2694
farmbytheriver.com
An original land-grant farm, still in the same family since King George III. Horses, cross-country skiing, and fishing on the property.

TO LEARN MORE ABOUT THE EASTERN WHITE MOUNTAINS

White Mountain Attractions Association
200 Kancamagus Hwy.
North Woodstock 03262
(603) 745-8720 or
(800) 346-3687 outside NH
visitwhitemountains.com

Mount Washington Valley Chamber of Commerce
2617 White Mountain Hwy.
North Conway 03860
(603) 356-5701
mtwashingtonvalley.org

Fox Ridge Resort
1979 White Mountain Hwy.
(800) 752-2538
redjacketresorts.com/
fox-ridge-resort
Motel-style rooms are large, with nice decorative touches and balconies or terraces with views. Swimming, tennis, conveniently located close to the outlet shops.

Green Granite Resort
1515 White Mountain Hwy.
(603) 356-6901
Family owned and one of the most attractive, hospitable lodgings in town, with indoor heated and outdoor pools, an exercise room, and a sauna.

GORHAM

Joe Dodge Lodge in Pinkham Notch
361 NH 16
(603) 466-2721
outdoors.org/lodging
-camping/lodges/pinkham
The Pinkham Notch Visitor Center offers rustic lodging and three meals a day at reasonable prices.

JACKSON

Christmas Farm Inn and Spa
3 Blitzen Way
(603) 383-4313
christmasfarminn.com
A charming country inn and resort with a full service spa situated on 15 acres.

The Mountain Club on Loon
Loon Mountain Rd.
(800) 229-7829
mtnclub.com
A modern hotel that maintains the atmosphere of a ski lodge; complete with indoor parking, balconies, and pools.

WATERVILLE VALLEY

Black Bear Lodge
23 Black Bear Way
(603) 236-4501
blackbearlodgenh.com
Two-room suites with kitchenettes. Ideal for families, with pool in building and moderate rates.

The Valley Inn
(603) 236-8425
valleyinn.com
A full-service hotel with the warmth of an inn, moderate prices, and some real bargain specials. The restaurant offers hearty standards—steak, fried chicken, burgers—in a pub-like setting, at moderate prices.

More Places to Eat in the Eastern White Mountains

CONWAY

May Kelly's
3002 White Mountain Hwy.
(603) 356-7005
maykellys.com
Hailed as "An Old World Atmosphere Irish Bar and Restaurant," May Kelly's offers comfort food from across the pond, featuring May's own recipes like May's Meatloaf Dinner, along with favorites, such as Paddy's Original Steak, fish-and-chips, and the Ploughman's Dinner.

Muddy Moose Restaurant & Pub
2344 White Mountain Hwy.
(603) 356-7696
muddymoose.com
Open every day at 11:30, the Muddy Moose is an affordable, family-friendly restaurant and watering hole, replete with wildlife decor, representative of what you might see wandering the North Country.

LINCOLN

Gypsy Cafe
117 Main St.
(603) 745-4395
gypsycaferestaurant.com
Just down the road from Loon Mountain, in the center of Lincoln, the cafe serves a worldly, eclectic menu with especially interesting Latin dishes, such as Cuban pork—a grilled tenderloin with habanero-orange mayo. Moderate.

NORTH CONWAY

Stonehurst Manor
3551 White Mountain Hwy.
(603) 356-3113
stonehurstmanor.com
A New Hampshire Farm to Restaurant member, Stonehurst serves a changing menu to take advantage of as much locally grown produce as possible. Breads are baked at the inn, which is well-known for its innovative pizzas.

NORTH WOODSTOCK

Cafe Lafayette Dinner Train
3 Crossing at Riverplace
(603) 745-3500
cafelafayettedinner
train.com
A restored, 1952 Pullman dome car travels at a stately speed along the Pemigewasset Valley while passengers enjoy dinner and a changing panorama. Service runs in the spring, summer, and early fall.

WATERVILLE

Wild Coyote Grill
98 Valley Rd.
(603) 236-4919
wildcoyotegrill.com
Serving dinner every day and weekend lunches, featuring such specialties as pork chops encrusted with walnuts and flavored with a hint of apple, or chicken marinated before slow roasting.

WATERVILLE VALLEY

The Campton/Waterville/Loon Mountain area is right on the border of our division between the Eastern and Western White Mountains, with North Woodstock and Thornton right on the line. Be sure to look in the "More Places to Eat" pages of the next chapter for dining and lodging options in these two towns close to Lincoln and Waterville Valley.

The Western White Mountains

The summer social season on this side of the *White Mountains* involved not only guests at the grand hotels—Profile House, Forest Hills, Sunset Hill, and the resorts of Bethlehem—but an increasing number of wealthy people who built their own summer estates, especially in Sugar Hill and Bethlehem. When the era of hotel summers ended, these families continued to return. Some retired here, giving the area a permanent cultural tradition that shows today in regular art and music events.

This land is beautiful, and the mountains a little less craggy than the Presidential Range to the east. Towns here have less of a seasonal air about them, being year-round communities with their own economic base. Downtown stores cater more to local needs than to tour-bus shopping expeditions. Hospitality is warm, and visitors return to the same inn year after year.

Country stores, covered bridges, farms, and mountain streams punctuate the miles of forests bordering the winding country roads. Only the stone walls that wind through the woodlands remind us that much of this land was once cleared for farming. This is a place for relaxing, exploring, and savoring.

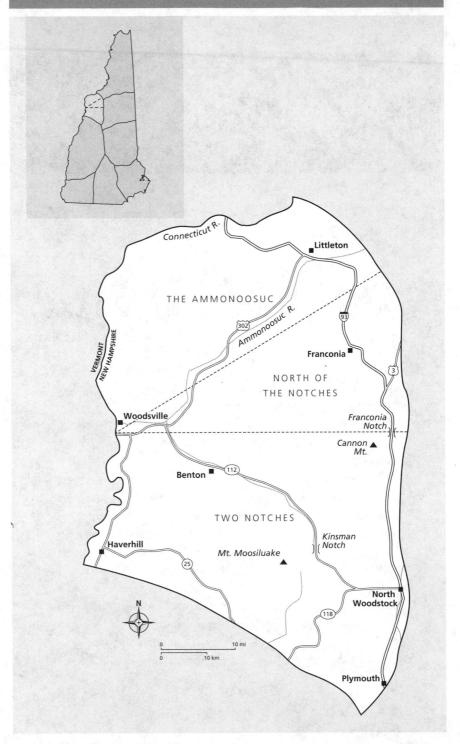

Two Notches

The **White Mountain National Forest's** westernmost segment begins just south of Sugar Hill and Franconia. Route 116 continues past the Frost Place to the town of Easton, high in the hills and completely surrounded by the national forest. South of Easton on Route 112 is a wild and beautiful notch almost completely overshadowed by the fame of neighboring Franconia Notch.

The road through **Kinsman Notch** winds and curves and climbs until it reaches tiny **Beaver Lake,** a high mountain tarn, rock-bound and icy cold. In its center rises a rocky, pine-clad island. The landscape here is wild and almost desolate under the slope of Mount Blue—but nowhere near as forbidding as it must have looked to Asa Kinsman and his wife. With their household goods on a two-wheeled cart pulled by oxen, they discovered that they had taken the wrong track to their new home in Landaff. Instead of turning back to go around the mountains that lay in their way, they hacked a path through the notch. If you take a turn you didn't plan on or miss the road you wanted, just remember the Kinsmans and take heart.

At its top the notch opens out, giving excellent views down the valley to the east. The narrowness and curves of the road at the top give a real sense of this being a pass, more so than some of the better-known notches. For some reason we can't understand, **Agaziz Basin** is never listed among the natural attractions of the White Mountains, whereas less interesting gorges and waterfalls are. It's also easier than most to get to, right beside Route 112, just west of **North Woodstock.** In the summer, there's a sign. Off-season, look for a parking lot on the south side of the road. One of the safer of New England's gorges to visit, the site includes a bridge over the falls.

Lost River really isn't lost; it just plays hide-and-seek for a while among glacially jumbled boulders, falling into huge rock chambers and through caves. Boardwalks and stairs make the trip easier, and you can simply walk through, or you can wriggle through the "lemon squeezer" or other tight passages that the claustrophobic should probably avoid. It's a beautiful area, and at the top is a garden with examples of woodland wildflowers, some of them quite rare. You can see the garden without paying the $12 admission to go through Lost River. Also at the entrance is a re-created "mining sluice" where kids can pan for real semiprecious stones that they can keep. Open mid-May to late Oct 9 a.m. to 5 p.m. and until 6 p.m. in July and Aug. It's on Route 112 West in Kinsman Notch; (603) 745-8031; findlostriver.com.

Farther along Route 112, the entire family can experience the real thing, panning for gold in the Wild Ammonoosuc River. Stop at **Twin River**

Campground (603-747-3640) to buy an inexpensive pan and join other "prospectors" in the shallow river to find a few flakes to take home.

Dinner on the *Cafe Lafayette Dinner Train* is not the usual pretty-views-with-mediocre-food tourist train ride. In fact, the scenery is not spectacular—no broad mountain vistas but a lovely woodland trip along a rocky river. And the meal served on this leisurely ride is excellent, prepared on the train and artistically presented. Each of the antique rail cars has been restored, bringing to life the aura of railroading's glory days. As dusk falls, outside lighting casts a spell on the passing woods. The dinner train runs May through June and late Oct, Tues, Thurs, and Sat; July through mid-Oct, Tues, Thurs, Sat, and Sun. Boarding time is 5:15 p.m. (4:30 p.m. Sun), and the trip takes about two hours. Located on Route 112, 0.25 mile west of exit 32 on I-93, North Woodstock; outside New Hampshire call (800) 699-3501, in New Hampshire call (603) 745-3500; or visit cafelafayettedinnertrain.com for fare information and trip times.

Using the same tracks along the Pemigewasset River is the child-pleasing *Hobo Railroad,* which leaves from a station just off I-93 exit 32 in Lincoln, at the beginning of the Kancamagus Highway. The onboard hobo clown doubles as a crossing flagman and stops traffic on Route 112 before taking up the role of onboard entertainer with magic tricks and spoofs, all designed to delight the youthful passengers onboard. The conductor tells about the train line's history in the logging days as you roll past views of the river framed in the maple and birch trees. In the 1850s, when the whole of northern New Hampshire was filled with lumber camps, the Boston and Maine Railroad built its line from Boston to Montreal through Plymouth. Loggers in the woods along the Kancamagus Pass floated the logs they had cut all winter down the Pemi to Plymouth, where they were loaded onto southbound trains. In 1880 the railroad was extended to Lincoln, and paper mills were built there to process pulpwood as it was cut. But chemicals from those mills killed everything in the river, until the Clean Water Act gave the mills a choice in 1975: Clean up or shut down. The Lincoln mills closed, and when the B&M abandoned the track, locals turned it into a tourist railroad. The Hobo Railroad operates daily through foliage season, weekends only in the spring, with departures at 11 a.m., 1 p.m., and 3 p.m. Before traveling a long distance, it's always a good idea to confirm times; call (603) 745-2135 or visit hoborr.com.

Tucked away in the White Mountains, the *Woodstock Inn, Station & Brewery* is among the most visited NH inns. Consisting of approximately thirty-nine guestrooms in five unique buildings, including two Arts and Crafts–style cottages with nicely preserved interiors and one a Cascade lodge, a classic old Adirondack-style lodge, furnished entirely in beautiful handcrafted rustic furniture. In the common room big cushy sofas face a huge river-stone fireplace with a birch mantel. In the guest rooms, king-size beds are made of peeled birch logs and accessories are museum-quality Arts and Crafts reproductions. Don't think rustic in terms of comfort, though—these rooms have heated bathroom floors and whirlpool tubs. The Woodstock Inn even offers a few dog-friendly lodging options; however, these do require advance notice. Rates start at $96 and range upwards of $250, depending upon accommodation style and season.

As the name implies, the Woodstock Station is the former train depot, which now offers lunch and dinner, and live entertainment. Considered a dining destination favored by both locals and visitors, make grabbing a meal at the Station a priority on your White Mountains adventure. Officially the third brewery to have opened in New Hampshire, albeit more than two decades ago, the original seven-barrel system at the **Woodstock Brewery** has since expanded to a thirty-seven-barrel production, distributing upwards of a dozen seasonal and yearly brews to stores and restaurants around New England. Enjoy a few on-site, but be sure to keep an eye for Woodstock Brewery beers wherever your travels through New Hampshire take you. The Woodstock Inn, 135 Main St. (Route 3), North Woodstock; (603) 745-3951 or (800) 321-3985; woodstockinnnh.com.

Franconia Notch, until May 2003, was the home of the state's symbol, the *Old Man of the Mountain.* It was to protect the fragile ledges of this famous stone profile from the dangers of blasting that I-93 was stopped just below the notch and resumed just above it. The Old Man may have slid into the notch,

An Old Friend Slips Away

In May 2003, New Hampshire was stunned by the loss of its symbol, the *Old Man of the Mountain,* which fell into Franconia Notch. For almost everyone it was a loss that was personal and deeply felt.

For 10,000 to 12,000 years, he looked out from his cliffside, but it wasn't until 1805 that workmen Nathaniel Hall and Luke Brooks, who were repairing the road through the notch, discovered him. Over the past two centuries, a few dedicated people, especially E. H. Geddes from 1916 to 1937 and Niels Nielsen and his family from 1954 to 2003, made a tremendous effort to shore up the cluster of huge loose ledges that made up the face. But nature and the immutable laws of physics have won out, to the great loss of New Hampshire and the people who loved the profile.

But the Old Man will not be forgotten. A special state commission is considering ways to commemorate him, and an expanded museum is likely to open in Franconia Notch.

but he is far from forgotten. You can learn more about the Old Man's geology at the small, free ***Old Man of the Mountain Museum,*** at the beginning of the path that leads to Profile Lake. Along with pictures of volunteers dangling on ropes in front of the Old Man's nose, you'll see a varied collection of memorabilia picturing the profile and Profile House, the grand hotel that once looked out across ***Echo Lake,*** at the head of Franconia Notch.

Most of the museum's collection of souvenir plates, cups and saucers, engravings, stereopticon views, and silver spoons are at least a hundred years old, many dating from the late nineteenth century—the "golden age" of the White Mountains grand hotels. Connected to the museum is a tiny shop where you'll find the new generation of Old Man of the Mountain souvenirs. You can also buy huge, top-heavy cones of the White Mountains' local homemade ice cream from Bishop's in Littleton.

The Old Man of the Mountain Museum is located at the head of Franconia Notch, near the base of the aerial tramway, and is open daily from mid-May through mid-Oct; oldmanofthemountainlegacyfund.org. For more information about the museum (or anything else in the White Mountains) contact White Mountain Attractions at (603) 745-8720; visitwhitemountains.com.

Also at the head of the notch, by the base of the aerial tramway, is the *New England Ski Museum.* Permanent and changing exhibits tell the story of this sport with historical equipment, photographs, art, and even changing fashions in skiwear. Open daily Memorial Day through the end of March, 10 a.m. to 5 p.m. Admission is free. The New England Ski Museum is in Franconia Notch; (603) 823-7177; skimuseum.org.

The *Rim Trail* can be reached from the top of the aerial tramway (look for one of its original 1930s cars at the Ski Museum) or via the *Kinsman Ridge Trail* from the head of Franconia Notch. It offers hikers panoramic views into the notch and across the Franconia and Presidential Ranges along the exposed rim and from the observation tower at the end. Notice the scar on the steep facing slope of Mount Lafayette, caused by a 1959 landslide that covered the road through the notch with 27 feet of debris. Even today, the physical forces of weathering and erosion continue the work of the glaciers in changing the landscape of the notches. Be sure to watch for peregrine falcons that nest on Eagle Cliff below, where golden eagles once laid their eggs.

A trail from the glacial formation known as *The Basin* leads to *Cascade Brook* and *Kinsman Falls.* Although these cascades are less than a ten-minute level walk from The Basin, they are never crowded and provide a fine place to picnic or just explore. The ledges over which the brook slides and drops have been worn into graceful curves, potholes, tiny flumes, and gorges by the brook. In places the water spreads over the granite in a smooth sheet; elsewhere it falls in ribbons from pool to pool. You can climb through the woods along the trail or up the sloping face of the ledges. When water is high or the weather rainy, it's better to stay on the trail and avoid the slippery rocks.

Below The Basin (turn left when the trail forks right to Kinsman Falls) is a pretty trail along the river, past a narrow little flume. The brook is the upper part of the Pemigewasset, well named by the Abenaki, who described it with their word for "swift." It is the prime watershed (river into which smaller streams empty) for Franconia Notch and for much of the hill country it flows through as it moves south, draining over 5,000 square miles. The river begins at Profile Lake, at an altitude of 1,900 feet. About 60 miles downstream it becomes the Merrimack River, which finally empties into the Atlantic Ocean, after a 185-mile trip, at Newburyport, Massachusetts.

EVENTS IN THE WESTERN WHITE MOUNTAINS

Frostbite Follies
early Feb, Franconia
(603) 823-5661, (800) 237-9007

Lilac Time Festival
late May, Lisbon
(603) 838-6673

Fields of Lupine Festival
June, Sugar Hill and Franconia
(603) 823-5661, (800) 237-9007
franconianotch.org/celebration-of
-lupine/

**Music in the White Mountains
Summer Festival**
July–Aug, Lincoln and Sugar Hill
(603) 869-3154

Quilt Festival
mid-Oct, Sugar Hill and Franconia
(603) 823-5661, (800) 237-9007

North of the Notches

Over the hills, on Route 117, lies **Sugar Hill,** stretched along the top of a ridge overlooking some of the White Mountains' most beautiful scenery. It's the kind of genteel town where people wave to you from their front porches as you go for an evening walk. **Harman's Cheese & Country Store** should be your first stop, for fine aged cheddar that bears no resemblance to the grocery store stuff. Harman's sends cheese and first-run New Hampshire maple syrup to people all over the country who don't really believe there is a town named Sugar Hill. The secret of their cheese is that they buy fine cheddar and then age it themselves. You'll find New Hampshire jams and jellies, soldier beans, common crackers, and whole-wheat pancake flour here, too, and all grades of the New Hampshire maple syrup that gave Sugar Hill its name. They also sell Vermont syrup for those people who won't believe that maple trees grow all over New England, New York, and Quebec (but the proprietors snicker a little behind their counter when they do). Call Harman's Cheese and Country Store at (603) 823-8000 or visit harmanscheese.com to confirm hours, which can vary by season.

Across the street is the historical museum. Housed in three buildings, the exhibits show, through an exceptional collection of old photographs, artifacts, carriages, and furnishings, the daily life of early settlers and Sugar Hill's heyday as a summer resort. Here are the kitchen from a stagecoach tavern with its original furnishings, a blacksmith shop, the ornate wagon of a local hotel, and a genealogical library. A small admission fee is charged. Open Thurs, Fri, and

Sat late June through Labor Day, 1 to 4 p.m; (603) 823-5336; sugarhillnh.org/library-and-museum/sugar-hill-historical-museum/.

Within walking distance of both of these is **Hilltop Inn.** This is one of those places that friends hesitate to tell you about because they are afraid it will become so popular there won't be room for them. The 1895 Victorian home is decorated with period furniture but offers every modern comfort. Big beds, plenty of pillows for late-night readers, flannel sheets, and antique linens are just a few of the luxuries. But the real charm of the Hilltop Inn is its owners, Meri and Mike Hern. Their offbeat sense of humor and irrepressible enthusiasm make old friends out of strangers from the first rumble of Mike's contagious chuckle. Meri's breakfasts are so good, with fresh-baked breads and elegant main dishes, that we keep hoping to be snowbound there so she'll have to cook dinner for us, too. It's possible, since the inn is open year-round. Rooms range upward from $45 in low season. Hilltop Inn, 1348 Main St., Sugar Hill 03585; (603) 823-5695 or (800) 770-5695; hilltopinn.com.

Since its heyday as a summer resort, Sugar Hill has had a flourishing arts community and hosts the **North Country Chamber Players**' annual summer festival in the meetinghouse in July and August. Members of this organization hold first-chair positions in major orchestras. For a complete schedule of concerts, write Box 99, Franconia 03580, or call (603) 444-0309 or visit northcountry chamberplayers.org.

The **Sunset Hill House** was one of the grandest of the White Mountains resort hotels, on the crest of a hill with mountain views in all directions. A boardwalk connected it to the village so that ladies could stroll up to watch the sunset without soiling the hems of their gowns. The main building is gone now, but a second one dating from 1882 has just been restored to an opulence that made the original hotel famous. Guest rooms are beautiful and comfortable, with a view from every window. The dining room overlooks the Presidential Range, which on clear evenings is bathed in a rosy reflection of the sunset known as alpenglow. Dinner guests may have trouble giving the menu the attention it deserves until after dusk claims the mountains, but the flavors of dishes such as duckling sauced in chutney, brandy, and almonds can compete with any view on equal terms. There is no off-season here, with sleigh rides, cross-country trails, golf, hiking, and maple sugaring available from the front door and ski slopes minutes away. Sunset Hill House, 231 Sunset Hill Rd., Sugar Hill 03585; (603) 823-5522 or (800) 786-4455; sunsethillhouse.com.

In the valley of the Gale River, east of Sugar Hill, **Franconia** was once the center of an iron industry that thrived from 1811 until the 1850s. The ore came from mines close to Sunset Hill House; the vein was the richest then known. The giant stone iron furnace where ore was smelted still stands by the river,

The Day the World Didn't End

The Millerites were followers of William Miller, a clergyman of the early 1800s who prophesied the end of the world on October 22, 1844. Sugar Hill had a particularly active group of Millerites, many of whom were so convinced by his preaching that they raised no crops that year, secure in the knowledge that there would be no winter to provide for. Others sold or gave away their livestock as the day approached and devoted themselves to prayer and fasting.

On the ordained day, they gathered at the cemetery on the little rise at the west side of town, which you can see above you as you head toward Lisbon on Route 117. They wore long, flowing white robes, the proper dress for ascending to their eternal reward. The end of the story is probably no surprise to you: The world didn't end on October 22. But other locals had a lot of fun over them, especially with one gentleman who was giving his unsaved neighbors a last-minute exhortation that morning, fell asleep afterward next to a small pile of hay. The objects of his sermon lit the hay on fire, and when the man awoke to the smell of smoke and crackling of fire, he was certain the end had come and he'd gone to hell.

near the LaFayette Regional School on the east side of Route 116, just south of its junction with Route 117. An interpretive center and outdoor panels explain the process that turned ore into wrought-iron bars. Inside the building, which is open irregular hours, is a scale model of the furnace, cut away to show its interior. This is the only iron furnace remaining in the state.

South of the village, off Route 116, the **Robert Frost Place** is a small weathered farmhouse with its mailbox marked R. FROST. Along with Robert Frost memorabilia and autographed first editions, there are a slide show, a nature trail marked with lines of his poetry, and a rare collection of the poet's less-known work: Christmas card verses. Open late May to July 5 Sat and Sun 1 to 5 p.m.; Wed through Mon, 1 to 5 p.m., July through Columbus Day. You can walk the trail after hours but mustn't disturb the poet in residence. Donations are suggested. The Frost Place is in Franconia; call (603) 823-5510.

The Ammonoosuc

Bethlehem, now a quiet town stretched out along a ridge, was once a major resort capital of the White Mountains. Along its main street stood thirty of the biggest and the grandest hotels, a summer-long procession of splendor and gaiety. They are gone now, but the elegant cottages that surrounded them are still there—some serving today as bed-and-breakfasts—and so is the pure, pollen-free mountain air that attracted the first visitors.

Its quiet streets and airy location make Bethlehem a good base for exploring the national forest, where the ban on commercial activity leaves no lodging for those who don't enjoy camping.

There are, it is said, more architectural styles in Bethlehem than in any other New England town. It's easy to believe. But the most unusual must be *The Bells,* a pagoda-shaped, three-story cottage on Strawberry Hill Street. For a self-guided tour that reveals some of Bethlehem's lively architectural and social heritage, get a copy of the booklet *An Illustrated Tour of Bethlehem,* sold locally for $2.

The Rocks, west of Bethlehem on Route 302, is a late-nineteenth-century farm estate now in the care of the Society for the Protection of New Hampshire Forests. The double stone walls, the buttresses, and the lower story of the Victorian barn were built of stones cleared from the rolling pastures and meadows that surround the house and barns. A free leaflet describes the sights along a 2-mile self-guided trail, past a highly original sawmill-pigpen and a beehive, and on through forest and wetlands. Another self-guided trail, this one through the Christmas tree plantation, describes the growing of trees and some of the estate's history as it leads to a scenic overview.

Seasonal activities are planned on weekends year-round, with a Halloween festival, and hay-wagon tours of the Christmas tree plantation (along with cut-your-own sales), a winter forest festival with logging demonstrations, snowshoe tours, maple sugaring, and a wildflower festival. Nature trails and gardens are free and open dawn to dusk. Maps are available describing cultural history, the process of growing Christmas trees, and the forest habitats. There are fees for special programs, and registration is necessary for some. The Rocks, Route 302, Bethlehem 03574; (603) 444-6228; therocks.org.

Off Prospect Street and also managed by the same society is the *Bretzfelder Memorial Park,* 77 acres of forest, pond, mountain brook, and picnic areas connected by walking and cross-country trails. A leaflet tells about the various trees, and signs along the trails explain the natural history and ecology. The story of Mr. Bretzfelder and his favorite tree (the tree is still alive even after major surgery) is told on a sign by the entrance. On Wednesday evenings in July and August at 7 p.m., take an evening ramble to explore some aspect of the park—its nocturnal animals, wildflowers, or other subject. No admission is charged; call (603) 444-6228 for dates and a description of the programs; therocks.org/bretzfelder.php.

Whether or not you've booked a room at the beautiful, secluded *Adair Country Inn,* don't miss a dinner at the *Adair Restaurant.* Featuring locally-sourced ingredients, culminating in savory dishes to satisfy a variety of tastes (and price points), the Adair Restaurant offers seating in the traditional dining room, library bar, or, weather permitting, on the patio. Pre-dinner cocktails and appetizers are on offer beginning at 4 p.m., and the library bar is open at 5 p.m. Wed through Sat. Located at 80 Guilder Ln, in Bethlehem; (603) 444-2600; adairinn.com.

Those with dietary restrictions will want to check out the offerings at *Cold Mountain Café.* Between its commitment to farm-to-table fare, and the abundance of gluten-free, vegetarian, and vegan options, there is truly something for everyone. As one customer observed, "Every town should have a restaurant like the Cold Mountain Café." Indeed! Open Mon through Sat from 11 a.m. to 3 p.m. for lunch, and 5 to 9 p.m. for dinner service. The Cold Mountain Café is closed on Sundays. The café is located at 2015 Main St. (Route 302) in Bethlehem; (603) 869-2500; coldmountaincafe.com.

Stop in to *Rosa Flamingo's* for creative comfort food, as determined by the seasons and sourced locally whenever possible. Diners looking for outstanding pizza and wings won't be disappointed, and the same goes for those with a serious sweet tooth. The restaurant is closed Mon and Tues, but dinner is served all other evenings, starting at 5 p.m., with pizza and panino available from 4 to 11 p.m. Rosa's is located at 2312 Main St.; (603) 869-3111; rosaflamingos.com.

Maplewood was not just the largest and grandest of the local hotels; it was a village of its own with a Victorian railroad station, farms to provide food for its dining rooms, a sugar bush that once yielded one hundred gallons of syrup each spring, a golf course, and a casino with a ballroom, movie theater, and bowling alley. The hotel is gone, but the village of Maplewood is still on the map. The restored casino with its stone tower still guards the golf course, and four wonderful old "cottages"—great hulking things with porches and gabled windows—are situated in a row just east of the casino.

Beyond them is a little shrine by the side of the road with a lovely story to tell. From the beginning of the century until 1949, underprivileged boys from a Boston industrial school were brought up in the summers to work as caddies at Maplewood. In 1958 a number of the former caddies, many of them prominent and successful, built the shrine. To this day these men gather at Maplewood for reunions.

Not far from Bethlehem, on its way to Whitefield, Route 142 drops down a long, steep hill. At the very bottom, just as the road curves to the left, is the tiny brown workshop of a man who has been honored by the president and whose work is on permanent display at the Smithsonian Institution. *Newt Washburn* is a fourth-generation Abenaki basket maker, one of fewer than half a dozen who have continued in this art. He designs and makes his own tools, the knives and splitters with which he turns an ash log into a finely woven basket. On a

Something for Every Taste

The Art Deco *Colonial Theater* on Main Street is being restored and brought back to life as the town's entertainment center. Its schedule features art and foreign films, live music and performances, and even a matinee for parents with babies so they can enjoy the movie without their children disturbing patrons who don't have kids. For a current schedule, call (603) 869-3422 or visit bethlehemcolonial.org.

full-size basket, each splint is the thickness of a growth ring separated from the log, but for smaller baskets Newt splits each splint in half to keep its thickness in proportion to its width. Newt will show you the whole process, from log to basket, and his scrapbook, too. This is a rare chance to order museum-quality Abenaki baskets, although there is no stock for sale ready-made. Newt Washburn's workshop is in Bethlehem Hollow; call (603) 869-5894.

As you arrive in Littleton on Route 302, *Bishop's Homemade Ice Cream Shoppe* is in a white house on the right. If you can think of any excuse to stop and try this ice cream, do it. You can sit at picnic tables on the lawn or inside the upbeat green-and-white ice-cream parlor while you enjoy the old favorite flavors—both blueberry and maple are extraordinary—a wide variety of homemade yogurt flavors, or one of their unique recipes. For calorie watchers or those with cholesterol problems, there are sorbets rich with the taste of real fruit. The Bishop's Bash is filled with chunks of brownie, walnuts, and chocolate chips. Open daily noon to 10 p.m. from mid-April until mid-Oct at 183 Cottage St. in Littleton; (603) 444-6039.

Opposite Bishop's, Mt. Eustice Road travels under I-93, just beyond which a short lane leads to the *Wallace Horse Cemetery.* Inside a small corral are three graves and a family stone; on the fence a placard explains the touching story of the team of matched bay Morgans, buried here with all their regalia, the only "children" of the Wallaces from 1889 until the death of the horses in 1919. As touching as the story recounted here are the pennies that visitors have placed on the stones.

Throughout northern New Hampshire you will see photographs of the White Mountains "the way we were" during the golden age. Most of these were reproduced from stereoscopic view cards, which, when seen through the double lenses of a special viewer, jumped into a three-dimensional landscape or scene. They were the forerunner of the Viewmaster and were a prime source of home entertainment. The major manufacturer of these cards was the *Kilburn Brothers Stereoscopic View factory* in *Littleton.*

Look where any river in New Hampshire drops more than a few feet in a short distance, and you are almost certain to find evidence of an old mill foundation or pieces of a former dam. You'll find them on small streams, often in places long overgrown with forest.

In Littleton you can see one of these brought back to life. At **Littleton Grist Mill,** between Main Street and the river, you can see the giant water-wheel that turned more wheels inside the understory of the mill, connected by belts to a series of other wheels and belts, only a small part of a complex system that once powered a fulling mill, three gristmills, and several others. The cogwheels are made of wood; with teeth more than 2 inches in diameter. You can buy flours ground at the mill, along with whole grain cereals and mixes for pancakes, scones, and breads, in the mill shop. The mill is at 18 Mill St.; (603) 444-7478 or (888) 284-7478; facebook.com/LittletonGristMill. It is open daily May through Dec and Wed through Sat in winter and spring. Admission is free.

In 2003, the National Trust for Historic Preservation named Littleton a Great American Main Street Community. One look at the 6-block Main Street, book-ended by the 1895 town hall at one end and the 1832 white Congregational church at the other, will tell you why. One side is lined with classic brick

A Real Deal

The White Mountain Attractions Association offers an irresistible bargain on admissions to seventeen of the most popular places in the mountains. For about half the price of the normal entrance fees, you can buy a *White Mountains Value Pass,* a single pass that admits two adults to each of the member attractions. Since nearly all the biggies are members of the White Mountains Attractions Association, the pass pretty well covers the North Country. But unlike most season passes, these are transferable, so two different households can share one, or you can loan it to friends.

The attractions include natural wonders (the Flume Gorge, Lost River Gorge, and Polar Caves) and New Hampshire's low-key kids' park and recreation sites—Santa's Village, Six Gun City, Story Land, Clark's Trading Post, Whale's Tale Water Park, and Fields of Attitash. In addition are the major mountaintop rides: the Cannon Mountain Aerial Tramway, Loon Mountain, Wildcat Mountain Gondolas, and—worth a big chunk of the cost by itself—the Mount Washington Cog Railway. Other scenic rides, including the *Conway Scenic Railroad,* Hobo Railroad, and Mount Washington Auto Road, are also included on the pass.

The number of these passes sold is limited, so it's a good idea to order them early—they are mailed on April 1 each year. The value of the admissions is about $600, and the cost of the pass is about $295. They are good until each attraction closes at the end of the season. Order from White Mountains Attractions, PO Box 10, VPB, North Woodstock, NH 03262; (800) 346-3687; visitwhitemountains.com.

mercantile buildings, interrupted by the white Doric-columned facade of 1850 Thayers Inn and the 1940 metal-wrapped Littleton Diner. The other side is more eclectic, ranging from the 1909 Beaux Arts Masonic temple and 1935 Federal Court Building to the last of the nineteenth-century homes that once looked down on Main Street from shaded lawns. The last remaining one is now the Community House, and its elegant interior is preserved and open to the public.

Learn about the architecture and history by picking up a copy of the sixteen-page walking tour booklet, which identifies and tells the story of more than twenty historic landmarks. Main Street was the original route of an 1820 coach road, and Thayers Inn was built to house the increasing traffic along it. The rest of the town grew as mills took advantage of the power generated by the 144-foot drop in the Ammonoosuc River, some 60 feet below Main Street.

The *Village Book Store* is the place to find, along with bestsellers and an excellent children's section, a tremendous array of books about the White Mountains. A stairway from the bookstore leads down to *the New Hampshire League of Craftsmen*'s stunning new gallery, overlooking the gristmill and the Ammonoosuc. Back up on Main Street, *Chutters* claims the world's longest candy counter, 112 feet of sweet stuff that includes all the long-ago penny candy favorites. At *Rae's Smoke Shop,* as much museum as shop, you can buy handy cigar boxes without having to buy the cigars that came in them.

Step inside *Parkers Marketplace* to see some of the original interior of the *Parker Mansion,* home of the business partner of Sylvester Marsh, builder of the Mount Washington Cog Railway. From the library lawn, a statue of the fictional character Pollyanna encompasses the scene with outstretched arms. She was the creation of local author Eleanor Porter, and her exuberant spirit is a good match for Littleton's own. This lively Main Street has taken a lot of local initiative to maintain in the face of the North Country's long-term economic woes.

Tim and Biruta Carr, owners of *Tim-Bir Alley* restaurant, are back in Littleton, after several years in Bethlehem, now in a classy setting on Main Street. Tim-Bir Alley provides an exceptional, if expensive, dining experience. The menu changes daily, featuring what might include sole with wild mushrooms and shrimp in a Chardonnay sauce, salmon in a sunflower-seed crust, or maple-glazed pork tenderloin. Fresh-from-the-oven biscuits and small breads arrive with the salad that accompanies each

sweettalk

If you "collect" world record holders, be sure to stop in *Chutters.* The *Guinness Book of World Records* says they have the longest candy counter in the world, and who are we to argue? The address is 43 Main St., Littleton; (603) 444-5787; chutters.com.

entree. Desserts are equally memorable, such as plum-and-almond tart and maple cheesecake. No credit or debit cards are accepted. Tim-Bir Alley, 7 Main St., Littleton; (603) 444-6142.

Fossils are not common in New Hampshire, and one of the few places where they are found is atop a rock formation overlooking Littleton. The *Kilburn Crags* are the result of great masses of layered, fossil-bearing rock being heaved into an almost vertical position. The fossils aren't just lying about; it takes some effort to find them, but serious geology buffs may find brachipods and ferns here. To reach the crags, continue on Route 118 past the Dells (a pleasant picnic area). Half a mile after it separates from Route 135 in a left turn, look for a sign on the left side of the road with a small pull-out for parking. There is no trail, but you can walk along the edge of the field to an old woods road. Follow it to the top, just over half a mile of steady but not difficult climbing. If fossils don't interest you, the view down over Littleton is worth the climb. Watch for moose, which are plentiful here.

Avoid the interstate here by taking Route 18 to the Connecticut River, which forms both the Vermont border and a huge lake behind *Moore Station Dam.* One of the major power-generating dams in the northeast, it has a visitor center with displays explaining the dam, as well as a picnic area and boat launch on the reservoir. The center is open June to mid-Oct, Thurs through Mon. For launch information contact the Connecticut River Joint Commission at (603) 826-4806; crjc.org/boating.

Route 135 plays hide-and-seek with the Connecticut River through valley farmland to *Woodsville.* You can either return to the Littleton area on Route 302 or take Route 112 from Bath to Franconia and Kinsman Notches.

In *Bath* be sure to stop at the *Brick Store,* which has been open in the center of town since 1804 or maybe even earlier. Without being "ye olde general store," this emporium manages to retain the feel and much of the merchandise of an old country store while remaining a useful shopping place for local residents. Top shelves are lined with old tins, a thread cabinet, and other vintage store memorabilia, and the homemade fudge is displayed in a glass case. There's a wheel of cheddar on the counter and four shelves of buffalo-plaid wool shirts, a hot item here in the winter. Notice the slanted counter fronts that make room for hoopskirts. If you stop here for a sandwich (if you don't find one you like in the fridge, they'll make one up for you), enjoy it sitting on the front porch with a view of Main Street and the old Mobil sign with the red Pegasus. Open weekdays 6 a.m. to 9 p.m., Sat 7 a.m. to 9 p.m., and Sun 8 a.m. to 9 p.m. The store is on Route 302; (800) 964-2074.

Behind the store is the *Bath Village Bridge,* a covered bridge so long that motorists are asked to turn on their headlights when entering it. Built in 1832 at a cost of $3,500, it still has its original arches. Be sure to notice its construction (all covered bridges are not built in the same way), a fine example of a Burr arch structure. At 400 feet, it is the longest in New Hampshire and one of the oldest still in use in America.

Bath has two other covered bridges, one of which is just off Route 112 in the village of Swiftwater. Farther along Route 112 and the Wild Ammonoosuc (don't let this confuse you—there are three different Ammonoosuc Rivers in the area), where the road parallels the river for a stretch, there is a spot where hopeful prospectors have had moderate luck panning for gold. You may see their vehicles parked along the road. Route 112 leads to Kinsman Notch.

Northeast of Bath on Route 302 is *Upper Village,* a cluster of eight homes remarkable enough to make almost anyone ease up on the gas pedal. The most imposing are three grand brick mansions built in the early 1800s. Also set in the carefully manicured grounds, which cover both sides of the road, are other homes and huge, yellow clapboard barns with steep-pitched roofs, all in pristine condition. You expect to see a sign with the name of a museum, but these are private homes. Jeremiah Hutchinson moved to Bath in the winter of 1781 with his wife and twelve children. As you might imagine, it took two sleighs to bring them. There's no place to stop safely, but look as you pass at this family village of extraordinarily well-preserved Federal-style homes, unlike any other in the state.

ALSO WORTH SEEING IN THE WESTERN WHITE MOUNTAINS

The Flume
Franconia Notch
(603) 745-8391
nhstateparks.org/visit/state-parks/flume-gorge.aspx
Open daily 9 a.m. to 5 p.m. mid May through late Oct. By definition and observation, the Flume is a deep natural chasm with sheer granite walls.

The Aerial Tramway
cannonmt.com
Carries passengers to the top of 4,200-foot Cannon Mountain, daily mid May through Oct.

Clark's Trading Post
Route 3, Lincoln
(603) 745-8913
clarkstradingpost.com
Open spring and fall weekends, daily in July and Aug. Spotless and good wholesome fun for kids, with enough to keep adults amused, such as steam train rides and a Victorian main street. The bears clearly enjoy performing as much as the audience enjoys the show.

Just south of Lisbon, on the east side of the road, is another group of historic homes, although of a much different sort. Early mills frequently provided housing for their workers, whose wages were often too low for them to afford adequate housing on their own. The company houses were built in rows, all alike. Most of the houses are long gone elsewhere, but eleven of them stand here in their original row.

Lisbon offers another view of the state, one that you have glimpsed from the hardscrabble farms on the back roads. This is a town with lots of guts and little money, but every year it looks just a little bit more prosperous. They have a **Lilac Time Festival** toward the end of May. A real hometown event, it has pancake breakfasts, chicken barbecue, races, a golf tournament, a quilt show, a flea market, crafts, bands, singers, and a Saturday night dance. It's a lovely and less crowded time to visit, before summer attractions have opened. For this year's dates and schedule, write the Lisbon Chamber of Commerce, Lisbon 03585; (603) 838-2862; lisbonnh.org.

Beyond Lisbon is Woodsville and Route 10, which heads south overlooking the beautiful Connecticut River Valley and the Vermont and New Hampshire farmlands that line it. **Haverhill** is the first town, and although **Haverhill Corner Historic District** is not as well known as neighboring Orford's Bullfinch-inspired **Ridge Houses,** it has some fine early homes that befitted its position as the northern terminus of the first Province Road from the seacoast. You'll see magnificent examples of Federal architecture along Court Street, including fan doorways and double chimneys. The road dwindles to a lane and then a trail, but you can trace bits of it elsewhere in the state. Equally fine brick buildings stand above the town common and bandstand, where you are welcome to use the public picnic tables.

Just north on Route 10, in **North Haverhill,** you'll pass **The Big Scoop** (603-787-6588), a bright pink cabin with picnic tables at the corner of Hazen Drive. The name says it all, and we can't imagine how they can make five scoops balance on a cone.

More Places to Stay in the Western White Mountains

BETHLEHEM

The Grande Victorian Cottage
53 Berkley St.
(603) 869-5755
Grand it is, with ten guest rooms decorated in antiques. Some have private baths; rates moderate.

The Mulburn Inn
2370 Main St.
(603) 869-3389 or (800) 457-9440
mulburninn.com
The former Woolworth estate, filled with architectural details, including fine woods, curved window glass, and an Art Deco bathroom; rates moderate.

FRANCONIA

Lovett's Inn by Lafayette Brook
1475 Profile Rd.
(603) 823-7761
lovettsinn.com
A National Register property restored as a B&B, with an eclectic dining room.

NORTH WOODSTOCK

Jack O'Lantern Resort
1668 Daniel Webster Hwy.
(603) 745-8121
jackolanternresort.com
A family resort with golf, tennis, and swimming. The moderate rates at the inn, motel, or cottages can be with or without meals at the resort's two dining rooms.

More Places to Eat in the Western White Mountains

FRANCONIA

Franconia Inn
1172 Easton Rd.
(603) 823-5542
franconiainn.com
Well-prepared dishes; moderate. Breakfast is served, too.

LITTLETON

Littleton Diner
145 Main St.
(603) 444-3994
littletondiner.com
The really old kind of diner, before stainless steel streamlined their look, right in the center of town. Their breads are baked with whole grains, ground

TO LEARN MORE ABOUT THE WESTERN WHITE MOUNTAINS

Franconia Notch Chamber of Commerce
421 Main St., Franconia 03580
(603) 823-5661 or (800) 237-9007
franconianotch.org

Waterville Valley Region Chamber of Commerce
Campton
(603) 726-3804 or
(800) 237-2307 in New England

White Mountain Attractions Association
200 Kancamagus Hwy.
PO Box 10, North Woodstock 03262
(800) 346-3687
visitwhitemountains.com

within earshot of the diner, at Littleton Grist Mill. Inexpensive.

Miller's Café and Bakery

16 Mill St.
(603) 444-2146
millerscafeandbakery.com
A cafe with a deck
that looks out over the
Ammonoosuc River just
downstream from the dam.
Big sandwiches, freshly
made soups, and salads.
Closed Mon; seasonal

hours, please call ahead of your visit to confirm.

SUGAR HILL

Polly's Pancake Parlor

672 NH-117
(603) 823-5575
pollyspancakeparlor.com
Freshly made and served
with real maple syrup
(their own). They grind the
organic whole grains right
there, too.

Sugar Hill Inn

116 NH-117
(603) 823-5621
sugarhillinn.com
Four-course prix-fixe
dinners, by reservation
only, might include such
dishes as agnolotti filled
with porcini mushrooms in
a sage butter or a savory
navarin of lamb and spring
vegetables. Tastings at
4:30 p.m. (you'll need to
reserve these, too) feature
comparative wines, beers,
cheeses, or caviar.

The North Country

The North Country isn't for everyone. The nearest mall is hours away; if the local grocery-store-cum-tackle-and-bait-shop doesn't have it, you won't find it here. Nightlife consists of swapping fishing or birding stories in front of the fire or soothing muscles tired from canoeing, hiking, or skiing. If there is a Jacuzzi in this part of New Hampshire, it's well hidden.

But if the sight of a moose with a full rack of antlers drinking from a pool at the side of the road makes your heart beat faster, and if the cry of a loon is your favorite song, this is your Serengeti. You'll meet people here with character, not the "ayuh" and hayseed-style characters but the real stuff. There is a ready wit born of the sense of humor necessary to those who choose the backwoods as home. It's tent-and-canoe country, with a few fine lodgings for those who prefer their adventures to end in time for a full-course dinner.

Route 3 stays close to the ***Connecticut River,*** which at Stewartstown ceases to be the border between New Hampshire and Vermont. Travelers who have seen the Connecticut River flowing through southern New England will hardly recognize this meandering little brook as the same river. Just north of Stewartstown is a sign marking the crossing of the forty-fifth

THE NORTH COUNTRY

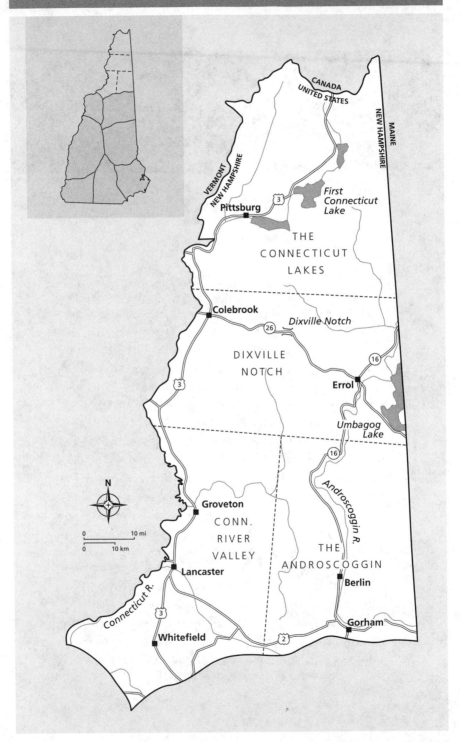

CANADA
UNITED STATES

VERMONT
NEW HAMPSHIRE

NEW HAMPSHIRE
MAINE

First
Connecticut
Lake

Pittsburg

THE
CONNECTICUT
LAKES

Colebrook

Dixville Notch

DIXVILLE
NOTCH

Errol

Umbagog
Lake

N

Groveton

Androscoggin R.

CONN.
RIVER
VALLEY

THE
ANDROSCOGGIN

0   10 mi
0   10 km

Lancaster

Berlin

Connecticut R.

Gorham

Whitefield

parallel. From that point north you are closer to the North Pole than to the equator.

Connecticut River Valley

The *Mountain View Grand Resort* has been a part of the White Mountains for over a century, but its recent rebuilding and renovation has restored its elegance and charm. It sits like a palace in a sea of green forest high above the valley floor, providing views that go for miles. Like most resorts, the Mountain View offers a wide range of activities, including a golf course with the most distracting views in New England. Accommodation rates start at $289, but look for special packages that can save you money. Mountain View Grand is at 101 Mountain View Rd., Whitefield; (603) 837-2100 or (866) 484-3843; mountain viewgrand.com.

A bit farther down Mountain View Road, *The Spalding Inn* strikes just the right balance between elegance and informality. First opened in 1926 on the site of a former hotel, the inn accommodates guests in bright, airy rooms in the main lodge, in a converted carriage house that was part of the former hotel, and in trim cottages close to the pool and tennis courts. Unusual in White Mountain hotels, the Spalding has a fine bowling green (they'll show you how to play) and a real British-style court for lawn croquet. But the view across the lawns and gardens from the wide front veranda may tempt you to spend your time just watching the flowers grow. Special arrangements allow guests to use the adjacent Mountain View golf course.

The dining room menu changes nightly and might include the inn's hallmark dish, Duck Bombay. Be sure to mention any special diet, since the chef is especially creative in designing alternatives, both at breakfast and dinner. Birders will find binoculars and field guides handy by the terrace window and will enjoy the bird photographs taken by the innkeeper's daughter. Another daughter's paintings decorate the walls of the parlors, and the innkeeper herself is responsible for the tasteful decor featuring her own collection of antiques. Rates are moderate, and include a full breakfast. The Spalding, 199 Mountain View Rd., Whitefield; (603) 837-9334.

A short distance away on Route 116 is *Jefferson,* an unadorned town set along a ridge facing the mountains. Only the outbuildings remain of the Waumbek Hotel, which once dominated its crossroads, but there are still accommodations in town at the *Jefferson Inn.* A new ell has been added to the original 1896 Victorian house with its tower and wraparound porch, along with woodwork and other architectural details that either match or fit the style of the original house.

The Lost Virgin

In 1759, after repeated Indian raids from Canada had left New Hampshire farms and villages in flames, Robert Rogers of Dunbarton led a group of his famous Rangers on a raid on the village of St. Francis, home of a group of Indians converted to Catholicism by the French, who encouraged Indian raids by paying a bounty on white scalps during the French and Indian Wars. The Indians were busy celebrating their most recent raid when the Rangers attacked, killing and scattering the Indians. Leaving, they carried with them a pair of candlesticks and a large silver image of the Virgin Mary from the church, rich from ransomed captive settlers.

On their return, the Rangers were forced to break up to avoid their pursuers, and the group with the Virgin, trying to cross over Jefferson Notch, floundered in the thick forests and rough terrain of the Israel River. Searches for the treasure were fruitless and were abandoned until the gold candlesticks carried by another band turned up on the shores of Lake Memphremagog in 1816. The silver Virgin is still missing, although tales abound of her appearing aglow in the night to lost hunters in the area. Keep a sharp lookout for the statue in the Jefferson Notch area, but don't get lost in the still-thick woods.

Quilts warm most of the beds, and antiques are mixed with more recent furnishings, creating a nice balance of comfort and style. Families will enjoy the inn's suites and ample recreation space, as well as the two sociable horses in the barn. Couples will find cozy rooms stylishly decorated by the energetic owners, who have added a historical theme and their personal art collection. The delicious European breakfast dishes have to compete with the birds outside the window for your attention. More than twenty-five species visit here, including indigo buntings. Reasonably priced from $115 to $145 in peak season. The inn is open all year at 6 Renaissance Ln. (Route 2), Jefferson 03583; call (603) 586-7998 or (800) 729-7908; jeffersoninn.com.

Meet some veterans of the Iditarod and their friends at *Muddy Paw Sled Dog Kennel* in Jefferson, where in the winter you can visit sled dogs "at home" and learn harnessing, hookup, and sledding commands before taking to the trails—with an experienced musher, of course. This is one of the rare places that actually teaches visitors how to drive a dogsled, instead of just taking them for rides. Of course there's nothing wrong with just going for a ride, and they're happy to do that, too. As for the dogs, they're happy as long as they are running with a sled behind them, a fact that's clear to see from their excited yipping when the teams are being selected and their crestfallen faces if they're not on one. Muddy Paw Sled Dog Kennel, 32 Valley Rd., Jefferson; (603) 986-0697; dogslednh.com.

Just before reaching Lancaster, Route 3 passes over a shoulder of **Mount Prospect,** a low peak easily spotted because of the stone tower at its summit. The tower and the stone-and-stucco "lodge" beside it were built by a man to whom the North Country and everyone who travels there owes a tremendous debt. John Wingate Weeks was a US senator and cabinet member to two presidents but is remembered most as the father of the White Mountain National Forest. It was the "Weeks Law" that authorized the government to buy and preserve forest areas in the East.

The tower and buildings are now in a state park encompassing 420 acres on the mountain. The lodge contains an outstanding collection of local birds, historical displays on the White Mountains, and a gallery of photographs that reflect Weeks's prominent role in world affairs and the friends who visited the estate. Free lectures on historical and ecological topics are held at the lodge on Thursday evenings throughout the summer. The lodge and tower are open from 10 a.m. to 5 p.m. Sat and Sun from mid-June until Labor Day. Admission is $7 (ages 12 and older); $3 (ages 6–11); New Hampshire residents free. For a current schedule of evening programs call (603) 788-4004 or (603) 788-3155, or visit nhstateparks.org.

Just north of the park is **Lancaster,** seat of Coos County, where descendants of its original settlers, who came in 1764, still live. Lancaster has completed its section of the **New Hampshire Heritage Trail,** which will one day provide walkers with a route from the Canadian to the Massachusetts borders. The 15 miles through Lancaster are not only complete, but they have a free brochure mapping the route and describing the historic houses along the way through the center of the town. One of the buildings is the Stone House on Main Street, once the only granite house in the state and built from a single boulder (there went another glacial erratic) in 1836.

Also on the route, and on yours as well, is the **Wilder-Holton House** at the junction of Routes 2 and 3, the first two-storied house in the North

EVENTS IN THE NORTH COUNTRY

North Country Moose Festival
late Aug, Colebrook

Lancaster Fair
early Sept, Lancaster
(603) 788-4531

Logging Competition and Fall Festival
June and Sept, at Northern Forest Heritage Park, Berlin
(603) 752-7202
Lumberjack competitions, log building demonstrations, and other activities.

Country, built in 1780, on the National Register, and now the historical society museum. Inside, along with fascinating information on the bizarre story of the *Brunswick Springs Hotel*, just over the river in Vermont, the museum has a children's room with dolls and a sled, a closet filled with vintage clothing, and household utensils, including a hand-operated vacuum cleaner. Every alternate Sunday from the end of June until the end of September a flea market is held on the lawn, where you can sometimes find amazing bargains. The house is open on flea market days and other times by appointment; call (603) 788-2073 or (603) 778-3004.

Leave Lancaster on Route 135 south to find the *Mt. Orne Covered Bridge* across the Connecticut River. The double-span truss bridge was built in 1911 to replace another that was destroyed in a logjam in 1908. This section of the river was filled with logs every spring, carrying them from the northern forests to lumber mills and shipping centers on the spring melt-off.

Route 135 follows the river closely, past farms that take advantage of the rich soil deposited by floodwaters. At Dalton, a long iron rail bridge crosses the river, and almost under it is a put-in popular with canoe and kayak paddlers. This is in the middle of a 125-mile stretch of flat water, one of the longest and most scenic stretches of easy river paddling in New England. About 7 miles south of Dalton village, a lane to the right leads down to the river where, alongside a scenic riverside picnic area with tables, there's another boat launch.

Following the Connecticut River from Lancaster in the other direction, Route 3 heads north, past northern New Hampshire's largest antiques shop. *Potato Barn Antiques Center* holds a little bit (or a lot) of everything, especially vintage clothing and hats and old tools. Some rooms are like museums, with display shelves filled with examples of lanterns or lamp chimneys or woodworking planes. It's open Apr through Dec Thurs to Mon 9 a.m. to 5 p.m., Jan through Mar Fri to Sun 10 a.m. to 4 p.m. Potato Barn Antiques Center, Route 3, Northumberland; (603) 636-2611; potatobarnantiques.com.

Farther north, just before Route 3 reaches *Groveton,* Route 110 branches to the right (east) and travels along the upper Ammonoosuc River. To the north lies the *Nash Stream Watershed,* an area whose future has been the subject of an intense battle among land developers, the state, and several conservation groups. Forty thousand acres of it have finally been secured as public lands, a mixed habitat for hawks, falcons, and smaller birds in a forested valley. Access is via Emerson Road, about 2 miles east of Groveton. Follow it another 2 miles to a fork and then go left. After about 4.5 miles of dirt road, a right fork leads uphill to Little Pond Bog, a fine spot for fly fishing high above the valley. In the winter this area is crisscrossed by cross-country ski trails.

Flat Water on the Connecticut

North of Lancaster the Connecticut River runs for a mellow 9 miles or so, providing a pleasant three- or four-hour paddle that is only slightly assisted by the current. The only white water in sight is upstream from the put-in, which is just across the river in Guildhall, Vermont. Cross the bridge about 7 miles north of Lancaster, not far past the fairgrounds on Route 3 at Northumberland. The put-in is downstream below the bridge. Take out at the state boat-launch ramp just below the bridge at Lancaster, on the New Hampshire bank. Except for the put-in point, you'll be in New Hampshire all the way, since the river is New Hampshire's. Of course, spring runoff creates a whole different set of conditions; so don't expect gentle, flat water on any river then.

If you continue straight ahead less than half a mile instead of taking the right, you come to **Pond Brook Falls,** a series of waterfalls known to very few people outside of Groveton and Stark. Just after crossing a culvert you will see a pull-out area to the right. Park there and follow the trail a short distance to the lower falls (watch for moose tracks—this is a favorite path for them, too). You'll hear the falls before you see them, and then you'll see only part of them. Continuing uphill, the path ends at a second falls; from here the best route is over the sloping granite ledge alongside the rushing water. Except during spring runoff, there is plenty of room on this 50-foot-wide span of rock for both you and the brook.

Keep going upstream for an ever-changing series of falls, some gushing through narrow chutes and others spread in a filmy veil across a wide ledge. As you reach the top of each, you look up to see another of a different size and shape. This is New Hampshire's sampler of waterfall styles. Do be careful after a rain or in the early spring when the rocks are wet, since they can be quite slippery to climb. On wet days, go through the woods next to the falls, where the footing is more secure.

Back on Route 110, continue on to visit **Stark,** a mountain town clustered around its covered bridge under Devil's Slide, a 700-foot precipice. During World War II, Stark housed a camp for German prisoners of war. The remarkable story of how these men, taken prisoner in North Africa, became friends of local farmers during their long winters together is told in *Stark Decency* by Allen Koop. East of the village, on Route 110, a state sign marks the site of the camp. In the field behind the trees, the fireplace in the dining hall, holding messages from children of former prisoners, is all that remains to tell the tale.

The well-kept house with a terrace overlooking the river, just over the covered bridge in Stark, is the **Stark Village Inn Bed and Breakfast,** offering three antiques-furnished guest rooms and a great deal of homey comfort to travelers. Hiking, canoeing, fishing, climbing, cross-country skiing, and bicycling begin at the doorstep of this restored farmhouse, and photographers could spend the day sitting on the front porch capturing the river and the bridge in all their different moods and lights. A full country breakfast is cooked on the big black woodstove in the kitchen; in summer guests can eat on the terrace overlooking the river. Low rates make this a bargain as well as a treat. 16 Northside Rd., Stark 03582; (603) 636-2644.

Rock hounds take note: At *Diamond Ledge* on Long Mountain and also on the south slope of *Percy Peak,* about 200 feet below the summit, amethyst is found in the surface rock; topaz is also found at Diamond Ledge. You will need to get thorough directions locally or use a topographic map.

Between the towns of *Stratford* and *North Stratford* on Route 3 is *The Foolish Frog.* This unexpected roadside museum is the personal three-decade collection of Carol Hawley and Francis McMilleon. The museum contains hundreds of frogs made in every imaginable material, ranging from plastic toys and novelties, to beautifully carved Indonesian frog deities, a frog-shaped flute from Colombia, baskets, batiks, puzzles, pottery, bottle stoppers, potholders, and mechanical banks. It's fascinating to see how this creature has been interpreted by artists all over the world. A small section displays frogs for sale, including several unusual toys. A discreet box stands near the door for donations, which help the collection to grow. Open May through Oct at 302 Route 3, Stratford Hollow; (603) 636-9843.

The Connecticut Lakes

The town of *Pittsburg* is geographically the largest in New Hampshire, more than 20 miles wide and covering more than 360 square miles. The entire tip of New Hampshire, from the Maine to Vermont borders to the international border with Canada, lies within its boundaries. The whole town was an independent nation for three years beginning in 1832. Claimed by both New Hampshire and Canada, and with no decisive action taken by either to settle the issue, the Indian Stream Territory was left in chronic limbo. Tiring of this, and not wishing to be governed by either contender, the citizens voted their independence at a town meeting. This finally brought them to everyone's attention. After three years and a few altercations among the local militia, a Canadian sheriff's posse, and a small company of New Hampshire militia, the Republic of Indian Stream became the town of Pittsburg.

Within Pittsburg's borders lie all four of the Connecticut Lakes and Lake Francis, and mile after mile of forests, mountain streams, bogs, and assorted wilderness lands. Pittsburg's main (almost its only) road borders each lake in turn until it finally climbs the "height-of-land" to the Canadian border station. ("Height-of-land" is a term commonly used in the North Country to describe the high point of any of the area's many ridges.) At nearly any point you may see deer or moose by the roadside.

What is unique here is the series of pristine waterbodies. Uninhabited by man, these provide habitat for wild shorebirds found in few other places. Loon populations are increasing here. You can put in a canoe on nearly any pond, and you are welcome to roam over the woods roads built by the timber companies as long as they are not barred. The whole area abounds with trout.

Coon Brook Valley, a long, wide, marshy area cut by a woods road, is a sure place to see moose at almost any time of day. To find it, look for a road marked MAGALLOWAY TOWER entering Route 3 from the right. Go a few yards north and take the road entering from the opposite side of Route 3. Just drive in and park in an open spot—you may even see moose before you park.

For an adventure into the outer reaches of the wilderness, but one that requires only a short hike, search out *Garfield Falls.* Take the above-mentioned gravel road marked MAGALLOWAY TOWER, following the tower signs until you reach the height-of-land. At this point a dirt road to the tower goes off to the right, but you should keep going. About 2 miles after you pass Paradise Camp on your left, you will go down a hill and see a road bearing off to the right (the road straight ahead of you may be blocked just below this). Follow the road to the right 1.1 miles to where it makes a sharp left turn and crosses a bridge. Take the dirt road right at the turn.

It's narrow, but unless there have been heavy rains, it is easily passable without four-wheel drive. In another 1.1 miles the road opens out into a yard (an open area where logs are stored). Park there and follow the trail into the woods on the left side of the road. It may take a minute to find it if there have been logging operations there recently, but it is close by a tumble of large rocks.

Garfield Falls is only a five-minute walk from here, through a forest carpeted in the spring with trillium, clintonia, bunchberry, wood sorrel, and occasional moose droppings that look like piles of nutmegs beside (or in) the trail. The falls will be to your left, dropping off the facing side of a chasm into a pool almost directly under your feet. It comes through a zigzag chute and then bounces off the boulder with such force that it has worn a depression in the face of the cliff as well as a cave at its base where its velocity creates a whirlpool. Below the falls the river is split by a giant boulder, from which you can get an excellent view of the falls—and the deeply undercut bank that you were just standing on!

This is not a trip to begin with bald tires, with a near-empty gas tank, or in a downpour of rain, but it is quite an easy one. The distances aren't great, just slow to cover. Before you curse the timber companies for their cutting throughout this area, remember two points. First, you are traveling on their roads, which are the only access to these areas in case of forest fires. Second, their cutting, done with the techniques that they now employ, creates a far more inviting habitat for birds and animals than dense forest provides.

A little farther up Route 3, just above Second Connecticut Lake, another timber road to the right leads to **Scott Bog** and **East Inlet.** The road curves down into a valley and across a stream to a rough T, where you should go left to find Scott Bog or right to find East Inlet. The latter is a former log drive impoundment from which logs were floated out on the spring thaw. In 1987 Champion Paper Company donated 426 acres of pristine pond and moose pasture here, including a tract of virgin spruce and fir, to The Nature Conservancy. The Scott Bog–East Inlet area is considered by birders to offer the best sightings in the North Country, with spruce grouse, Canada jay, sixteen warbler varieties, and the rare black-backed woodpecker. Sightings of eighty to ninety species in just a few days are quite common here.

Wandering around on these woods roads is a lot easier and less nerve-wracking with the inexpensive map "Roads and Trails, Connecticut Lake Region," printed on waterproof paper and available at most stores in the area.

The Connecticut River, barely a trickle now, crosses the road above Second Connecticut Lake, and the tiny **Deer Mountain Campground** (603-538-6965) sits on its northern banks. Its twenty campsites are rustic: no hot showers, flush toilets, or camp store here, but there is plenty of quiet, and the riverbanks are alive with birds. The **Moose Falls Flowage,** just north of the campground, is a good place to put in a canoe. The campground is open from May until the end of Oct and is administered from nearby Lake Francis State Park; (603) 538-6965; nhstateparks.org.

Third Connecticut Lake has a boat ramp right off Route 3, but Fourth Connecticut Lake takes a bit more effort. Only about an acre in size, it is reached by a trail from the US Customs station at the Canadian border. The trail, which is actually the cleared swath along the border, is "steep and rugged," as the map warns. Because it is rocky, it is not a hike for street shoes. Park and sign in at the customs station, where they will give you a trail map. It is only about 0.5 mile to the 75-acre site that Champion Paper Company donated to The Nature Conservancy in 1990. Be sure to walk around the upper part of the lake to find the spot where the first few drops of the mighty Connecticut River trickle from the rocks.

The best way to enjoy this area is to settle in for a few days, and the best place to do that is in a comfortable log cabin or lodge overlooking a lake. ***The Glen at Bear Tree,*** at 118 Glen Rd., a former private estate, looks as though it had grown there with the tall spruce trees that line the shores of First Connecticut Lake. The big lodge, which has been welcoming guests for more than thirty years, is a convivial place, with a huge stone fireplace and comfortable Adirondack log and maple furniture; you can also opt for the seclusion of your own cabin. The atmosphere here is comfortable, not cute. There are no frilly curtains or designer sheets, but you won't be roughing it either.

All meals are included in the rate ($100 to $190), and they'll pack you a box lunch; they will even fill your thermos with hot coffee when you leave for your day's adventure. Dinners in the dining room are generous, including such entrees as Wednesday's special: haddock filet with shrimp and scallops, served with vegetables, pilaf, and wine. The whipped cream on your chocolate cream pie is real, and the vegetables in the salad bar are crisp and fresh. Meals prepared to suit special diets are treated with the same careful attention. Non-guests are welcome to dine there with reservations. But you can expect one distraction while you're eating: The bird feeders outside the dining room windows swarm with hummingbirds.

Its owner, Betty Falton, sets the warm tone at The Glen. She helps guests choose places to hike, fish, bird, or just wander around, suggesting routes and telling about her own favorite nooks and crannies. Betty keeps rental boats moored on various lakes so you won't have to haul them around, or you can bring your own. She loves her "neighborhood," but she stresses that this is not the place for everyone's taste. "If you can't walk to the brook without seeing something interesting, you don't belong here," she is quick to tell prospective guests.

When the full moon rises over Mount Magalloway, reflecting in the lake and outlining the spiky silhouettes of the fir trees around the lake, it looks like the stage set for *Rose Marie.* If the lure of the wilderness charms you, there's no finer place to enjoy it. The Glen is open from mid-May to Oct, when you can call for reservations at (603) 538-9995 or visit atbeartree.com/the-glen.html.

South of Pittsburg you have a choice of roads. Route 145 covers the same route, but in a straighter line. At least on the map it's straighter—if you ironed out the hills, the length would probably be the same. The view from the hilltops, past hillside farms and forests to the skyline of mountains to the south, makes it a nice change from Route 3's river-bottom route.

Fishing friends of ours rave about the hearty homemade food at ***Tall Timber Lodge,*** a rustic backwoods sporting resort of cabins and a B&B-like

lodge, with licensed guides on staff, a fly-fishing school on summer weekends, and fly-tying classes in the winter. Thanks to a bottom-release dam, the waters are cool even in August, which allows three months of prime trout fishing. It's a rendezvous for snowmobilers in the winter; 609 Beach Rd., Pittsburg; (603) 538-6651 or (800) 83-LODGE; talltimber.com.

Don't think that just because this area is remote, it doesn't have fine dining. *Rainbow Grill & Tavern,* the restaurant at Tall Timber Lodge, brings regulars who think nothing of driving an hour or more for the mesquite-grilled duck or venison sausage with blackberry-cognac sauce. Fish and sauces are interchangeable to suit individual taste, though to ours, the boneless trout sautéed in lemon butter needs no further embellishment. The Drambuie-based Highland Sauce plays well with the filet of Atlantic salmon that has been basted in olive oil as it's grilled. Wed through Sun evenings the Rainbow Grill serves a full dinner menu; other nights a shorter tavern/dinner menu. Rainbow Grill, 609 Beach Rd., Pittsburg; reserve at (603) 538-9556.

South of Pittsburg, *Stewartstown* has several landmarks, including the marker identifying the *45th Parallel,* the point exactly midway between the North Pole and the Equator. In the little village of *West Stewartstown* is a unique furniture and home decor store. *Northern Rustic Furniture* works with craftsmen to provide beautifully designed furnishings for northern living, items as small as wrought-iron hooks or as large as beds crafted of peeled logs. Beautifully grained tree burls are hollowed to form waste baskets, while shelves and frames are edged in white birch. The large showroom displays furniture for all rooms, from bentwood chairs and a dramatic red-cedar dining table to peeled log futon frames, bunk beds, and a king-sized pine canopy bed. Decor accessories include hand-wrought iron chandeliers and an eye-grabbing stag-horn wine rack. The genial owners are a goldmine of information about the area, too (they were the ones who introduced us to the Rainbow Grill). Northern Rustic Furniture, 866 Washington St. (Route 3), West Stewartstown; (603) 246-7025.

Across the street, *The Spa* has grown from a 1927 family diner to a full restaurant serving three meals a day from an extensive menu. Whether it's a heaping plate of ham and eggs with home fries for breakfast or seafood platter at dinner, it will be good and very reasonably prices. The pies are all made right there. The Spa, 869 Washington St. (Route 3), West Stewartstown; (603) 246-3039; spa-outbackpub.com.

Beaver Brook Falls drops almost onto Route 145, about 2.5 miles before you reach *Colebrook.* You will see small parking areas on both sides of the road before you see the falls. Be prepared for a surprise, especially if it has rained recently—somehow one doesn't expect the 35-foot straight drop of a waterfall to appear out of the woods, particularly on the side of the road. Below, a series of cascades spill from pool to pool. At the foot of the falls is a small park with picnic tables and a swimming hole. If you aren't going into the tip of the state, you can get to the falls via Route 145 out of Colebrook (the sign is marked CLARKSVILLE), making the 5-mile side trip before going on to *Dixville Notch.*

notyourtypical dayinmay

On May 2, 1798, a man crossed the Connecticut River just south of Colebrook on foot, across the ice. Locals observed stoically that the breakup was a tad late that spring. At least the mosquitoes, usually thick by May, didn't bother him.

Dixville Notch

Unlike most of New Hampshire's other notches, which run north and south, Dixville lies east and west. Route 26 follows the Mohawk River all the way from Colebrook to the notch itself. About 3 miles outside of Colebrook, look for East Colebrook Road going up the hill to your left. The road continues upward, giving fine views over the notch.

For many visitors, the goal and the reward of the long trip to this far-off tip of the state is staying at the world-class grand hotel set just below the head of the notch. *The Balsams* is unique in so many ways that we'll mention only a few. Once one of many large resort hotels where city families came to spend the summer before the days of air-conditioning, The Balsams is still thriving, having weathered the tough financial climates as well as it has weathered its natural climate. It has turned the harsh winters to advantage by opening a family ski area and miles of cross-country ski trails, keeping Lake Gloriette cleared for skating, giving snowshoe lessons, and offering the free use of snowshoes.

Its success is even more surprising because of the hotel's remote location, but therein lies another unique feature. Unlike the other big hotels that were built in the busy White Mountain circuit, The Balsams stands alone, with none of the tourist attractions of the more heavily traveled routes. It is a gracious and highly civilized oasis in a vast wilderness, and its owners have turned that fact to their advantage. They have provided so many activities, sporting opportunities, social events, and gastronomic pleasures that it would take a week to enjoy them all. In the summer, you can enjoy golf, hiking, walks with a staff naturalist, fishing in the lakes and streams, boating, canoeing, tennis, moose watching, swimming, dancing, movies, cooking lessons, a daily sports program, and the opportunity just to sit on the wide veranda and look at the mountains.

Long gone are the days when the White Mountain resort hotels depended on having a captive audience at dinner; today all these grand dames use their dining rooms—and menus created by their award-winning chefs—to lure guests. But The Balsams has put food first for decades, putting it on the New England culinary map. The resort's signature display of the entire menu each evening is a welcome feature, so you see exactly how each menu item is served. Near the front of the dining room, guests can circle a table with plated samples of each item on the menu—the soups, the salads, the appetizers, and the main dishes.

Dinner might begin with the choice of chilled Peaches and Cream Soup, crab cake with guacamole, ginger-poached Gulf shrimp, or gnocchi in roasted tomato cream garnished with thin spears of asparagus. Entrees also change nightly, perhaps including roasted chicken with strawberry-rhubarb chutney or sashimi-grade ahi tuna with mixed Asian greens. Chocolate mousse, apple tarte with cinnamon ice cream, or a simple bowl of perfect raspberries might be offered for dessert.

Unlike many luxury resorts where families can eat together in the dining room only before the normal dinner hour, The Balsams welcomes all its guests, whatever their age, to all its facilities. Children are welcome to join fly-fishing lessons, for example, and a whole menu of spa experiences are geared to a child's attention span. To help youngsters through the dining experience, a class in dining room manners is part of the regular daily Camp Wind Whistle program for ages 5 and up, and included in the hotel rate. The camp provides activities for kids and free time for parents all day if they want it, and baby-sitting is available. But we find that many families choose as we do, to play together.

Non–hotel guests are welcome to visit the historic room where the residents of Dixville gather every four years at midnight to cast the nation's first ballots for the presidential election. The Balsams, 1000 Cold Springs Road, Dixville 03576; (603) 255-2500; thebalsams.com.

Between meals at The Balsams, explore the notch. You can vary your level of exercise, beginning with a walk around the **Lake Gloriette** walking trail, a 1.4-mile loop, with the hotel's *Natural History Handbook* as your guide. This informative little book explains the geology of the notch and helps you identify its abundant wildflowers and birds. More energy is required for the climb up to **Table Rock,** especially if you take the rock-strewn trail that goes almost straight up from the notch. A more gentle ascent can be made by a trail beginning near the Balsam/Wilderness Ski Area entrance road. Table Rock overlooks The Balsams, the lake, and the notch, but it's no place for the acrophobic.

At the point where the trail drops steeply to Table Rock, another trail leads away from the ledges. If you follow it for a few yards you will come to a deep split in the rock face. This ice chasm has snow and ice in it even during the hottest summer days. Although there is no sign leading to it, you won't have trouble finding it; you just have to know it is there. Be careful: It can be dangerous if you get too close to the sharp edge.

After hiking, be sure to stop for a refreshing drink of pure mountain spring water at the newly built *Spring House,* an exact reproduction of the original, which was a popular destination for a Sunday drive. Many locals remember the spring as the scene of their first kiss or even the place of their marriage proposal. There must be something about the water.

The *Balsams Wilderness Ski Area* is part of the resort but is also open to non-guests. Its trails tend toward intermediate skiers and beginners, which makes it a good place for family vacations. A few more challenging runs are available for more advanced skiers. The resort has sixteen trails, 80 percent of which are covered by snowmaking. The slopes have a vertical drop of approximately 1,000 feet. Another of the great appeals of the resort is the Nordic facility: 15,000 acres of northern paradise with 95 kilometers of trails winding through them, making this one of the finest cross-country sites in the Northeast. Eighty-five kilometers of those trails are regularly tracked and groomed, most to 14 feet in width. Watch for moose, deer, and other wildlife and expect to see at least their tracks during your outing. For information check thebalsams.com.

The Flume is on the other side of the notch, and on your way there you can appreciate how wild this notch is compared to Franconia, Pinkham, and even Crawford Notches. It's a real notch, where you go over a hump in the road, through a cleft in the cliffs, and down a steep, winding road squeezed between two tree-covered walls. The difference is geological: The surface rock

Sharpen Your Winter Skills

L. L. Bean has partnered with several local resorts to create a series of winter activity workshops to teach snowshoeing, cross-country skiing, and orienteering. Four-day *Outdoor Discovery School* workshops are designed to teach beginners and to help more experienced winter enthusiasts improve their skills. The easy pace includes three days of training, one dedicated to each sport, and all equipment is provided (a good chance to try out the latest models and designs in Nordic skis and snowshoes). Visit llbean.com/llb/ods for schedules and rates.

here has been tilted on end so that its strata stand upright, causing the craggy eroded points of rock that give it such a wild aspect.

About a mile past the head of the notch look for a picnic area on the left. The geology changes back to granite here, as Flume Brook carves a gorge more than 200 feet long with sides so straight it almost seems to have been built from cut blocks of stone. It is 40 feet deep in places, as the brook drops from pool to pool and finally over the ledge. Walk along the rim, and in the spring look for trillium and white and pink lady's slippers beside the trail. They are protected species, so enjoy them in place.

Just a few yards down Route 26, this time on the right, is the road to a second picnic area. **Huntington Cascades** is reached by a short path to the brook and then a short walk upstream. The falls continue above the one that you can see from the base, but there is no trail up the steep slope beside the falls, so most visitors simply enjoy the lower section as it rushes in its curving path over the rocks. If you do go exploring here, be careful and stay away from the edge, which has been undercut by the brook. In case you wondered, the little cemetery by the entrance to the parking area contains the remains of some of the area's earliest settlers.

The 5 miles of road between Huntington Cascades and the town of **Errol** is a prime stretch for moose viewing, so drive slowly and keep watch. You can't miss the Errol International Airport, whose building is so tiny that its long name has to be abbreviated to fit across its facade.

Staying at **A Peace of Heaven Bed and Breakfast** is like having a small place in the wilderness all your own. Travelers who once stayed in Rooms with a View (now closed) will recognize Sonja and Charlie Sheldon, who now run this small, three-room B&B in Millsfield, between Colebrook and Errol on

Outdoor Adventures

Lucie LaPlante Villeneuve is a wilderness guide and outdoor educator, who knows the backwoods of New Hampshire's North Country and its nature, from the delicate springtime wildflowers to the moose that populate the forests. And she revels in introducing these woods, lakes, ponds, rivers, and mountains to those who would like to know them better. She can arrange, outfit, and guide day or overnight (and longer) canoe and kayak trips, snowshoe hikes with a picnic, winter survival training, and backcountry skiing excursions. She teaches orienteering, nature photography, archery, and camping skills and can lead moose-spotting tours on foot, skis, bicycle, or in a canoe or kayak. Her website is an excellent source of information—and pictures—on northern wildlife. To arrange or join a tour, contact **Outdoor ESCAPES** at (603) 528-0136 or visit outdoorescapesnh.com.

A Note About Our Less Appealing Wildlife

While May's lilacs are safe as the state's flower, there is talk every spring about changing the state bird from the purple finch (which we rarely see) to the mosquito or blackfly, which we see all too often. Unless you have allergies to their bites, these springtime insects are merely an annoyance. They don't carry malaria or yellow fever as their tropical relatives do, and slapping them is a source of moderate exercise.

But in the North Country, especially in May and June, it is wise to be prepared with long sleeves, long pants, and shirts with collars when these voracious creatures are at their worst—evenings and mornings and in the deep woods.

Everyone has a favorite brand of repellent; we favor Natrapel for most places, the only repellent we know of with EPA approval that comes with a propellant-free spray and a recyclable bottle. Natrapel is a New Hampshire product, created by people who know mosquitoes and blackflies intimately. For sources call (800) 258-4696, write Tender Corporation, PO Box 290, Littleton 03561, or visit tendercorp.com.

Route 26. Rooms are beautiful, as you would expect from Sonja, and all have private bath and come with full breakfast. One room has a separate entrance and is fully wheelchair accessible. Rates are a reasonable $90 for a double. They will also arrange special outing packages for guests, including biking, canoeing/kayaking, photography, snowshoeing, cross-country skiing, and other of the delights of the Great North Woods. Located on Route 26, Millsfield; (603) 482-3443; apeaceofheavenbandb.com.

At *L. L. Cote* you'll find anything you need for camping or outdoor sports, from a backpackers' stove and hand-tied fishing flies to archery targets and long underwear. In the back is the famed white moose. Open daily 8 a.m. to 5 p.m., and until 6 p.m. on weekends. It's easy to spot at 7 Main St., Errol; (800) 287-7700 or (603) 482-7777; llcote.com.

Each of the two roads leaving from the far end of Errol's main street will take you to the Maine border. Route 16, to the left, offers a pleasant drive along the Upper Androscoggin and Magalloway Rivers.

Both Route 26 and *Lake Umbagog,* whose southern tip it passes, continue on into Maine, and just before the border is New Hampshire's newest state park. In 1999 the state purchased the Lake Umbagog Campground, creating *Lake Umbagog State Park* and protecting all but 10 percent of New Hampshire's share of the lake's shore from development. The park preserves the nesting grounds of bald eagles, loons, and ospreys and retains the character of the campground's thirty-eight campsites, designed primarily for "canvas campers," and the thirty additional sites that can be reached only by boat. Cabins and sites with electric hookup are also available. The farthest of the "remote sites" is 11 miles from the main campground, about as far off the beaten path as you can get without carrying your camping gear on your back. Take your canoe or kayak and lose yourself for a day on this beautiful, pristine lake.

These sites are isolated, at least half a mile apart, and are not for beginning campers but for the woods-wise and the water-wise. They offer real camping that is very hard to find. You can rent canoes, kayaks, and boats at the campground. Open from Memorial Day to mid-September; you can reserve sites. Lake Umbagog State Park is on Route 26 in Errol; (603) 482-7795. For reservations for this and other state parks, call (603) 271-3628 or visit nhstateparks.org.

In Errol, **Saco Bound** rents canoes and kayaks, and operates a full transportation service so you can put in at one place and be picked up at a different location. In the summer they offer reasonably priced guided day trips complete with a barbecue lunch. They operate a whitewater canoe and kayak school at Errol, as well as a campground for their customers with sites spaced for multiday trips. Saco Bound is headquartered at 2561 East Main St. (Route 302), Center Conway; (603) 447-2177 or (603) 482-3817 during the season; sacobound.com.

The Androscoggin

South of Errol on Route 16 begins a scenic stretch where the road and the **Androscoggin River** travel side by side through **Thirteen Mile Woods.** The river is wide and for the most part gentle, and there are put-ins at several different points. If you have ever held a paddle, you will long to be on the water in this flat reach where the trees overhang the river. There is even a campground, the **Mollidgewock State Campground,** right on the river and designed primarily for canoeists. It is open from mid-May to mid-Oct. Be sure to call them at (603) 482-3373 for information or (603) 271-3628 for reservations, since its half-mile frontage on calm water and rapids is a favorite teaching area for groups learning whitewater techniques. More information is available at nhstateparks.org.

Motorists will find good places for a riverside picnic or to just sit and watch the river traffic go by. Below the Thirteen Mile Woods is another area frequented by moose, where it is not unusual to see them beside (or in) the road.

North of Berlin look for the stone cairns in the river, among the last reminders of the days of the logging drives that were common in this country during the nineteenth and early twentieth centuries. These mid-river cairns served as the point from which the great chain booms were secured. These captured and held a vast flotilla of logs during the annual spring release of the timber that had been harvested during the winter. As trees were cut during the winter, the logs were hauled into impoundment ponds. During the runoff, the dams holding these ponds were released. The water and logs broke into a wild frenzy of energy and wood that found its way downstream into the sawmills and paper plants of New England.

Berlin (pronounced with the accent on the first syllable) is a paper mill town; you can't miss the smokestacks of the James River Corporation. It has been a paper town ever since the first logging camp was established in 1825, although the first paper mill didn't open until 1852. At one time it was estimated that the paper produced in Berlin annually would cover a road 15 feet wide that would run nineteen times around the world. The mill brought immigrants from Canada and as far away as Russia. These ethnic groups have mixed and moved, but a few traces remain from the days when church services in the community were conducted in five different languages.

Berlin's lumbering and papermaking history is explored at **Northern Forest Heritage Park,** a growing museum that displays historic artifacts and photographs. Displays explain how the timber was cut, moved during spring log drives, and either shipped for use elsewhere or converted into paper. A regular schedule of festivals celebrates the wide range of ethnic groups drawn to the mills and lumber camps and the unique lifestyle they made together. Although its biggest era was the late 1800s, lumbering is still important to the North Country, and its modern operations are included, too. Other programs are planned in the summer, so it's wise to call ahead. The museum is open year-round, Mon through Fri from 10 a.m. to 7 p.m., and it is located at 961 Main St.; (603) 752-7202 or visit androscogginvalleychamber.com.

While in Berlin, inquire at the information booth about moose tours, which began at Heritage Park. These take visitors by van to some of the most likely locations for spotting moose, showing a video about the local logging heritage on the way. Tours are usually held every evening from mid-May through

And You Thought You Spoke the Language

You have already learned how to pronounce the name of the state's capital like a native, but the road map is filled with names that will expose you as a foreigner the minute you try to say them. In the North Country, Berlin and Milan are pronounced BURR-lin and My-lin, respectively. They had European pronunciations until World War I, when they changed for political reasons.

Columbus Day weekend. Call (603) 752-7202 or (603) 752-6060 for reservations, or take your chances by appearing at the park. Times vary according to daylight hours.

Saint Anne's church, a classic French-Canadian brick structure, rises like a fortress in the center of town, enormously tall, with an oversized statue on top. But far more unexpected is **Holy Resurrection Church.** Take Mount Forist Street, which intersects Main Street near the post office, and follow it up the hill. When we say up, we mean almost straight up what may well be New Hampshire's steepest street. Just before the street ends, go left on Russian Street, still going uphill, and look to your right. Six polished, gold-leafed, onion-shaped domes crown a gem of a Russian Orthodox Church on the corner of Petrograd Street. A double patriarchal gold cross surmounts each dome; the rest of the church is white. It sits above the city overlooking the smokestacks and rows of company housing below, a poignant and rare reminder of the homesickness of the many peoples who were propelled into this strange and new land.

For a fine view over the mountains to the west, take the **Cates Hill Scenic Route,** turning right off High Street onto Hillside Avenue. The road continues to climb until it reaches a ridge of cleared meadows with a backdrop of mountains. You can reach Hillside Avenue from Route 16 north of town by taking the road marked Coos County Home and continuing to the top of the hill.

On Jimtown Road, just off Route 2 west of Gorham, is a very pleasant campground at **Moose Brook State Park.** Its forty-six sites are well spaced in open forest, with a few at the edge of a field. An ingenious warming pool brings the icy-cold waters of Moose Brook up to a more suitable temperature before it flows into the swimming pool downstream. There is a picnic area near the swimming pool. Be sure to notice the architecture of the administration building, which is a classic of Civilian Conservation Corps (CCC) construction. The park is open from late May through Labor Day; (603) 466-3860; nhstate parks.org.

Across from the town hall on the common in **Gorham,** the **Victorian Railway Station** has been turned into a museum by the local historical society. The collection emphasizes the years when the railway was the lifeblood of the region but contains other memorabilia as well; including a stereoscope that visitors can actually use to view the collection of historic cards. Outside stands a fine collection of rail cars, including a beautiful steam engine and its coal car from the Grand Trunk Railway; 19 Railroad St. Call (603) 466-5338 or (603) 466-5570. Hours vary.

If you think that heading into New Hampshire's most remote northern corner means leaving fine dining behind, think again. There are a number of choices, one of which is just on the other side of Mount Washington. In a former bank building on Main Street, you'll find two restaurants run by the same family. Whether you choose to dine at *Libby's Bistro* or *SAaLT Pub,* you'll enjoy the same menu. Opt for SAaLT if you're looking for a more casual vibe; if the occasion calls for linens, Libby's is your best bet. No matter where you sit, you'll find dishes so good that people think nothing of driving the forty-five minutes from North Conway to have dinner there. We've driven even farther for a taste of James Beard semifinalist Liz Jackson's Forever Braised Beef or Truffled Tallegio Fonduta with roasted vegetables and polenta fries. The eclectic dining room, with its rich colors and well-spaced tables, sets the perfect background for a menu that's just as eclectic. On Friday nights in the winter, Liz (the "L" in SAaLT) features a particular cuisine, maybe Mexican, maybe Italian, or maybe a "Friday in Paris" menu that includes Hunter's Cassoulet and a shrimp and scallop stew with Normandy influence, served with a garnish of crispy fried mussels. The cassoulet brims with rabbit, duck, Cornish hens, and smoky bacon. Desserts get equal attention from this talented chef; the Chef's Table menu might offer coffee caramel pot de crème with hazelnut shortbread on a cold winter night, or on a summer evening finish with Liz's own citrus-Prosecco sorbet with pomegranate seeds, clementines, and cookies. For those fresh off the hiking trails that prefer a more casual menu and atmosphere, the downstairs pub is a cozy place for a drink or dinner. The quality matches the upstairs standard—the food is from the same kitchen. Libby's Bistro & SAaLT Pub are open Wed through Sun starting at 5 p.m. 111 Main St., Gorham; (603) 466-5330; libbysbistro.org.

Shelburne is best known for *The Shelburne Birches*, a stretch of Route 2 lined with beautiful white birch trees. These are striking at any time of year—their paper-white trunks contrasted against summer's green, autumn's yellows, or casting shadows on the snow. Just past the birches, the big white *Mt. Washington Bed and Breakfast* is enviably positioned to catch views of the summit of Mount Washington from the rocking chairs on its west porch. Two of the two-room suites have whirlpool tubs; all have private baths. The informal, comfortable atmosphere and the genial owners make this an ideal place to relax, and the delicious breakfasts fortify more ambitious guests for nearby hiking trails and kayaking in Reflection Pond. Mt. Washington Bed and Breakfast is located at 421 US-2, Shelburne 03581; (603) 466-2669; mtwashingtonbb.com.

The *Old Man of the Valley* in Shelburne is virtually unknown, despite a modest sign on the south side of Route 2 between Gorham and the Maine border. Park in the pull-out, which is just east of the sign. Walk back to the sign, where a short trail enters the woods. A short distance ahead is a large stone with the profile of a man on one side. Surely, you say, this has just been sculpted to look this way, but a walk around the stone shows a jumble of perfectly natural planes that form the face when viewed from the front.

More Places to Stay in the North Country

JEFFERSON

Applebrook Bed and Breakfast
110 Meadows Rd.
(603) 586-6008
applebrook.net
Eight rooms and two suites. Moderate.

Josselyn's Getaway Log Cabin
4 Blue Spruce Cir.
(800) 586-4507
Real log cabins sleep four to ten and have full kitchens.

PITTSBURG

Lopstick
45 Stewart Young Rd.
(800) 538-6659
lopstick.com
Housekeeping units with baseboard heat, open all year and convenient to snowmobile trail system.

Mountain View Cabins and Campground
2787 N. Main St.
(603) 538-6305
mountainviewcabinsand campground.com
Log cabins open year-round, located on the main snowmobile trail system. All have central heat, some with fireplaces or woodstoves, too.

SHELBURNE

Philbrook Farm Inn
881 North Rd.
(603) 466-3831
philbrookfarminn.com
A comfortable, old-fashioned place where families come year after year; breakfast and dinner included in price of stay.

Town and Country Motor Inn
1033, 20 US-2
(603) 466-3315
townandcountryinn.com
Well-kept motel with a swimming pool; moderate.

TO LEARN MORE ABOUT THE NORTH COUNTRY

North Country Chamber of Commerce
104 Main St., #206, Colebrook 03576
(603) 237-8939
chamberofthenorthcountry.com

Androscoggin Valley Chamber of Commerce
961 Main St., Berlin 03570
(603) 752-6060
androscogginvalleychamber.com

More Places to Eat in the North Country

BERLIN

Northland Restaurant & Dairy Bar
1826 Riverside Dr.
(603) 752-6210
North of town on the road to Milan, the Northland is a local institution with a pleasant dining room, reliably good food and low-to-moderate prices. In the summer the dairy bar serves up generous scoops of excellent ice cream.

ERROL

Northern Exposure Restaurant
12 Main St.
(603) 482-3468
Don't look for innovative nouvelle anything here, but expect well-prepared generous portions of favorites, plus a surprise or two—such as venison burgers. The pies are made in-house.

GORHAM

Yokohama Restaurant
288 Main St.
(603) 466-2501
Pan-Asian menu, with particular emphasis on Japanese food. Closed Mondays.

WHITEFIELD

Grandma's Kitchen
187 Lancaster Rd.
(603) 837-2525
Breakfasts and pies are what Grandma's is famous for, but the burgers are outstanding, the sandwiches generous, and the prices unbelievably low, which probably accounts for why it's usually full. Everything is prepared from scratch here, from hand cut fries to the sliced turkey in the sandwiches.

Index

About the Authors

Barbara Radcliffe Rogers and **Stillman Rogers** have, jointly and singly, written and illustrated dozens of books, most of them on travel, wildlife, and gardening. Titles include *It Happened in New Hampshire, Galapagos, Safari, Drive Around Portugal, Big Cats, Giant Pandas, Exploring Europe by Boat, Drive Around Italy's Lakes and Mountains, Travellers Milan and Italian Lakes, Adventure Guide to Canada's Atlantic Provinces, Adventure Guide to New Brunswick and Prince Edward Island, Adventure Guide to the Chesapeake Bay, Eating New England, Secret Providence and Newport,* and *The Rhode Island Guide.* They have written and illustrated several books in the *Children of the World* series and written several others in the *Enchantment of the World* and *Cities of the World* series, describing the lives and cultures of children from Argentina to Zambia. Barbara has written articles for *Yankee* magazine, *Country Journal,* the *Boston Herald,* the *Los Angeles Times,* and others, including a monthly column for *New Hampshire Magazine.* Stillman's photographs have illustrated hers and other articles.

Although **Amanda Silva** was born in Manchester, New Hampshire, she didn't return to the state until 2005, when she embarked on a Masters' Program at Dartmouth College. Up until then, she had spent her life relocating with her family across the United States and abroad. Whenever possible, her parents prioritized trips home to visit relatives in New Hampshire, where Amanda spent many summers on the seacoast. After graduating from Dartmouth in 2008, she began teaching at schools in southern New Hampshire and now works full-time as a writer. Amanda is surprised, but pleased to have returned to her roots.